BEYOND
"WHAT IF?"

Real Life Stories of How Purpose Turns Dreams Into Reality

Best Wishes /

[signature] 12/7/17

DEDICATION

Dedicated to everyone who knows, or is seeking to find, his or her life's Purpose and pursue it with Passion! May our stories spark your imagination and strengthen your confidence and belief in yourself.

TESTIMONIALS

"Having been a big fan of Napoleon Hill's lectures and teachings for many years, it was very inspiring to read a collection of stories that brought Hill's teachings to life. Real examples of people who endured struggle, financial hardship or personal tragedy and yet persisted until their definite purpose was realized. I will lean on these short stories in the years to come, on those days when I need more than a coffee to get me going, and I encourage you to do the same."

-Kevin Pressburger

President

Pita Pit Canada

"The stories in this book are a perfect example of what can be accomplished when determination is applied. Everyone should read this book and apply its helpful message to their lives. It was an inspirational read."

-Gary Chappell

CEO/Chappell Enterprises

"Beyond "What if?" is a great book that features Napoleon Hill Foundation Certified Instructors and Students, sharing stories from their lives that will inspire you. We all experience difficult times in our lives.

The human spirit that keeps us going is what this book is about. Refusing to give up and give in is what allows us to see success in our lives. These authors have shared their stories with us to help us achieve more from our lives by giving us examples of what they have faced and overcome.

The principles shared in the book can guide anyone's life no matter where they are in their life journey."

-Daniel Hanzelka (Reset Warrior) Business Success Coach

http://www.danielhanzelka.com

"I have long been a fan of Dr. Napoleon Hill, and his many teaching to define and discover your infinite purpose.

The stories compiled in this book will guide you to areas of success within your life that you are perhaps unaware of.

Fear is the biggest obstacle in our lives, but through Hill's teaching we can discover that there is nothing to fear but fear it's self.

Courage is not the absence of fear...Courage is your actions in spite of your fear.

To all that read this book, I wish you continued success in your lives.

Thank you to all the contributing authors for having again, touched the very soul of success."

-Christopher Robins

https://trg-therobinsgroup.com/

"I have recommended Napoleon Hill's book Think and Grow Rich to over 500,000 audience members. My newest program, MindStore Online, was created to help you implement The Secret in Think and Grow Rich according to Andrew Carnegie.

The authors of Beyond What If have opened their lives to share how the have used the various Success Principles in their own lives. Those stories will give you hope, faith and courage to persist in pursuing your Purpose and Goals as you strive to get the most out of your God given skills, talents, and abilities.

These real life stories will clearly show you how to turn your dreams into reality."

-Jack Black

Creator of MindStore and MindStore Online

http://www.mindstoreonline.com

"This book focuses on how people have used the time-tested principles of Dr Napoleon Hill. Full of inspiring stories of everyday people, you realize that Dr Hill's work will be relevant for as long as the human race exists and that it will help all who adopt his philosophy."

-Janet Jones

Founder of www.happinessmillionaire.com

"If only Napoleon Hill's teachings were a scholastic requirement for schools throughout the world as our communities would truly benefit with the understanding and application of the 17 Principles of Success.

The stories, insights and lessons within Beyond "What If?" demonstrates the positive impact for creating success in all aspects of our life. These Principles transcend and help all those reach within themselves to create and maintain a better life. I am a better person for it. I know others will find the same."

-Anthony Marquart

President of Royalty Developments Ltd. & Queen City Sports & Entertainment Group Ltd. (Regina Pats)

"Beyond what if is one of the most exceptional contemporary manuscripts. The writing in this book is profound and deep. These depths will be received at different spectrums depending on the conscious awareness of the observer. The thoughts are well articulated giving simplicity to the complexity of sound reasoning. These words are meant to be read more than once and revisited often. The sharp minds, humble wisdom, and passion for humanity is admirable and the trajectory of this world changing legacy is inevitable."

-Rob Fajardo

Sofro Media Group, www.sofro.com

ACKNOWLEDGMENTS

With great esteem we are thankful for each other's chapter contribution and for being vulnerable and transparent so that others may read and learn from our life's journey in this book. You have embraced the torch lit by Dr. Napoleon Hill and are now givers of truth; your personal truth to inspire others on their life's journey. This book would not have been possible without a team of skilled project managers who are all specialists in their right. Their unique contributions and dedication would make Dr. Napoleon Hill proud. In no particular order special thanks to:

Tom "too tall" Cunningham for patient, stern and loving project management, which kept us all on track and motivated to bring forth a timely and beautifully written book. We thank you for consistently finding time in your busy schedule to be a mentor, friend and everyone's go to guy. For countless hours of editing, and making sure all the submissions and resubmissions were given careful attention we are extremely thankful.

Brad Szollose for a vibrant cover design that literally jumps off the page and is indicative of the emotions shared by each chapter contributor. For endless iterations until perfection was reached we are grateful for your creativity, patience and dedication.

John Westley Clayton for being a formatting wizard of twenty-five chapter submissions and resubmissions. For the hours of content uploading and formatting we thank you for serving as "publisher extraordinaire".

Jim Stovall for your belief in this project, for your unwavering support and for finding time in your busy schedule to write a special forward. You are always so unselfish with knowledge and generous with time and for that we are eternally grateful.

Jeremy Rayzor for your creative genius in sifting through many suggested titles and coming up with a title that encompasses the essence of all that this book seeks to offer its readers.

Dave Doyle for writing the text copy for the back cover. Know that we sincerely appreciate your generosity of time and talent.

Don M. Green (Executive Director & Humanitarian of the Year 2000), the entire Board of Trustees and staff from the Napoleon Hill Foundation for determination and dedication in perpetuating Napoleon Hill's success philosophy. Thank you for allowing each of us to honor Dr. Hill's work by sharing how being a student has impacted our lives.

Sincere appreciation and heartfelt respect to Judy Williamson (Director), Uriel "Chino" Martinez, and Alan Chen for being great role models and stewards of the Napoleon Hill World Learning Center. You three are the most accessible, authentic, and humble torchbearers the World Learning Center could have. Your dedication and hard work in keeping the World Learning Center vibrant and relevant has made it possible for many students across the globe to become friends, benefactors, and now champions of Napoleon Hill's success philosophy.

To our families and friends whose support and life experiences have made each chapter possible. Thanks for taking this journey with us by being patient, understanding, and when necessary a cheerleader.

Last but certainly not least, an endless debt of gratitude to Dr. Napoleon Hill whose timeless message continues to inspire, and empower millions of people all around the world. Because of your unwavering belief and dedication to the science of success philosophy millions of people better know their purpose and their Creator.

FOREWORD
By Jim Stovall

I have long believed that we should never take advice from anyone who has not demonstrated that they have what we want. Anyone who wants success in their life should vigorously follow the words, lessons, and example of Napoleon Hill. One need look no farther than the ongoing work of my friend and colleague Don Green and The Napoleon Hill Foundation as well as the contributors to this book to see the success, legacy, and impact of Napoleon Hill continuing to grow. Napoleon Hill, throughout his life and beyond, showed us that if you learn something, you can change your life; if you teach something, you can change someone else's life; but if you teach people to teach, you can change the world.

As the author of over 30 books myself with 10 million copies in print in two dozen languages around the world, I'm embarrassed to admit that when I could read words on a page with my eyes as you are reading this, I don't know that I ever read a whole book cover-to-cover. After losing my sight, I discovered audiobooks and high-speed listening. That discovery has opened the whole world to me, and in the last 25 years, I have averaged reading a book a day.

In the field of success, there are many good books, a few great books, and Think and Grow Rich. Any book can be judged by the impact it has upon those who read it. Through my own books, movies, syndicated columns, TV interviews, and work on stages around the world, I have met hundreds of high-level performers and successful people from every arena of human endeavor. Among the several questions I ask all these luminaries is "What book impacted your life the most?" Invariably, the most common response I receive is Napoleon Hill's transformational book Think and Grow Rich.

He launched a movement in the success and development field that many other authors and thinkers have built upon. While I enjoy reading the work of Hill's disciples and find it enlightening and inspiring, every year or two, I find myself going back to the well and drinking from Think and Grow Rich. Within these pages, you are going to read messages from people who have been impacted by Napoleon Hill's work and who are, in turn, using that impact to change the world.

If you are familiar with my work in any way, it's probably due to a little novel I wrote entitled The Ultimate Gift. There have been three other books in that series and a movie trilogy based on the stories. The third film in the trilogy, The Ultimate Legacy, deals with the value of a person's life being measured by the value they create in the lives of others both now and in the future.

The book you hold and the work of its contributors, along with Don Green and The Napoleon Hill Foundation, are a testament to Hill's legacy and a signal that we should all pay heed to the success principles contained in this volume.

My success journey with Napoleon Hill began in a strange and unusual way. As a young man, I had no desire other than to be an All American football player and then make my living playing in the NFL. The coaches and scouts who monitor such things assured me that I had the size and speed to live out my dream, but during a routine physical to play another season of football, I was diagnosed with a condition that would cause me to lose my sight. I never played football again but became an Olympic weightlifter and got to finish my athletic career as our national champion in that sport. I did, indeed, lose my sight slowly throughout my 20s, and by age 29, I was totally blind.

During those years, my father introduced me to a man named Lee Braxton who became my first mentor. Mr. Braxton had a third-grade education, and through his entrepreneurial endeavors, became a multimillionaire during the Great Depression. He then gave away the majority of his fortune and devoted the rest of his life to charity. When I met him, he was well into what, for most people, would be retirement years. He was still very driven and made it clear he wasn't going to waste much time on an almost-blind weightlifter unless I performed. At our first meeting, he gave me a copy of Think and Grow Rich and told me to read it all before our next meeting.

As I began devouring Napoleon Hill's work, I got so excited I wanted to ask Mr. Braxton some questions before I read on. He simply told me to finish the book or don't come back. I remain eternally grateful for his stern and firm advice. Mr. Braxton and Think and Grow Rich were the basis for all my success.

I didn't realize until a quarter of a century later when Don Green became a friend and colleague that Napoleon Hill and my mentor Lee Braxton had been lifelong friends, and Lee Braxton delivered Hill's eulogy.

The connection I feel to Napoleon Hill through Lee Braxton is one that remains with me to this day, and as you read these stories and lessons by the dedicated contributors who created this book, you will begin to forge your own connection with each of them and Napoleon Hill.

I want to be a part of that connection for you as you read this book, so from this day forward, any time you're discouraged, depressed, or despondent, and any time your goals and dreams seem dim and distant, reach out to me at Jim@JimStovall.com, and you will find a fellow traveler with an encouraging word and advice to go back to the well of wisdom that is the work of Napoleon Hill.

Jim Stovall

Bestselling Author

INTRODUCTION
By: Tom "too tall" Cunningham

Napoleon Hill and W. Clement Stone used to have a friendly difference in opinion about which Success Principle was the most important. Stone was well known for his Positive Mental Attitude and naturally felt it was the most important key to success. Napoleon Hill, influenced by Andrew Carnegie, Henry Ford and Thomas Edison believed that having a Definite Purpose, or Definite Chief Aim, is the most important of all his 17 Success Principles.

Napoleon Hill Foundation Certified Instructors and Students of the Foundation's PMA Science of Success course and Certification process are a diverse and closely-knit group. Men and women from many countries take the Foundation's online course and many of them attend the Leader Certification trip as one of the final requirements in the Certification process.

My wife, Kim Cunningham, and I have many of the authors in this book because we have attended 6 trips at the time of this writing. Most recently I travelled to Cambodia to speak at the Cambodia Science of Success International Conference. Timothy Chhim, the Napoleon Hill Foundation licensee for Cambodia, assembled an international team including; Jeremy Rayzor, creator of Napoleon Hill board games Achievus and Ticket To Wealth, Apple Suwanna Mitchell from Thailand, Ruth Neslo from the Netherlands and Taylor Tagg and Chief Dwaine Perry from the United States. That International Convention is an example of the diversity of the people spreading the news and educating people about the 17 Principles of Success.

The stories shared in Beyond What If: Real Life Stories of How Purpose Turns Dreams Into Reality will encourage you to persist in discovering and knowing your Definite Purpose and give you ideas about how best to Pursue Your Purpose with Passion! Once you are doing that, and continue to do that, your What Ifs will be transmuted into I Can and I Will.

Our Publisher, John Westley Clayton, is also a Napoleon Hill Foundation Certified Instructor. John Westley works with each of the authors for format, edit and creates their chapters and bios. He also Published Refusing To Quit, the first book written by Foundation Instructors and Students.

I would love to hear from you and learn about your personal Definite Purpose and help you with your goals. Please email me at tom@tom2tall.com or visit the book website at www.beyondwhatif.com.

Tom "too tall" Cunningham

Producer and Publisher

Founder of Journey To Success Radio

MWR Life Inspiration Ambassador

www.mwrlife.com/tootall

CONTENTS

LEFT IN FEAR, RETURNED TO CHEERS

By: Timothy Chhim

"A quitter never wins and a winner never quits."
-Napoleon Hill

Even though I had a zero percent chance of escaping the Khmer Rouge's death row in Cambodia, I tried not once, not twice, but three times. What if I had quit after taking only one chance?

Like millions of Khmer people, I was supposed to die from either execution, starvation, disease, or overwork. After being evacuated on April 19, 1975 from Phnom Penh, the capital city of Cambodia, and trudging along the highway for many days, the Khmer Rouge took yet another census, which included our background information. Honest, naïve, and not knowing their true intentions, we told the truth. They then segregated us and gathered about 70 students and soldiers of the Khmer Republic at a time, telling us we would be returned to Phnom Penh to help rebuild the country. By now it was the middle of May, and the news gave us hope and security.

Along the way at different times, three people—a young man, a middle-aged woman, and an elderly man—gave me clues that my group was being taken to Ghost Mountain to be beaten to death with a bloodstained garden hoe. Thinking they were already the victors of the civil war and believing no one could be that cruel, not even those black-pajama-and-checkered-scarf-wearing revolutionary people, I did not

1

believe the three strangers—not until it was almost too late. Chills ran down my spine as I sat outside in a drizzling rain with a plastic sheet over my head among over 70 other people, positioned in front of an abandoned pagoda and listening to the communist cadres with their stern faces, venomous words, and murderous eyes making revolutionary speeches. I began to think hard. Clarity set in after I examined my surroundings, calculated the activities of the communist cadres, and evaluated their body language. My stomach turned. Fear, anger, and frustration overwhelmed me.

My mind went back to my family as I faced death. I thought about my parents and siblings who believed in the words of a fortune-teller who said I was a person of "great merit and fortune"—that I would "do great things for my family and country." They often reminded me about it. A person of great merit and fortune who would do great things for his family and country could not die. I felt my blood rush from head to toe. I had to act and act fast! My hopes, dreams, and desire to live kicked me so hard in the ass that I got up from the ground and jumped as high as I could over the heads of two scared and confused-looking women who were sitting in front of me. I spun on my feet without seeming to touch the earth. As I headed for the forest on the east side of the abandoned pagoda, multiple rounds of gunshots echoed around me. My burning desire to stay alive grew as I heard the loud popping explosions and saw the impact of flying bullets striking the trees and the wet ground to the sides and in front of my path. Zigzagging to dodge the bullets, I tripped and fell a few times. Discarding the plastic sheet I had used to protect my head from the drizzling rain, I finally reached some thick bushes, which seemed to stretch kilometers into the distance.

I drifted along to many places and approached death row two more times, all the while guided by the voice of my deceased father, before I reached Preah Vihear and ultimately the Cambodian–Thai border. There, I vowed I would return to rescue my countrymen. I did not know when or how, but I would return.

I was supposed to die, but that didn't happen. I believe my life was spared for a specific reason—that I had a definite purpose to help others succeed and to save their lives. I have had faith and belief in this purpose for 40 years, from the time I decided to escape the death row of those failed leaders of the Khmer Rouge who were responsible for the murders of their own citizens.

On April 8, 2016, I returned home to Cambodia nearly eight years after my last trip in 2008. I have been given a great opportunity as a refugee to live, work, and serve communities in the United States, my adopted country since 1976. I realize I have always had a chance to help save the lives of Cambodian people and to help rebuild my native country, which I escaped in the summer of 1975. Something unexplainable has been burning inside me for many years now—the burning desire to find freedom for the mind, body, and spirit and to be free of hunger, fear, and want—not just for me but also for my fellow countrymen. Such a strong desire had led me to experiment with many different ways and means to bring about my personal success and the advancement of all Cambodians—a recurring dream that led me to jump out of the Khmer Rouge death row and dodge rounds of bullets even when I knew the chance of surviving was nearly zero.

I have always wanted to help my fellow countrymen become successful in their lives, thinking that when they become self-reliant and productive, Cambodia, too, would reap the same benefits. To this day, Cambodia remains one of the poorest countries on the planet. That includes the poverty of thoughts and the quality of general education.

Since June 2015, I have spent many hours every Saturday evening (Sunday morning in Cambodia) teaching Dr. Napoleon Hill's Science of Success Principles via Skype to more than 100 students at the International Education Institute (InterEd) in Phnom Penh, Cambodia. A week before the end of 2015, InterEd's Chairman, Dr. Samnang Sorn, one of Cambodia's finest French-educated professors and one of his board members, Mr. Suykry Path, who used to work and live in the

United States, and I agreed to bring to Cambodia the 17 Principles of Success written by the late Dr. Napoleon Hill. Dr. Hill was the well-known author of the best-selling book, Think and Grow Rich. Some 70 million copies of his book have been sold throughout the world, and he helped many people become successful through his research and teaching. Think and Grow Rich has helped me achieve many of my own goals. I firmly believe Dr. Hill's principles will help change many other lives as it has changed mine. Dr. Sorn, Mr. Suykry and I had been preparing for the grand opening of this class for a few weeks and decided to hold an International Conference to officially open Cambodia Science of Success on April 9, 2016.

The grand opening would be hosted by officers of the Cambodian government, InterEd school officials, national and international organizations, and six of my colleagues: Napoleon Hill Certified Instructors from the U.S, Canada, the Netherlands, and Thailand. I was eager for the special 10-day trip, thinking that it was also a great occasion to meet and greet those hundreds of students and staff of InterEd, to say hello to my two older sisters and relatives, and to seek help for my only son, who was in need of a kidney transplant.

I was grateful to my friends and colleagues who volunteered to go to Cambodia for the first time with me, primarily to help me with the grand opening. Jeremy Rayzor from Montana was scheduled to meet me in Phnom Penh; Ruth Neslo from the Netherlands and Apple Mitchell from Thailand booked their flights to land on the same day. Meanwhile, Tom Cunningham from Toronto and Taylor Tagg from Memphis, Tennessee agreed to fly to New York's JFK airport to meet me and Chief Dwaine Perry of New York. At the last minute, my wife, Neang Kim, finally decided to join us on the trip to return to her hometown for the first time. Like me, her greatest hope was to seek help from any one of our relatives who, if the blood matched, was willing to donate a kidney to save our son's life. Neang had never returned to her birthplace since she left in 1975. I prayed that some of her relatives, if she could locate them, and my relatives would consider helping our 30-year-old son Anthony. Neang had donated one of her kidneys to save Anthony's life in 2010, but the kidney lasted only five years with many complications. His body has been fighting and rejecting the kidney, and he lives with constant chronic and severe pain. He has been on dialysis three days a week, eight hours a day. If he could not drive himself to the hospital, his older sister or I would take him.

Phnom Penh

We all arrived at Phnom Penh International Airport, a small airport in Cambodia's capital, at about the same time—around midnight on April 8 via Korean Air. The flight was more than 20 hours long but flying in a group helped relieve my anxiety. Little did we know that a great surprise awaited us. After checking out of the airport, dozens of students from International Education Institute, a school where I had been volunteering as a teacher, greeted us with great enthusiasm. They welcomed us at the exit door as hundreds of bystanders eyed us curiously. The well-organized reception overwhelmed us. I felt utterly pleased, motivated, and amazed by their friendliness, kindness, and most courteous compliments. Many of the students who came to meet us in the middle of the night had dressed up very beautifully in Khmer traditional outfits. What a surprise! I thought. They welcomed us with many lovely fresh floral garlands and bouquets of flowers as if we were dignitaries or rock stars. Every one of us was in complete shock. I could see it in their smiles, laughter and enjoyment. Such an extraordinary greeting made me proud of the many students and staff of the school in which I had taught Dr. Hill's principles for nearly a year. The principles do work! What beautiful things and beautiful people we have, I smiled as I thought to myself. Most importantly, they went the extra mile to make these arrangements for us.

Getting out of the airport was a little hectic as we were swarmed by the many unwanted helpers who expected a donation for their service.

Nevertheless, we got into our vehicles and proceeded along Phnom Penh's roads. The capital was busier and more crowded compared to eight years ago. Many more buildings and homes had been erected with no zoning or skyline restrictions. New buildings and dilapidated ones overlooked each other like heaven and hell. Garbage was piled high everywhere. Improvements had been made, but the city had a long way to go. Angkor Watt was not built in a day. It took days, years, and even centuries, I told myself.

We arrived after midnight at the Frangipani Hotel overlooking Mekong River and Khmer Royal Palace. The strange environment, unfamiliar accommodations, anticipation of the conference scheduled for 7 a.m. the next morning, and jet lag caused me to stay up all night. In the blink of an eye the morning came. Roosters crowed from the south side of our hotel and the familiar sound of mopeds and cars woke me up just as I was finally falling asleep.

A minivan was waiting for us in front of the hotel. As we stepped outside and into the van, the scorching April heat blasted me in the face with its intensity. The high temperature and low air pressure gave me a slight headache—my body could not handle the drastic change from New York's 40-degree weather to Phnom Penh's over 100-degree temperatures, barely cooled by the van's ineffective air conditioning. But my excitement and passion about the trip and my colleagues' enthusiasm for Cambodia and the International Conference soon helped me to forget all about the heat and my headache. Everyone seemed cheerful as the driver toured us around Independent Monument on our way to one of the best schools in Cambodia: The Royal School of Administration.

International Conference on Cambodia Science of Success

We arrived to an informal and warm reception hosted by a few high-ranking Cambodian officials. The organizers arranged for us to take our seats on a large red-carpeted stage facing hundreds of well-dressed students and teachers. I recognized a few faces from our Skype seminars. Though I felt physically exhausted from more than 24 hours of traveling, my mental and spiritual powers became stronger than they had been in a very long time. Before the meeting began, beautiful young women in their Khmer costumes and crowns took to the stage below us. The sound of Khmer traditional music and the graceful dance performed by skillful Khmer musicians and dancers filled my heart and soul with joy, and the inspiring classical music, singing, and dancing gave me goose bumps. The sights and sounds brought me back to that critical day—the day of my successful escape.

Sometimes I called it the miraculous escape—the escape millions of victims might have wished they would have attempted before their deaths. What if they all had the same inspiration as I did? Would the fate of the country have changed? What if I did not make the most important decision of my life then? The decision that only took me a fraction of a second? The decision that could end my life instantaneously if I did not succeed? Or the decision that could save my life and the lives of others? One thing is for sure, none of those students and teachers who were staring up at me on stage would have met me or heard what I had to say. I, too, wouldn't have met them or any of the wonderful people who shared the stage with me. I would not have discovered Dr. Hill's book, Think and Grow Rich, which inspired and shaped who I am today and helped me bring his research and teaching to others. I would not have formed a bond and friendship with people I had met at the Napoleon Hill Foundation Leader Certification trip to Ireland and elsewhere. I would not have been able to keep in touch with them via phone calls and Facebook. They would not have made the journey to Cambodia with me and would not have inspired those audience members with their knowledge and life experiences. Moreover, I would not have met or known the grandson of Dr. Hill, Dr. James B. Hill, Mrs. Judy Williamson, and Dr. Don Green. I would not have been able to form a mastermind alliance with Khmer–American and Khmer citizens in

Cambodia under a partnership called PMA Science of Success Cambodia, also known as Cambodia Science of Success. What if I did not escape death row and Cambodia—would someone else have brought those students at the InterEd the idea of "Definiteness of Purpose"? Judging from their eager smiles and glowing eyes, they yearned for more and were happy to see us there.

Just to think, a few weeks after I had escaped my last death row, I stood on top of the sacred mountain of Preah Vihear on the border of Cambodia and Thailand and turned around to look at my country for the last time, promising that one day I would bring something useful to help her grow and stop the pain and suffering of Khmer people. I had planned to revisit my death row site on April 13. I wanted to have my students and colleagues see and experience what I went through. In fact, Taylor expressed in the many phone conversations we had before the trip that he really wanted to see the site where the Khmer Rouge attempted to execute me. What a glorious feeling, to think back to that amazing day of my escape from darkness toward the light.

More gloriously, while the melodic pinpeat music traveled to my ears and the graceful blessing dance moved before my eyes, I knew then that I would be able to bring success principles home to Cambodia. I kept my promise. I had arrived. After teaching the principles online via Skype for many months, I had a chance to meet the many beautiful smiling faces of my students and hundreds of other enthusiastic students who came from many parts of the neighboring cities and provinces. I heard that one of the young women dressed as a man to travel from her village to the city to learn Dr. Hill's principles. What commitment! I felt proud as I looked at all of them. They seemed happy to meet us face-to-face, not just through monitors and digital images.

We had a great gathering throughout the entire program. The conference went well but it went too fast. All of the speakers shared their experiences with more than 200 students and most of our speeches focused on guidance to success. After the day was over, my colleagues,

Neang, and I returned to the hotel to spend the rest of the evening sitting on a rooftop patio, watching the beautiful sights of the Cambodian Royal Palace, Mekong River, and the Phnom Penh skyline. I was struck by how much better the country looked since that horrific time when I, among millions of Cambodians, was forced out at gunpoint on April 19, 1975. That same year, I began my journey to freedom, which left unforgettable scars on the minds, hearts and souls of myself and the entire population of Cambodia.

My Return Home to Kampong Chhnang

April 9 passed too quickly, but April 10 ushered me into another spectacular day. It was a combination of good and bad memories that would stay with me forever—good because I was going to see my place of birth again and bad for my flashbacks to the time when two million innocent people died from one of the worst tragedies in the history of mankind.

Neang, Tom Cunningham, Taylor Tag, Jeremy Rayzor, Dwaine Perry, Ruth Neslo, Suwanna Mitchell and I went to Kampong Chhnang as planned. I wanted to visit my two older sisters who had miraculously survived Cambodia's wars and the Khmer Rouge massacres. I will someday tell their stories of survival. We traveled by two touring buses for about 100 kilometers via National Route 5, a small rough highway connecting the capital city to the northwestern part of Cambodia.

Cambodia's landscape along National Route 5 had changed drastically in 40 years. The long Chroy Changvar bridge linking Phnom Penh and Chroy Changvar island had been reconstructed and a new one was recently built to make it look like a twin bridge. When the Khmer Rouge soldiers forced us out of the capital among some two million evacuees in April 1975, they directed us to walk north on National Route 5 to exit the city. I saw the Chroy Changvar bridge had been badly destroyed, apparently by the Viet Cong force from the early days of the war. During that mass exodus, hundreds of decayed bodies of soldiers lay abandoned on the road, over the sidewalks, and inside the ditches alongside the highway. I saw stiff corpses sitting in their upright positions, being eaten by swarms of maggots and flies. Many residential and commercial buildings were destroyed. Shops were ransacked or looted. Now, 40 years later, the same highway was filled with many types of vehicles: trucks, cars, motorcycles, and bicycles.

Traffic was bustling and nearly impassable. People had constructed buildings, houses, huts, and shops on both sides of the dusty highway. All buildings were covered with brownish powder and piles of trash could be seen scattered between the houses. It appeared the trash had not been collected for days. It made me more appreciative of New York where people cared deeply about the environment. American people lived spaciously and freely from dust and garbage. I glanced at Tom and Taylor quickly and noticed they were looking out at the many unorganized buildings lined up on the right side of the highway. I wondered what they were thinking about Cambodia.

Suddenly, Neang was trembling and screaming, "Oh God!" She turned quickly away from the window. I looked over to see a traffic accident and a person lying in a pool of blood. We could not hear any sounds from inside the insulated bus. Crowds of people encircled the body. In America, an ambulance, police cars, and other authorities would be at the scene right away. A helicopter would whirl over the traffic jam to take the critically injured person to the nearest hospital. People would be told to back off, the area would be sealed, and the body would be covered up if the person had died. Ambulance, hospital, skilled paramedics, skilled doctors, and a professional police force were hard to come by in Cambodia. Bicycles, motorcycle, cars, vans, buses, trucks, and other forms of transportation all shared the same congested road. I tried not to take in the horrific scene and focus on the negative aspects of this developing country.

The traffic still moved slowly. I maintained my positive thoughts of arriving on time for the ceremony. It felt so surreal for me to travel on the same road in a different time. This time it was 40 years later and I had a chance to experience my journey again. The bus crept along, reaching the area of the road where I had wanted to give up my pursuit of freedom. I had seen many people die from gunshots, sickness, and diseases along both sides of that same area when we evacuated. I, too, became severely sick and thought my life was going to end. What if it did end? Then, like I had imagined before, I would not have met my students and they would not have met the talented people on the bus whom I befriended and brought with me to guide and inspire them.

After being caught in traffic for about 30 minutes, our buses reached the true countryside. I did not see the dense forests I used to enjoy when I was young. The ground had turned grayish, desolate, unorganized, and and in need of cleaning and proper care. I imagined one day Cambodians could turn Cambodia into one of the most beautiful countries if they could make the environment clean and green as it was during my childhood years. However, in the 1970s during the raging war, rubble from buildings damaged by the many gun battles, hundreds of trenches surrounded by sandbags, and giant bomb craters could be seen along both sides of the highway. By 1973, the Khmer Rouge rebels cut nearly all highways including Route 5 into many pieces. They mobilized people from the villages to physically dig out many large portions of the highway in order to prevent the government force from moving to and from the northwestern part of Cambodia. They cut off the roadway connection between Kampong Chhnang and Phnom Penh for many months until the country fell into communist hands. I only made it to Phnom Penh to study and find work thanks to a Cambodian military pilot who accepted my small payoff and allowed me to fly with his screeching pigs. What if I could not have gone to the capital at that time? Where would I be now? What would I have become?

While I gazed through the window daydreaming, I could hear Dr. Sorn talking on his loudspeaker. He informed us about Cambodia's history—a long, historical background of my hometown when, many years ago, Cambodians from my district revolted against the French. I recalled my late father, God rest his soul, telling me quite often about his and his friends' involvements during an incident in the mid-1920s. My father died mysteriously from food poisoning in the wilderness in 1972, during the Cambodian war of 1970 to 1975. He, my mother, and siblings left our village of O Ta Sek as American bombs obliterated it. The devastation forced everyone in our village to seek shelter away from the battlefields. My mother returned my father's ashes to Watt Trapaing Teuk Trachak or the Cold Pond Temple, a Buddhist monastery that he helped build in the 1960s. I found out about my father's death later in 1973. I never had a chance to return home to see my family members or my birthplace again after I left for Phnom Penh.

The Cold Pond Pagoda

My sisters and my relatives had prearranged to have my homecoming reception ceremony done at the Cold Pond Temple. I couldn't be more excited because one of my wishes during the April trip was to take my friends and colleagues, as well as my students, to visit my birth village and to see some particular places and learn more about my story and the history of Cambodia. Many of them wanted to know more about the success of my journey after facing unimaginable obstacles while leaving Cambodia and entering Thailand over four months—a brief story I co-authored in a bestselling book titled Adversity to Advantage. It was thanks to Dr. Sorn and the InterEd staff for arranging for all of us to visit the Cold Pond Temple one day after we had successfully finished the International Conference on Cambodia Science of Success. He appropriately turned our trip into an educational journey where all postgraduate students at InterEd could discover more about Cambodia's Kampong Chhnang—a province located 90 miles north of the capital.

As our buses reached a red dirt road leading to the temple on the right side of Route 5, I saw a small four-door sedan police car waiting there to lead us to the temple. I was informed that some provincial officials had also arrived to participate in the homecoming reception ceremony. My heart began to race rapidly and excitement surged inside of me. My childhood memories returned as I saw some familiar landmarks. I tried to conceal my feelings by joking about the bouncy dirt road, but deep inside of me I felt as if I had traveled back in time when my family was together and living our lives in peace. I could imagine my father riding on an oxcart teaching me Khmer history and Buddhist morality. I could hear the sound of my mother's morning wake-up call asking us to get ready for school. I could feel the love of my four sisters when they used to give me piggyback rides to and from school and I could smell the April sun scorching the dry earth. The dirt road also reminded me of the devastation from the many gun battles between Cambodian armed forces that fought against each other and against the Viet Cong and North Vietnamese.

On my left was a hill with a few huge stones resting on top called Phnom Deurm Phka. In the early 1970s, the hill represented one of the few higher grounds controlled by Cambodian government forces who had launched their artillery attacks on the Khmer Rouge rebels in the nearby areas on regular basis. The tug of war between the government and the rebel forces caused my parents' village of O Ta Sek, including their own home, to be completely destroyed by an American air raid. Survivors ran to the wilderness, far away from the artillery range. My mother and sister were trapped for hours inside a trench that had been buried by a huge bomb explosion dropped by an F-111 less than 100 feet away from our home. Although some landmarks remained untouched, the rest of the environment had been transformed. I did not recognize much of the new landscape along the dirt road because all of the thick forests had been cut down. I just hoped the new sight would not totally erase my childhood memories.

Somewhere in the area alongside the dirt road, the Khmer Rouge soldiers used the location to execute their enemies: those who were seen as traitors for being on the side of the American-backed government or those who were educated. Several mass graves filled with the countless skulls of Khmer Rouge victims were found in the white sandy areas alongside the dirt road. After the Khmer Rouge won the war on April 17, 1975, they evacuated the residents from the capital. My Uncle Say's family, who I was staying with at the time, and I did not leave until the next day. They directed us to return to our original hometown. Thanks to the universe and my decision to seek freedom rather than returning home during that time, I was spared from torture and execution. What if I had returned home then? One of the skulls could have been mine. Any person who knowingly worked for the Cambodian government or was considered an intellectual such as a teacher or student would be executed. My skin crawled when I thought about the mass graves nearby. I found myself in the reverie of my past as I relayed to my friends and colleagues the stories of my birthplace.

The bumpy bus ride didn't bother anyone as I had feared. Everyone still wore their cheerful faces since leaving the city. We finally arrived at the temple in the late morning, taking more than two hours to travel from Phnom Penh. But the long, bouncy ride began to pay off when we heard the rhythms of Cambodian folk dance and traditional music fill the air. The folklore band made up of a group wearing different costumes and amusing and exaggerated facial masks, as the Khmer New Year's symbol, greeted us at the entrance to the temple. My heart beat faster as I looked out the window, seeing them dancing at the large gate of the temple. Everyone else on the bus seemed to be thrilled too.

Completely overjoyed during these moments, I forgot about the unusual heat wave. You could crack open an egg on a rock and it would sizzle. I could feel the extreme heat as we stepped down from the bus. It forever reminded me about the mass exodus ordered by the victorious Khmer Rouge many years ago. April 1975 and April 2016 differed like day and night. In 1975, the Khmer Rouge humiliated us and kicked us out of our home at gunpoint, and in 2016 I was welcomed home in style. This time I returned home with nearly 100 friends and colleagues riding in two big beautiful air-conditioned buses and several other vehicles. They consisted mostly of my Cambodia Science of Success students at the International Education Institute led by Dr. Sorn, the president of InterEd, and his family members. Dr. Sorn was the one who helped arrange the trip and kept everyone on the bus well informed about the history of Kampong Chhnang.

I felt motivated by my friends—Napoleon Hill Certified Instructors and others—and the InterEd students who came along. They were my hope to help open the Cambodia Science of Success program, a program that can help many Cambodians become self-reliant and achieve personal growth.

As we approached the temple grounds, I heard the folk music getting louder. Beautiful multicolor Buddhist flags were flying on and around a huge and beautiful gate carved with Khmer artwork. Several hundred people were waiting for us inside the temple. Many adults and children lined up on both sides of the entrance. They joined the traditional dancers in singing and clapping to welcome their national and international guests. I smiled with delight upon seeing everyone on the buses looking as happy and excited as I was. Wearing his bright green neon shirt and blue Khmer krama (checkered scarf), Tom Cunningham limped toward a young policeman standing in uniform to say hello. Jeremy Rayzor sported his blue-checkered shirt and checkered scarf, Taylor Tagg was dressed in his bright, short-sleeved, red chemise with blue scarf hanging around his neck as well, and Dwaine Perry wore his relaxed Native American shirt. They were the biggest and tallest men among the crowd. They looked very comfortable with the people and appeared to enjoy the gathering as well. They strolled along the white sandy pathway, taking pictures. Meanwhile Ruth Neslo and Suwanna Mitchell joined students from Phnom Penh to dance along the causeway to the rhythm of the Cambodian folk dance called Chhyamm. Neang and I followed Dr. Sorn and his wife to greet everyone at the gate. We shook hands and hugged as many people as we could. It was one of the most joyful festivities I have ever experienced, primarily because I was witnessing genuinely happy people who came together to help celebrate my homecoming.

I scanned the large crowd standing under the shade of a sizable mango tree, looking for the most important people I wanted to meet—my two sisters as well as the people I knew from the past. I didn't recognize any of them. I believe the adults I used to know years ago had either grown too old for me to recognize or had passed on. When Neang and I reached the gathering, the people stretched out their hands to us. One of them was my older sister, Salom. I hugged and held her briefly for fear I could not contain my tears. Then minutes later I saw my other sister, Sen, who due to her shortness and small size, was hidden behind other people I couldn't identify. I noticed that both of my sisters appeared much older than I had expected since seeing them in 2008. Like many people who gathered around us, they looked frail and weak.

Decades after the war, I could still see scars from past atrocities in their facial expressions and emotions. I could feel and see the suffering in their eyes and in their frail and deformed bodies. My oldest sister, Sen, who stood five feet tall, was limping back and forth. My other sister, Salom, much taller, was very weak and thin as a rail. If a strong wind were to blow against her, she would fall. Fighting through the crowds to reach me, they finally got to hold me and hug me for the first time in eight years. Both of them were trying to hug and comfort me as they did when we were much younger. I could not stay close to them for long. So many emotions rushed through me and I could not fight my tears. After some 50 years later, the condition of my sisters, the villagers, and many of their children was no better than that of the 1950s and 1960s.

Under extreme heat from the scorching sun and earth, there stood many small children lined up to greet us. I saw awe in their cute faces.

They probably had never seen touring buses with nearly 100 strangers, including foreigners, arriving to visit their village. They reminded me of myself when I was their age. I, too, was shocked to see outsiders and modern vehicles coming into my village. For my two sisters and me, I remembered our good times together when I was a little boy walking on winding pathways though the jungles for many kilometers to the elementary school. They used to shield me from the rain and hot sun. As I looked at them during the reception ceremony, from the beginning to the end, I felt as if someone had stuck a dagger in my chest. I wanted them to be strong and healthy. The only feeling that kept me inspired was their happiness. They smiled. They were definitely happy to see me and also seemed proud to see me bringing two busloads of people to help celebrate in our village and in the temple that our late father helped build many years ago.

Time did not permit us to stay together long, just like the space in this chapter does not permit me to write more about the rest of my homecoming trip. My journey back home brought me so many good, bad and sad memories. However, before I say goodbye to you, my readers, I want to share the part that affected me the most during the entire fantastic voyage to my past.

The Glass Chamber

When we returned to Phnom Penh on April 11, we visited the most heart-wrenching site: Tuol Sleng Genocide Museum. The stifling heat had reached 105 degrees. My body was dehydrated from sweating, and I constantly drank water to keep my body cooled and my throat from becoming parched. The heat and hot air inside the small building that the Khmer Rouge had used as a torture center caused throbbing pain inside both of my temples. It was so hot that I did not know if I had a fever. My head hurt and my heart raced as I looked at the many haunting pictures of hundreds of prisoners who were tortured and killed inside a school compound known as Tuol Sleng. I looked at the black and white headshots of terrorized victims and saw them looking back at me with hopelessness, despair, and physical, emotional, and spiritual pain. They were on their own. No one came to rescue them. They reminded me of the many faces of innocent people who were lined up on death row with me when the Khmer Rouge sent us to be executed in 1975. Many people believe the Vietnamese orchestrated the massacres in disguise. Whatever the case might have been, millions had died during more than 10 years of fierce fighting from 1970 to 1980.

Ruth, Suwanna, Taylor, Jeremy, Dwaine, Neang, and I were accompanied by a couple of local Cambodian guides as we ventured into the museum to learn about the torture and killing of millions of innocent Cambodians. Tom had opted out to avoid the emotional stress caused by witnessing the devastation of Cambodian lives. It turned out that Tom was right. The sight alone could trigger nightmares. After viewing how Cambodians were brutalized and slaughtered by the Khmer Rouge, most of us could no longer stomach the scene. I caught Ruth, Suwanna, and Neang weeping under the shade of a tree just outside of the rooms that contained hundreds of pictures, bones, and skulls. Taylor and I stood silently on the verge of tears inside a room where the bones and skull were stockpiled inside a glass chamber. I swallowed my tears. We prayed for all lives: dead, injured, and living ones. Taylor offered his condolences: "We pray for the lost souls here and offer condolences and love for all involved. Forgiveness is the key to health for living. Let us remember the sacrifices our brothers and sisters have made by living this example. Let us pray and live in peace." I read his card after he left the room. I was about to break down in tears myself.

I remembered the rainy day when I was slated to be executed. I was reliving that moment, the moment that helped shape my past and future. It taught me about having faith in the higher power and faith in myself. The moment when a quick decision was made after some facts were mysteriously given and considered. A moment that could result in me either standing outside of the glass chamber, sobbing, or being among the other skulls. All I could write on the back of one of the many condolence cards, hung on a handmade wooden tree inside the prison on April 11, 2016, was to ask those souls to help save and heal the living Khmer people through LOVE: "May your souls return to engrave in Khmer heart and soul and make us love one another forever!" Thank God. My skull is not here! I thought to myself. What IF I hadn't escaped?

My full memoir, the first of the Blue Horizon Trilogy, will be finished this year. Please be on the lookout for it. May you and your family be blessed with freedom, knowledge, love, health, and wealth. Thank you.

Timothy Chhim

BIO

Timothy Chhim is a motivational speaker, best-selling author, Napoleon Hill Foundation Certified Instructor and licensee. He is the owner of an Allstate Insurance Agency in Nanuet, New York. He was born into an impoverish family in Kampong Chhnang, Cambodia. From a young age he has always dreamed of freedom and strived for a better life for himself and his countrymen. Tragically, the Vietnam War spread into Cambodia, forcing its leaders to take sides and the people to be divided. The battle between communism and capitalism raged on from 1970 to 1975. Devastatingly, the former won. Timothy became one of the millions of people who were forced out of Cambodia's capital at gunpoint by the Khmer Rouge on April 17, 1975. After several screening processes, Timothy was singled out as an educated citizen and as a Khmer Republic official. He was slated to be executed in the jungle among more than 70 people.

Timothy's desire for freedom emboldened him. Believing in his destiny to achieve greatness for his family and countrymen, as foretold by a seer, he decided to escape the Khmer Rouge's death row by jumping out, zigzagging, and dodging many rounds of bullets to make his way toward the dense forest. Timothy escaped his execution two more times before he journeyed for a few weeks through the jungle that teemed with human predators, dangerous animals and landmines. He finally reached Thailand on August 18, 1975—4 months after his evacuation from Phnom Penh.

Father Arthur Pedersen of Grace Church, Jersey City, N.J. sponsored Timothy and his wife Neang to New Jersey in October 1976.

Timothy Chhim can be reached at 845-642-3232 or at Timothychhim@aol.com

LIFE'S MAIN IDEA

By: Jeremy Rayzor

Let your heart be your path and your mind be your guide.

We were taught in Elementary School how to find the main idea in a story. This could be a challenge because it requires some critical thinking to understand it at first. In retrospect, most individuals are not taught in school about how and why one must find their life's main idea. We may have only been asked... "What do you want to be when you grow up?" Others may have been born into a family who has acquired generations of experience in a certain profession and they may be greatly influenced by the family to follow the same path, even though they may not prefer it. Fortunately, many others and I have learned about this important discovery for one's life because we have studied Dr. Napoleon Hill's 17 Principles of Success. The main idea of this life is to enjoy it by discovering and pursuing your Definiteness of Purpose, Dr. Hill's first principle of success.

Dr. Hill teaches us through his writings that the lack of having a Definite Purpose, also known as a Definite Chief Aim, means a person is merely drifting throughout their life without a specific purpose or aim. Defining a Definite Purpose is a major challenge for most people. This may be either due to their unawareness of the principle or because they have not devoted the time and contemplation that is necessary for discovering their purpose. As a brief example: My purpose is to live my life in the direction of my heart's desire. This desire is creating a source of revenue and happiness for my family. This desire is pursued with the guidance of my mind and my passion for educating through the value of play.

An individual is certainly fortunate who has discovered their purpose early in life but it is never too late for a person to define or rediscover their purpose, at any time during their life. Dr. Hill says that after many years of experience and responsibility, individuals usually realize their purpose after 40 or 50 years of age. This may be because they have worked many jobs or have changed professions due to their unhappiness in their previous work. An undiscovered purpose is most commonly due to the fear of failure in a venture they only wish they would pursue. What is missing is they have not found or followed their passion yet, a labor of love for their time. An individual's passion could be a combination of parenting, teaching, business, writing, inventing, art, and/or any other creative work that fulfills their purpose.

The realization of a Definite Purpose is how that person continues to feel fulfilled by doing the work or having such responsibilities over a long period of time. They know there is nothing else they would rather be doing with their life. They see many obstacles and responsibility ahead of them but this does not stop them. Why? Because their desire for expression and recognition for their passion is greater than the struggles they may face.

The Everlasting Reward

My childhood took place in the City of East Chicago, Indiana. This area is a rough neighborhood due to gang violence and drugs. My brothers Jeff, Jason, and I had the gift of having loving and supportive parents. Because we had a strong home life we stayed away from gangs. In the late 1980's gang violence in the area was increasing. During this time, my twin brother Jason and I were in elementary school and Jeff had graduated from high school. Because Jason and I are twins we went everywhere together and we liked doing the same things. If you saw one of us you saw the other. We had to stick together to protect and watch after each other, due to bullying and the violence around us.

During our freshman year at East Chicago Central High School, I decided to visit the school's swimming pool to see if I should join the swim team. The next day, while walking in the halls of the school I crossed paths with the team captain Jon Meyers. He encouraged me to try out for the team. Later we would become close friends. Soon after, my brother Jason and I joined the swim team together, which was one of the best choices and commitments we made during high school.

Even though swimming was not a very popular sport at our school, we loved the E.C. Shark's team spirit that we built together with our friends on the team. During the freshman year season my coach and friend Jason Schwenk showed great confidence in me. He believed I could set a new school record in the 200 yard Freestyle (8 swimming laps) which was such a high goal for me to attempt. I believed in his faith in me which helped me to believe in myself. I am grateful for my friends and family who also encouraged me.

With applied faith I strived for this monumental goal. After three years of intense practice and hard work I was getting closer but not close enough. At the end of my junior year I still needed to drop 10 seconds (Not easy to do!) to break the school record. I was determined to set the new record during my senior year even though I was not aware, at the time, of Napoleon Hill's powerful quote "What the mind can conceive and believe the mind can achieve." Before my final swim season started, I was struck by adversity. I badly injured my right knee playing tackle football with my friends at the park and could not bend or walk on it. This was a poor decision on my part.

I felt a horrible feeling that my dream of breaking the school record was over when I was told by my doctor that I needed surgery. I firmly decided to postpone the knee surgery until after the swim season. The doctor's optimistic response was that swimming would be great therapy for my knee. I was young and had a goal in mind, to break the school record. The odds were high that I would either possibly further the damage to my knee or not recover enough so I had very little chance of accomplishing my goal. I refused to quit even though I knew it was not a safe decision.

I had to practice twice as hard to make up for the power I had when using my right leg. This required a high level of self-discipline. I had to build the power of my left leg to push off the starting block and off every flip-turn, remembering to use only one leg. After lots of practice, the end of the season approached. I swam my personal best time two days before my last high school swimming race. After practicing hard all season, I dropped only 3 seconds off my best time. I was disappointed because I was only able to drop my fastest time to 7 seconds away from the record. I only had one chance left and it was in two days.

I remember the night before the last chance. I recall laying in my bed visualizing the race over and over in my mind and finishing the race strong. I felt the excitement of accomplishing my long endured and sought-after goal and that is exactly what I did, breaking the school record by half a second and that record still stands today. I was ecstatic! Knowing that I was able to accomplish what I set my mind to, against great odds, was an everlasting reward.

How I realized and pursued my purpose

While growing up in East Chicago my family liked to play tabletop games together. We played some of the classics board games like Sorry, Monopoly, Scrabble and many other types of games. I also liked to play card games with my brothers and friends. Activities like this kept us entertained at home and not playing so much around the neighborhood, as this could become dangerous. As I grew older this type of entertainment stuck with me. I realized many benefits beyond just having fun playing games. It was also a way to develop strategy skills, decision-making, learning from the consequences of decisions, and interacting face to face with one another.

During the end of my senior year of high school my brother Jason and I were playing with a deck of playing cards. I thought about how amazing it would be to create our own rules for a new game so we created a game called "Switch-Up". We had fun playing this new game with our friends and family. This was when I realized the passion I had for creating entertainment for other people's enjoyment and relaxation. Soon after, I created several other games with playing cards. This became a fascination of mine. I soon realized that I needed to design my own cards but did not know how to do it at that time.

My brother and I attended Vincennes University in Southern Indiana after graduating high school in 2000. I became a certified welder, machinist and then completed an Associate's Degree in Applied Science, majoring in Tool and Die Making. During college I made a great decision to take an elective course in Graphic Design to learn how to use Adobe Programs. Because of this single decision I was now able to convert my game ideas into playable prototypes, leading me to the next level of game inventing. After the first prototype I made I decided to submit it to a game agent who represents several ideas from about a thousand submissions a year from around the world. This agent only presents concepts they feel would be great for the largest game companies in the industry. Unfortunately, my idea was not selected which was heartbreaking to me but, I did not give up on this passion of mine.

After this temporary defeat, I began thinking about starting my own company but I did not know how to start a new business. Everyone I knew at the time had no experience in starting a business. The year before graduating college in 2004, I acquired a summer job where I worked an internship at a machine shop owned by a family operating in Chicago Heights, Illinois. Because I demonstrated such great work ethic that summer, the company wanted me back fulltime after college. I happily accepted the job at a good hourly wage and went to work as a welder and machinist after graduation. At the same time, I continued thinking about my passion for creating games and dreaming of having my own family business. Not a machine shop... but my own game business.

Burning the bridges behind me

"Definiteness of decision always requires courage, sometimes very great courage. "
  - Napoleon Hill

While working at the machine shop I conceived a new game idea and wrote it down. This idea would become a game I named "Paper Football®" card game. Soon I attended a night class to learn how to become incorporated and co-founded a family business with my parents in 2005, which we named Rayzor Sharp Entertainment, Inc. After working for several months at the machine shop, I became very unhappy with where my life was headed. I realized that I was not satisfied with working overtime in a machine shop for the rest of my life. It was a good job, but I knew it would not fulfill my life because it was not my passion. Therefore, my "Paper Football®" Card Game would become the first game Rayzor Sharp Entertainment, Inc. would self-publish.

Then I made the biggest decision of my life to follow my passion, my purpose as a game inventor. I had to burn the bridges behind me so I gave my boss three weeks' notice. During our discussion, his last words to me were... "When you become a successful business owner I would like to invest in your company". I was 23 years old at the time when I made that courageous decision. When my parents found out that day my mother was upset and my father was surprised! Shortly after meeting with several occasions of temporary defeat, I tried contacting my previous boss to request my position back. I was fortunate that he never replied.

Now I had to find work that would also allow time for me to work on my business. So I became a part time substitute teacher in two school districts for the next two years, with the School City of East Chicago and School City of Whiting, Indiana. This was when I realized I also loved to teach. One day, I taught a classroom which I attended when I was young, at Westside Junior High School. This day would become a turning point towards my perspective for inventing games. I was teaching a math assignment and a student said, "Why do we need to do so much math!". After explaining to the students how important math is for our life, I suddenly received a new Idea. I should take on the challenge of inventing a math game that students would find fun. At the same time, they would also be practicing their math skills. At that time in the classroom, I scribbled an Idea, which would become my next game, which I named "Math Wiz" (also called Spiral Math®) the puzzle card game. On that day I planted a thought that would soon define my personal mission of "Educating through the value of play."

One fateful day during 2004 I received an unexpected call from my friend Rennie Rivera. We had known each other since middle school. He called to encourage me to read Napoleon Hill's book "Think and Grow Rich". When I read the book, I thought there should be a fun way to engage this remarkable philosophy with family and friends of different ages. This was the beginning of an educational game idea that I would name "Achievus®" The Napoleon Hill Cooperative Board Game. Playing Achievus instills the success principles through repetition and communication of the philosophy. While playing, players are working together to achieve a common goal. It reinforces the premise that the most important individuals closest to you should also understand success principles if you want to be positively supported and influenced by them. Later I became a Napoleon Hill Foundation Certified Instructor and invented a new card game called "Ticket to Wealth®" 100% Pure Mental Gold. This Napoleon Hill Leadership card game provides 100 multiple-choice challenges to learn, review, and apply the knowledge necessary to find happiness and prosperity.

To live for passion it takes action

Beyond all the decisions I have made up until this day, I now ask myself... WHAT IF I did not make the choices I made to follow my passion? I certainly would not have had the privilege to become friends with wonderful Napoleon Hill Foundation Certified Instructors and Students from around the world. I would not have had the thrilling experiences of traveling to 11 countries. This year I would not be traveling to the country of Cambodia to pursue my purpose of educating through the value of play. The educational games that I have created would not exist. I may still have been working at the machine shop but that was not a choice I was willing to live with.

Written in Napoleon Hill's book "Think and Grow Rich" he declares... "Indecision is a habit that usually begins in youth. The habit takes on permanency as the youth goes through grade school, high school, and even through college, without definiteness of purpose. The habit of indecision goes with the student into the occupation he chooses... If in fact, he does choose his occupation. Generally, the youth just out of school seeks any job that can be found. He takes the first place he finds, because he has fallen into the habit of indecision. Ninety-eight out of every hundred people working for wages today are in the positions they hold because they lacked the definiteness of decision to plan a definite position, and the knowledge of how to choose an employer."

I have learned firsthand that choices followed by action make the biggest difference in the journey of our life. The fundamentals of following one's passion and purpose in life are the same for everyone. I firmly believe the fundamentals are learned through studying and applying the 17 Principles of Success. I wonder where my journey will take me next and the friends I will meet along the way. Do not allow indecision to hold you back... apply your courage! The life that you experience is made from your own thoughts and decisions. What decisions will you make from this day forward?

BIO

JEREMY RAYZOR is a Napoleon Hill Foundation Certified Instructor. He has been recognized as a VIP member of The Cambridge Who's Who Registry of Executives, Professionals and Entrepreneurs. Mr. Rayzor is a passionate inventor of unique card and board games that educate through the value of play. He believes in family entertainment that encourages face-to-face communication. He is the inventor of "PrisMix®" a card game which players mix and match 12 prismatic colors to score points with prisms, "Math Wiz" (also called Spiral Math®) a puzzle card game which encourages practicing mental arithmetic in a fun approach, "Paper Football®" card game which players use strategic thinking and math skills, "Achievus®" a cooperative board game of positive interaction which offers a fun way to learn and review Napoleon Hill's 17 Principles of Success, and "Ticket to Wealth®" 100% Pure Mental Gold... a Napoleon Hill Leadership Card Game that provides 100 challenges to learn, review, and apply the knowledge necessary to earn the wealth of happiness and prosperity. Mr. Rayzor is the co-founder of Rayzor Sharp Entertainment, Inc. The mission of his business is "Educating through the value of play!" under the slogan, "Don't Be DULL! Be Rayzor Sharp!"

You may connect with Mr. Rayzor on LinkedIn and Facebook by first introducing yourself by sending him an email to jrrayzor@rayzorsharpent.com

Visit his company website at www.RayzorSharpEnt.com

OBSESSUCCESS
By: Paul Hatcher

The concept of having a definite major purpose for your life is nothing new. In fact, there have been volumes written throughout history stating that the starting point of all accomplishment begins with a definitive purpose.

I have known many people who have written out a specific, measurable, realistic goal. They have set a timeline to accomplish the goal and set up accountability partners to help them to achieve their stated purpose. Even though these people had great intentions, followed the steps, and were committed, they missed the mark. We find that the path to achievement is littered with countless failures. Something is missing.

Consider that as of 2015 the United States of America had a population of 321,442,019 and every year approximately 45% or almost 150 million people choose to make a New Year's resolution to accomplish some type of goal in the upcoming year. Consider also that of the 150 million who desire some type of resolution only 8% actually keep the resolution for the entire year.

The numbers are staggering. Ask yourself this question, "Why is it that such a small few achieve their desired goal, while the vast majority of others fall by the wayside and are washed away by the waves of this life?" Today is the day we answer that question.

Is there a word, a concept, or power that could serve as the catalyst to assist people in achieving their definite life purpose? Is there a process that they could turn to after they have attempted over and over again to achieve their definite aim but have continually come up short?

Let me introduce you to a new way of thinking, a new philosophy of achievement to help you achieve your definite major purpose in life.

You have never heard or seen this word until now and it is Obsessuccess.

Obsesuccess is exactly what is says, obsess and success.

These two words connect to form one word that is truly powerful. This word is not a secret but has been hidden in the shadows from the average man and woman. When someone makes its discovery and follows the philosophy they accomplish their definitive purpose for their life.

Here are just a few examples of men and women from all ethnic, religious and social-economic backgrounds, discovered this philosophy and achieved their definite life purpose.

In the Jewish Torah and the Muslim History of Prophets and Kings the story is told about a man named Nimrod. He is described as a great and mighty man on the earth. He was a skilled hunter and builder. Many stories abound about this man, in many historical and religious texts, but there is one significant thing that stands out about him, and that is the fact that he became obsessed with uniting the people of earth and building a tower that reached to the heavens to prove his power and authority. The interesting thing about this story is that when the Creator of the Universe spoke about Nimrod and the people and the tower they were building, He responded by saying, "Now nothing will be restrained from them, which they have imagined to do." In other words, the Creator is saying, when one has an idea in his mind and makes a decision to achieve it, becomes obsessed with it, believes it and applies discipline, nothing can stop him from achieving his purpose.

Over 2500 years ago a royal family in Nepal reigned over a small kingdom. The queen of that kingdom was named Maya Devi. She had a dream that a white elephant descended from heaven and entered her womb. The elephant shared with her that she would conceive a child who was pure and enlightened. When her time had come, she gave birth but instead of experiencing pain she experienced a vision where the gods took the child from her and gave him honor. The king and queen named this baby boy, Siddhartha. Today, he is better known as the Buddha Shakyamuni, the founder of the Buddhist religion. The man who would change the world through his practicing and teaching, made a decision, he became obsessed with it, he strongly believed it and utilized discipline to achieve his purpose. To this very day, you can see his definite chief aim throughout the world.

It was 336 B.C. when a 20-year-old Alexander III Philippou Makedonon became the king of Macedon. He would go on to become one of the greatest military commanders the world has ever known. When you study the short life of Alexander the Great, it is easy to see how was he able to use Obsessuccess to conquer the known world. He determined that his destiny was to become the emperor of the world and he believed it so strongly that it consumed his every thought. He took disciplined action, persisted onward, and sacrificed everything to dominate the world. When he believed he had achieved his obsession, he wept because there were no more lands for him to conquer.

If you ever travel to Italy, you will most likely go to Rome and Florence and see the work of Il Divino "the divine one", Michelangelo, arguably the greatest artist of all time. His work ethic and persistence is legendary. He would sleep in his clothes and boots when working on a project. He would eat and drink discriminately. He took pain staking lengths to ensure his work was done to perfection. He was completely obsessed and his obsession, belief and discipline provided us with the famous sculptures of David, the Pieta, the Sistine Chapel ceiling, St. Peter's Basilica and many other priceless works of art.

On February 21, 1848 the world was moved by the published writing of Karl Marx. His Communist Manifesto and written philosophy laid the foundation for modern sociology, social science, economics and progressivism. Marx died in 1883 after making a decision to live his entire life in a zealous struggle to change the world's social landscape. He believed in that change, and disciplined himself toward that end. Although he did not live to see the impact his writings had on the world, they have become ingrained in society and their merits and inferiorities are taught in universities around the world.

Harriet Tubman is an icon. She not only escaped slavery but also made it her life's mission to help others do the same. During her life she battled poverty, sickness, slavery, and inequality for women. One of the most powerful things about her life was her faith. She truly believed that all should be free, and that belief helped her to take disciplined action and overcome adversity. Whether she was being beaten, fighting illness, escaping slavery, risking her own life while freeing others, or standing up for what was right, she never wavered from her decision. Over a period of 11 years she led 70 slaves to freedom. Her entire life is an example of someone who was obsessed with her mission of equality and civil rights and sacrificed to ensure that her belief became a reality.

Brigham Young became the President of the Church of the Latter Day Saints and established Salt Lake City. He became the first governor of the territory and founded the University bearing his name. His vision included building new roads, creating and funding public welfare, establishing a militia and building new Temples across Utah along with the Salt Lake Temple that stands today. His decision to grow the Church of the Latter Day Saints became his ultimate obsession and he believed it would happen. His disciplined action, persistence, and sacrifice continues to echo through the world today through the Mormon's teachings and missions.

Thomas Edison may be the greatest inventor to have ever lived. Consider that when you walk into a room and flip the switch that provides light, that it was one man's decision, belief and disciplined action, sacrifice and persistence that made that happen. He failed over

10,000 times in experiment after experiment while trying to create the incandescent light. Though he failed over and over, he did not quit. He believed, and then disciplined his action even more. He was obsessed with discovering the incandescent light, and finally, he did. When asked about his 10,000 failures, he said, "I did not fail, I simply discovered 9,999 ways that do not work."

Marie Curie was a pioneer in the field of science. She overcame extreme poverty, worked her way through school and was dedicated to completing her education. She made her decision to persist regardless of the gender inequality of the day and became the first woman to receive a doctorate degree in France. She relentlessly studied uranium, its effects and radioactivity and because of her exemplary work in the field of physics she was the first woman to be awarded a Nobel Prize. She not only received the award for her work in physics, but she won the Nobel Prize again for her work in the field of chemistry by discovering the elements radium and polonium. She was the first person to ever win two Nobel prizes.

What does it take to overcome an empire? It takes a magnificent decision, a powerful belief, and a disciplined will. Mahatma Gandhi had all three. He led his nation to independence with a non-violent overthrow of an oppressor and did it without an army. He unified factions within his country through his message of peace and humanitarianism. He is remembered as an iconic leader, who exhibited incredible self-discipline, tolerance and influence. Gandhi's impact on the world and its leaders has been widely shared from Martin Luther King to Nelson Mandela to Barak Obama. Albert Einstein said that he was a "role model for the generations to come."

One man with one dream can change the world and that is exactly what the Reverend Martin Luther King, Jr. did with his life as a civil rights leader. He became a voice for all who had been mistreated just because of someone's color of skin. He led the equality movement and paid the ultimate price for his decision, his beliefs and disciplined convictions. His "I Have a Dream" speech that he gave in 1963 will be remembered and honored forever. Martin Luther King Jr. was killed by an assassin's bullet on April 4th, 1963, but his legacy is an undeniable one and he is one of the greatest leaders of all time. He is an icon, and his obsession for equality for all races and religions, and his consistent belief that it would happen, has impacted the world to this day and will continue to impact generations to come.

There is a mountain of evidence that Jesus Christ of Nazareth was born approximately 2000 years ago in a small town in Israel named Bethlehem. Most religious and secular scholars agree that He suffered a terrible death by crucifixion. Ancient writings say that Jesus claimed He was the Son of God and that He was sent to sacrifice Himself for the world. During His brief ministry of three years, He impacted the world unlike any other before or after Him. He utilized the Obsessuccess philosophy to achieve his definite chief purpose by making a decision to die for the world. His teachings on faith established the foundation for how we are to control our thoughts and beliefs. He took disciplined action to reach his purpose, persisted towards that purpose even though He was constantly persecuted, and made the ultimate sacrifice to accomplish His definite chief aim. His life is the ultimate model of this philosophy.

At this point, you may or may not recognize the people that I have presented to you, but regardless, each of them discovered Obsessuccess and achieved what they set out to accomplish in their life.

So, what is it that you want?

What is the true desire of your heart?

What is the definite purpose that you want to achieve in this life?

You get to decide. It is your choice. It is your decision. What is it that you REALLY want to accomplish? No limits. No boundaries. What do you want?

Obessuccess is a philosophy of achievement that is based on this decision that only you can make for your life.

Your ability to make this all-important decision is your greatest power.

First you must decide. Once you decide exactly what your definite chief purpose is for your life, you must desire it, but not just a normal desire. This desire is rooted in much more than just a thought or a wanting.

Obsessuccess is about an all-encompassing must. Your body must have food, water and air or it will die. In the same way your body must have these necessities to live, you must have your definite purpose, your Obsessuccess, or you will not be able to survive. There is no other option. You must achieve your decision.

Do not be like the masses of those who have great intentions but never achieve.

Follow the examples of the people you just read about and make the decision now. Do not wait. Do not put off the decision any longer. Decide what your definite life purpose is right now.

After making your choice, the next step is that you must believe. Belief is another term for faith and your faith must be strong. Jesus said, "If you have the belief (faith) of a mustard seed you can move mountains." Believing you are going to achieve your decision is critical.

You must keep all negativity out of your beliefs. The words "no", "can't", "won't" and the like cannot be in your belief system. You must believe it will happen. Do not doubt; just believe. The definition of faith is the substance of things hoped for, the evidence of things not seen. Even though you may not see it, it's ok, just believe in it. Your belief will make it become a reality.

The final step in the Obsessucces formula is discipline. This is the most difficult part of the philosophy and many fail at achieving their definite purpose because they cannot master this step.

The philosophy calls for discipline in three areas. The first is your actions. You must discipline yourself to do something every day that will move you towards your purpose. Do not get caught up in any specific action just take some type of action. As long as you act you will be amazed at how the universe puts itself on your side and begins to help you achieve your definite purpose.

Second, there is never something for nothing in this life. There must be a sacrifice on your part. The examples of the lives you just read about all had to sacrifice something in order to reach their definitive purpose in life. The Universal Law of reaping and sowing tells us that something must be given so that something can be received. Sow a seed and reap a harvest. Give a little and receive abundance. You must determine what you will sacrifice and discipline yourself to follow through, even though that sacrifice might be painful.

Third, you must discipline yourself in your persistence. Once you have made your decision about what you want and have believed for it, have disciplined your thoughts and actions, and prepared to sacrifice, recognize that adversity, negativity, problems, challenges and obstacles will begin to appear. When these enemies arrive and attack, you will be tempted to quit, and you will feel defeated. You will feel like you cannot go on, but you must. You are closer than ever to achieving your definite chief purpose in life. Do not quit, press on and remember that through every adversity there is a seed of an equal or greater benefit.

When you follow the Obsessuccess philosophy of achievement you can and you will achieve your definite chief purpose in life. To learn more about the philosophy, go to Obsessuccess.com.

BIO

Paul Hatcher is arguably the greatest retailer of automobiles in the United States today.

He has been selling cars for over 25 years and has been employed by Lithia Motors, the nation's 5th largest publicly held automotive dealer group in the nation, for the past 13 years.

During his tenure with Lithia Motors he has operated 6 dealerships, trained hundreds of sales and service personnel and has retailed a documented total of over 50,000 vehicles.

Paul has won numerous awards and has been called by his peers "the greatest retailer they have ever seen."

He is the author of the Easiest Job in the World and currently resides in San Angelo Texas with his wife of 25 years, Denise.

VISITING HOURS
By: Glen Ringersen

What comes to your mind when you think about visiting hours; hospitals, nursing, home and museums most likely? How may times have you visited these places? I like to think of visiting hours in another way. I would like you to focus your thoughts on the most important person you know, the one who uses your tooth brush every day, that person is you.

In reality many of us never visit with this person, to console yourself sounds ridiculous, but really the only person you can rely on is you. Your life is yours and you were put on this earth for a reason. That reason is not to tip toe through life waiting for it to end. Benjamin Franklin said most people die by the age of 25 and wait to be buried at the age of 75.

Life is meant to be lived, and to live your life you need to have a purpose. Most people have desires and soon see that these desires start out bright then burn out like a lighted match, with a big flash of light and a slow burn to the end of the strike of the match. Just like most of us, our desires are only wishes that fade away.

A burning desire is different. It is an all-consuming purpose that your conscious and subconscious mind thinks about while you are awake and while you sleep.

How does one find their purpose? This is different for everyone and it is not always easy to recognize your purpose. Napoleon Hill said to start with a plan, even if it is not a good one. Start where you stand. The timing will never be right so do not wait for circumstances or conditions to be in your favor. Revised plans will come to you and aid you as you start your journey.

Let me share with you two different stories about my own challenges with finding a purpose.

Years ago, I worked for a corporation and had an administrative position. I had a good salary, with vacation time and benefits, which gave my family and I great freedom. As the years passed, I coasted with a love for what I did. Times changed and the corporation went through audits and sought advice from outside consulting firms. This was the beginning of the slippery slope for hundreds of employees and myself.

Consultants came in and jobs were eliminated. Services were added to our daily responsibilities, and the workload became very heavy, with no light at the end of the tunnel and low staff morale.

I needed 3 more years to be vested, and I knew that I needed to visit with myself and find something that would bring the joy back into my life. I used to love my job, but it had begun to take a toll on my life, and the stress and frustration was beginning to affect my family life. My wife and I had recently purchased a new home and, with 3 children to raise, we needed to provide for them and we needed to continue to do so.

But what should I do? I needed my salary, benefits and consistency of my income to sustain my way of life. I had a secure job up until this point and, before I could think of moving on, I needed 3 more years before I could leave the job with a pension.

It was something I never thought of before. I planned on staying at this position until I retired. Now I was being forced to look at my life. I was coasting, never really giving it much thought. Like many people, I would get up and go to work, work all day, go home, eat dinner, watch some TV and then off to bed and start it all over again.

I did have something going for me. I listened to audio books, read books, and watched videos, all based on self improvement, such as Laws of Success by Napoleon Hill, Earl Nightingale Lead the field, Claude Bristol's The Magic of Believing and the list goes on and on.

I always filled my thoughts with positive progressive information to fill my life with good intentions of who I wanted to become. I was always reading, listening and practicing these teachings to enhance my life. I made time to visit my plan of action and strive each day to obtain my goals.

But now I was torn at work, the negativity was creeping in and the stress was overbearing, It was like the powers to be at work would tell me go to the left and when I did as they asked, they would then ask 'Why did you go left when you should have gone right?' It was like this every day, with the added pressure of never knowing what would happen next. Mind games were something they were good at.

I needed to do something quickly. Time was moving fast and a year had gone by in a flash. I needed to find a new purpose that would suit my life. I needed to really look into myself and discover what I wanted to be, have, and do. Have you ever looked into the mirror, I mean really stood face to face with yourself, and asked the important questions to yourself? What am I here for? What can I do to make a difference in my life, in my family and for the world? Try it sometime. When you do this often enough, you will see your mind's eye. The realization of who you are, and who resides in your body can be a scary experience at first but it is well worth the end result.

I did not sit back and wait for something to happen. I got involved with my life and worked on me. I made time to build my life with information that would assist me in achieving my plan. I sacrificed so I could bring into my life bigger and better things. I love what Bob Proctor says about sacrifice. He says that sacrifice is giving up something of a lower nature to obtain something of a higher nature. Like giving up fattening unhealthy foods, and lying around watching television and eating healthy, and exercising, to become healthier. Sacrificing is a good thing, if you look at the benefits that you will enjoy.

I needed to focus and get help and so I re-read Think & Grow Rich by Napoleon Hill. I went to networking meetings. I joined the Chamber of Commerce and made connections. One particular day, I met a young man at one of those meetings and he was promoting franchises for a company. We talked, I took his number, and we soon connected. He said that he could help find the right type of work for me by understanding who I am, taking tests and spending time with me over the phone on weekly calls and all at no cost to me.

What did I have to lose? I needed to do something, because my position at work was really bad. I had a plan to get out of that place and, even though my plan was weak, and I was not sure how it would even pan out, it was still a plan, and I slowly added to it to make it stronger. I did things to ensure my progress like joining groups and getting active, even though I did not know what I wanted to do.

Soon I was on my way and I was making strides on what I would be good at, and what I wanted to do. I knew I liked to fix things, help others, be my own boss, and deliver what I promise.

I chose a franchise, studied, and went on a ride along with other franchisees to get an understanding of how the system works, and the ins and outs of the business. I now had a new purpose and I was ready to go.

I had 6 months before I could be vested and that seemed like an eternity. Imagine knowing something that will change your life and not being able to share it with anyone at work. I had to keep it a secret from them, otherwise I might be let go and lose my chance of a pension. I had to eat crow for 6 more months. I also was taking a big risk with a new venture. I had to purchase the franchise, and have enough money for supplies and labor, and money for my house. Doubts were trying to creep in, and the fear factor was getting hold of me. My close friends and family were telling me that I was crazy to do this. They said I was getting older and should not take such a big risk.

I remember reading that persistence creates faith, and that faith is the only antidote to failure in the book Think and Grow Rich by Napoleon Hill. I persisted, and kept my focus on what I wanted. I did not listen to the naysayers, and there were plenty of them.

I had to walk away from a job that at one time was the greatest thing that ever happened to me. Times had changed and the place was deteriorating. People were turning against each other, and it seemed that there was nobody you could trust. I felt like I was in the evil empire and the common good had left the building. Soon my time would come and that time was ticking down, one week then 4 days, 3, 2, and then the last day was finally here. I left the building.

For the next 2 years I worked for myself, seven days a week, 12-14 hours a day and built my business. I had some rough patches with customers, employees, and financial hardships, but I was free to make my own decisions, my own choices and to live my life for myself. I had to answer to me. It was not always sunshine and rainbows but I kept my focus and kept my plan alive and gave my thoughts the ability to absorb the teachings of Napoleon Hill. I never lost sight of my goals, and it was begging to show. I was working on a big contract and put everything I had into it. It would make all those hours well worth the sacrifices I had made to make a better life for my wife and children.

Weeks went by and soon I received the phone call I have been waiting to hear. I landed the account now had to deliver what I promised. I knew that when they saw the work I would provide for them that I would be awarded other contracts. My purpose was in full swing and life was now on the upswing.

What happens if your purpose changes due to circumstances that are out of your control? I would soon find out. My life was going to change again and this time it would be life altering. Let me explain what happened to me and how my purpose changed as did my way of life.

It was a warm June day. I had just landed a few more contracts and was on my way home. I parked my car and proceeded to walk to my house. The colors of summer blooms were everywhere and I was just enjoying the early evening sun as I walked along to my home. Suddenly I heard the screeching of wheels and the engine revving and, as I turned to look over my shoulder, I saw a sports utility vehicle heading straight for me. I turned my head back around and did a stutter step trying to get out of the way but it was too late. I felt the impact of the grill as it struck my back, and my head snapped back onto the hood, leaving an imprint. I was pushed forward and everything seemed to go in slow motion.

As I flew through the air I was thinking to myself 'Why was this happening to me?' as my body hit the pavement. I was like a glass jar filled with jelly. I was broken but remained together in a jelled mess of bone and flesh. Then I felt the crushing of bones and crackling of my body as the first set of tires ran over my hips and legs and then mangled my legs and headed towards my ribs and chest area as it crushed everything in its path.

As I watched in horror I could do nothing as the second set of tires came within inches of my head. As the under carriage passed over my broken body, I could hear the sounds of metal now behind me as the vehicle came to an abrupt stop. I was left for dead, a broken man, with life slipping out of me, and the natural response from my body was to go into shock. I could see people running over to help me, and soon I was carted away in an ambulance.

In the hospital my family was called and was told they had better pay their last respects because I would most likely not make it through the night. For the next six weeks I was in a comma and on life support. I suffered crushed hips, a punctured lung, a broken back and a broken shoulder. I lost a mass of muscle and tissue on my left leg and I was on a ventilator. I was what some called a train wreck.

I had numerous surgeries and metal rods, plates, and screws were attached to my spine to hold me together. I had metal rods sticking out of my abdomen to hold my hips together, a tube in my chest, braces on my legs, and machines attached to my body.

As I laid there, friends and family came to visit me but I did not remember any of them. Months went by and numerous additional surgeries, x-rays, cat scans, MRI, and blood tests were taken. I had to learn how to speak again, learn to feed myself and hold up my hand to hold a fork. I had to start my life all over again. The pain I endured was unbearable and was something that I do not wish on anyone.

I was transferred to a rehabilitation facility where I spent the next year of my life, re-learning everything that we take for granted. Learning to walk again, sitting up, and using the bathroom. I was on IV and every eight hours they had to change the bag for a new one.

What would you do if this were you? So many people tell me that they could never have done what I did. Why then am I so lucky? All the extra time that I had when I wasn't rehabbing was spent studying. I had my wife bring in my books, tapes, and CD's and I applied them to my life. My goal, my Purpose was to get out of there and go home. One year away from my familiar surroundings was a hard thing to swallow. I wanted to get out of there as soon as possible. My body needed time to heal and it could not be rushed.

Before this incident, I had memorized the Self-Confidence Formula from the Law of Success by Napoleon Hill, and applied it to my life. I recommend that everyone commits it to memory and applies it. It starts out by saying 'I have the ability to achieve my definiteness of purpose, and therefore I demand of myself persistent aggressive continuous action towards its attainment.' This is what I believed for my purpose however my purpose was no longer for my business because I had already lost that business due to my injuries.

I was forced to change my purpose in order to save my life, to better my condition and health. If I did not do this, I believe I would have succumbed to my injuries. I believe applying the Self-Confidence Formula to my life actually helped saved me on that fateful day.

I had suffered so much pain to get my life back on track, and at times I wanted to give up and let go of my life. I sacrificed through the pain to obtain a better outcome for my life. I am glad I visited with myself and made the time to improve it. I made time to better my life and I am happy that I did.

I had over 50 surgeries from that day until now. I am left with a bum leg, which I have braces on, and a cane to help me get around. Had I listened to the medical professionals that said I would never walk again I might have believed them and stayed in a wheelchair for the rest of my life.

How many times do people tell you that you cannot do something? So many people have opinions for your life and think they know what is best for you. That will never work for me. I have my own way of looking at things and do not let others determine what I can and cannot do. Yes, I will never run, jump, or skate again. I realize that, but I do not listen to those who never tried to accomplish what I want to accomplish. I search out those who accomplished what I want to accomplish, those who are in the know.

I was thrown into two separate choices for my definite purpose, my job and then my health. I could have waited for something to happen or take the steps to direct my life and wait for someone else to take control of my future. In other words, to just play it safe and close my eyes to what lay ahead. I am in charge of my life and want it that way. When you visit with yourself and reevaluate your life, and make a plan for the next 5, 10, 20 years, you will have a purpose and success will follow you. Be proactive with your life and never succumb to what others say you cannot do. Life is meant to be lived, not to play it safe.

My life is not over yet and I will continue to learn and apply the principles of those great teachings of Napoleon Hill and other great leaders. I leave you with this statement from Napoleon Hill.

"Definiteness of Purpose is the starting point of all achievement. Remember this statement. Definiteness of Purpose is the starting point of all achievement. It is a stumbling block to 98 out of every 100 persons because they never really define their goals and start towards them with Definiteness of Purpose. Think it over – 98 % of the people in the world are drifting aimlessly through life without the slightest idea of the work for which they are fitted. They have no concept whatsoever of even the need for such a thing as a Definite objective towards which to strive. This is one of the greatest tragedies of civilization."
- Napoleon Hill.

BIO

Glen Ringersen has been studying the works of Napoleon Hill for over 25 years, and has applied these principles to advance his career, family, spiritual and physical health. As a result, Glen was able to accomplish things that others deemed impossible.

In June 2004, Glen was in a tragic accident that nearly cost him his life. While he did escape the grip of death, he lost everything as the months turned into years in hospitals and rehabilitation facilities. It was only through his strong Will and Faith that Glen managed to pull his life out of the downward spiral, and apply Definiteness of Purpose to his life once again.

Doctors had told Glen, he would never walk again, but Glen refused to allow others to define his abilities. Today Glen is walking. He attributes his recovery to his application of the Philosophy of Napoleon Hill. It was during this time, that Glen became a Life Coach and began to help others overcome their obstacles and gain success.

In addition to Glen's many accomplishments, he is a Distinguished Toastmaster, the highest level of achievement obtainable from Toastmasters International, a world-renowned communication and leadership organization. As an added testament to his leadership ability, he was also awarded Toastmasters Division Governor of the Year. Glen even formed a Toastmasters club based on the philosophy of Napoleon Hill's principles, a proven method for success.

Certified by the Napoleon Hill Foundation as licensed instructor, Glen Ringersen continues to apply the rules in Napoleon Hill's book Think & Grow Rich to all areas of his life.

Glen can be reached at email...themindmovers@yahoo.com

WHAT IF... YOU DO NOTHING!

By: Steve Martin

I have always believed that every person born into this world is born with at least one gift, something that makes them special and unique to the world. I have always believed that we were all born for greatness. There has to be a reason, a purpose. After all, I think it would be disrespectful for us to just assume we were created to be average! I cannot bring myself to believe that we were all put on this earth to be average but I believe that we have been educated that way, not only in our schools and universities but also in our lives through our experiences and relationships.

Have you ever wondered who you are? Or why you are? Possibly even what you are? I have asked myself these questions for decades. I have determined throughout my years of triumph and struggle that the gifts given to me by the universe are simple yet powerful ones. I have two gifts; my first gift is that I am never satisfied with good enough and I am continuously looking for more; more excellence, more success, more understanding, more significance, more purpose, more love, just to mention a few. As long as I breath I will never be happy with good enough. I truly do consider it a gift to always stay hungry for more. My second gift is my ability to immediately recognize the things I do not want in my life. I have the ability to recognize negativity very quickly and run away from it the same way a person would run away from a dangerous wild animal.

In the last 8 years, from 2008 to 2016, I have been given another gift, the gift of opportunity. This gift allows me the opportunity to work with and learn from people. Over the last 8 years I have spoken with thousands of people from more than 50 countries and counting. This tremendous opportunity has allowed me to travel the world listening to and having conversations with all types of people. People from different religions, backgrounds, education, lifestyles, economic conditions, and beliefs. All this being said, how is this a gift?

As I have shared already, I have an obsession with more; a true hunger to receive more. I have come to the realization that for me to achieve more and receive more, I must do more, give more, and be of better service to more people. It has become clear to me what it is I must do everyday to achieve my goals. This clear vision, this definiteness of purpose, was not always clear to me and in fact, for a long time, I had no idea.

Allow me to give you a little history on how I used to see things very clearly. I started my career after a dream of becoming a world famous professional athlete was cut short by injury. I am grateful that I was given the ability and opportunity to compete at a national level and win two national championships. The experiences of sport and teamwork in my life has taught me many great lessons. Many of these lessons have made me who I am today.

I will always be grateful to my teammates, mentors, and coaches. Once the dream of making a living as a professional athlete came to a screeching halt it was time to move on. I was 20 years old and the world was at my feet waiting for me to conquer it, or so I thought. I began my career as an entrepreneur in the family owned and operated business with my Dad. I am very grateful to him and his tremendous commitment to providing for his family his entire life. He worked hard all day, every day, with no holidays and no time off. I had the idea that together, him and I could grow the company and become big!

Remember my gift, the one where I always want more? Well as it turned out bigger is not always better. In fact, in our case, bigger just meant more liability, more responsibly, more headaches. It did not mean more profit. In fact it was just the opposite. It was at this point early in my career that I realized that being your own boss is not all it is cracked up to be. I was, however determined to become successful. I would do whatever it took, work as long as it took and make it work. I was determined to have more and to never give up on my dreams.

As time passed, it started to become painfully obvious to me that this type of business was really not what I wanted to do with my life. It was a harsh environment, which was not very positive, and in fact, was full of negativity and stress. I never stopped believing that I could will my way to success; I, however, doubted the business model by which I was going to do this.

Remember my second gift, the ability to run from negativity? My subconscious was screaming at me to run and not look back. The negative environment I was in was not going to get me what I desired most; money and freedom! It was at that point in my life that I made a decision to find a better way to reach my goals. What did I need to do to become rich and free and to live my life with who I wanted, where I wanted, and as long as I wanted, in order to be a true champion of my life?

I decided I would go to the bookstores and find the answers I was looking for. It seemed like a simple idea: if you want what other people have, learn to do what other people do. My first step was deciding what I wanted and desired and I decided that money and the time freedom to enjoy it was my first answer. Was there a book that could answer my questions? How could I get rich, and have the time freedom to enjoy it with the ones I love? The answer was a resounding yes. There are thousands of books and articles on how to become rich and famous. How would I find the right one? I did not have time to read all of them and I needed to get rich now! After all I was 25 years old and not getting any younger.

Then, like a lighthouse on a dark stormy night, I found the book that changed my life. So simple yet brilliant was the title that it answered all my questions in the title alone...THINK and GROW RICH. Of course I was doing everything but this one thing, "THINK". I never realized that such a book existed. It became my instruction manual to success. The book contained easy to read, simple instructions, and great stories and examples of success.

Can you imagine the richest person in the world at that time sitting down with you to offer you a job? Exciting right? Well it depends on the job and the compensation of course! Let's think about that for a moment. Bill Gates asks you to stay at his house for the weekend because he enjoys your company and is intrigued by your line of questioning. The weekend comes to an end and Bill has a proposal for you to consider. The task is simple enough; gather information using a certain line of questioning. The questions relate to what people do, how they live, who they associate with, and what do they continuously think about? In summary, answer the question "Why do some people become wealthy and some do not?". Bill continues by mentioning that he wants you to talk to no less than 500 of the wealthiest people in the world who are of course his friends. He will supply you with a personally signed letter that will guarantee you a meeting with those friends. The purpose of the meetings is to gather information and organize it in a way that people from every country in the world can understand it and apply it to their lives so that they as well can live a life of freedom and significance, in short become rich! We will call this book 'Think and Grow Rich', a beautifully simple title that everyone will want.

Wow! Are you excited? I most certainly would have been!

Before you accept this amazing offer, they're a few more details. This study you are so willing to take on will take a minimum of 25 years to complete. One final detail; your time and expenses will not be taken care of by me. In fact, the job does not come with any form of compensation whatsoever. Mr. Gates finishes his proposal by simply asking for an answer - on the spot! Can you imagine if this was you? Well this was the story of a newspaper reporter named Napoleon Hill.

The year was 1912. The billionaire was Andrew Carnegie, the 3rd richest person in history. The answer was 'yes' and it took 37 seconds for him to decide. That is all it took to change the lives of countless generations to come. Twenty five years later, in 1937, the book Think and Grow Rich was published and became the all time best selling business book in history, with over 100 million copies sold worldwide. It was a decision made swiftly since Carnegie was timing him and was only going to allow only 60 seconds. It was a journey that lasted the rest of his life and is now passed on to all of us. Can you imagine what you would have done?

What if you do nothing with the information in this book and in this chapter? Do you think things will change if you are not willing to change? Do you think things will get better if you are not willing to get better? It is time for you to take charge of your life. Your success is your responsibility, it is time for you to step up and take action! Where are you going? Do you have a plan? What do you want? Do you want it so bad you can taste it? These are powerful question only you can answer.

Napoleon Hill wrote that a burning desire is the starting point of all achievement. Every human being who reaches the age of understanding of the purpose of money wishes for it. Why money? Because money makes peoples lives better. I am here to tell you that it does. I have lived without money, and I have lived with money. I strongly suggest you live with money because life is much better. In most cases however, people spend their entire life worrying about their lack of money and not focusing on how to attract more money into their lives. The simple solution is to stop wishing and hoping for money. If it is not coming, it's because you do not truly believe it will. Change the way you think about money. It is not evil. You are worthy and deserve to live a better life. You cannot eat money, you cannot drink money, you cannot dress in money, you cannot live in a house made of money, and you cannot help anyone without money. You can do very little without money. The purpose of money is to make your life better. Do you truly want better?

Your actions create your results. Desire is the key to your amazing life, the life you imagine and visualize. In life you do not get what you want, you only get what you picture in your mind. Focus on your deepest desire and never stop picturing what it will look like. See it, smell it, feel it, and turn your desire into an obsession, a magnificent obsession, a white-hot burning desire.

Put pen to paper. Now that you understand the first step towards riches as stated by Hill, it is time for you to sit down and draw out your future. What does it look like when you have your deepest desire? Do you have a purpose? Are you on purpose, or are you just existing day after day? It is time for you to turn desire into gold.

These simple steps to follow is in fact where most people fail. Most people never start anything. In fact the start is where most of us accept defeat as our reality. I read a very powerful statement once that impacted my life. "Every test in our lives makes us bitter or better, every problem comes to break us or make us. The choice is ours whether we become victim or victor!" Be very clear on two things "vision" and "mission". Too many people refuse to set high goals for themselves for fear of failure. Success is simply going from one failure to the next without loss of enthusiasm. Remember, as I mentioned earlier, we were all taught what to think but not how to think. It is time for us all to take charge of our lives.

Definiteness of purpose...Picture in your mind the exact amount of money you desire. Remember to dream BIG, because it is very expensive to dream small. Determine exactly what you intend on giving in return for the money. It is a law of the universe that no one can expect to receive without first giving. Put a date on your success, an exact date when you will be in possession of the money you desire. Put a plan together on how you will achieve your goals. Do not spend a lot of time here. It is best to start immediately right where you are. If you have the will, you can develop the skill. Your burning desire will show you the way. Write out on a piece of paper the exact amount of money you desire, when you will be in possession of it, what you will do in exchange for it, and the plan for its attainment. Lastly and the most important part, read your statement out load at least 2 times a day, once when you rise and once before you retire for the evening. Your definiteness of purpose is simply put, the knowledge of what one wants, and the burning desire to possess it.

All the things we do come down to the habits we develop as we go through life. It is the things we do that produce our lifetime results. Habits are transferable, both good or bad and success will come when you learn to apply your habits to the proper activities. Motivation gets you started, habit keeps you going. Focus your attention on doing the things you need to do today and do not put off today what you believe you can do tomorrow. Procrastination is the opposite of decision.

What is Power? Power is required to accumulate money. Power is required to keep and multiply money once it is accumulated. Power is essential for success. Power is organized and intelligently directed knowledge. Knowledge is converted into power by organizing it into definite plans. True power, the real measure of actual power, is your capacity to create results in this moment, right now. Napoleon Hill said it best "Success is the development of the power with which to get whatever one wants in life without interfering with the rights of others" Become committed to serving others because service to others is the measure of true greatness. To simplify this, I have always found that success occurs when your dreams are bigger than your excuses.

In closing, I would first like to thank you for believing enough in yourself to make a change. We are all blessed to be given choices in life. I appreciate the choice you made to invest your time in this book and in these chapters. The small amount of time we invested together in these chapters will make a difference in your life if the information is applied. I say this because, before I wrote about it, I applied it to my life, and today I am living the life I choose without any limitations.

"When you come to select your definite purpose in life, just keep in mind that you cannot aim too high"
– Napoleon Hill

"Your work is going to fill a large part of your life, and the only way to be truly satisfied is to do what you believe is great work. And the only way to do great work is to love what you do. If you haven't found it yet, keep looking and don't settle". – Steve Jobs

A successful life lives in all of us. I wish you success

Cheers

Steve Martin

BIO

Steve Martin is the proud father of two young men, soon to be great men, a grateful husband to his wife who is his best friend, and business partner for over 25 years. Steve's true passion is working with people.

By choice, Steve has been unemployed his entire life, believing that your success is your fault. A serial entrepreneur his entire life, starting at age 9.

Steve has started and developed multiple business around the world, taking those companies into the millions a month in sales. A "Burning Desire" and the willingness to always go the "Extra Mile" are the cornerstones to Steve's success.

As a Certified Napoleon Hill trainer, Steve speaks to thousands of people a year sharing with them the simple principles of success as taught by Dr. Napoleon Hill. His messages are simple, yet powerful – If you Strive for success and significance all one has to do is "Think and Grow Rich".

This is Steve's first attempt at writing and he hopes that some of his unoriginal, but highly effective thinking, may in fact move you to do something big in your life.

Never stop learning, loving and, living BIG.

Steve can be reached at 587-439-5800 or by email at steveshealthyjava@gmail.com

http://rtbglobalx.com/

A TINY LITTLE DETOUR

By: Daniel Mazzeu

It was a bright Monday morning and as I looked outside the airplane window, my eyes were delighted with the beautiful ocean and the clear blue skies. It was as if I were staring at a screen-saver of a Caribbean beach. The plane was about to land at the city of João Pessoa, a beach city in the northeast of Brazil, roughly 2,000 Km from my hometown of São Paulo, a fast-paced and insanely populated city.

Although I was in João Pessoa for business, I always enjoyed the atmosphere of that small city, which offered a large enough market for any business and still a great qualify of life. The city has a couple of great malls, little traffic and, most important of all, amazing tropical beaches.

My customer and good friend Helder Vaz picked me up at the airport and, as in previous business trips, we went to grab lunch. He knew my favorite restaurant was a place called Mangai, so we drove straight there.

We talked about the market challenges in the printing industry and Helder asked me if I had made a decision on what he called "The big 4"; Leaving my job, moving to João Pessoa, selling my property to invest and marrying Daniela. I said I was working on it, but it looked like I am going for the full package. He laughed and after a couple of hours of great conversation, he dropped me off at the Ibis Cabo Branco Hotel, located right by the ocean.

The scariest decision of the big-4, as my friend called it, was getting married. The word "marriage" gave me goose bumps and sounded like an insult. I had been successfully dodging this "bullet" in a sophisticated matrix-style for over 10 years. I intended to dodge it for a few more years, but my love for Daniela was growing and that was beautiful and scary at the same time.

An internal dialogue about marriage went on for a couple months and I finally decided to take the big jump and propose to Daniela. But how could I make the proposal something really special? She had asked a few times in the past to go parachuting, to which I responded: "NOPE, don´t like heights, thanks but no thanks!" To make it a really special day for her, I was willing to go the extra mile, in a vertical and a radical sort of way.

I researched parachute jumping on the internet and found out there was a city nearby named Boituva that offered it. I called them up and explained that it would be a wedding proposal and that we were both going to jump. I would jump first and as soon as Daniela landed, I would propose to her. The lady on the phone loved the idea and we set a date for the following Sunday. She suggested I bring a cooler for the champagne and the rings, of course.

Paradigms Blowing in the Wind

I woke up that Sunday morning deeply fearing what was about to happen. After all, it was the biggest day of my life, but multiplied by two. Since the entire event was a surprise, I told Daniela that we were going to a barbecue at a friend´s house in the countryside. She gladly agreed and as we drove by Boituva City, 80 km from São Paulo, Daniela cheerfully said, "Amor, this is the city where they do parachuting." I responded as if I were surprised: "Really? Wow, let´s go check it out just out of curiosity". As we got there, there were 5 or 6 companies, similar to little shops, forming a semi-circle right across from a tiny airport, with tiny airplanes. I thought to myself, "Holy Cow", how can someone with the least amount of love for life get into one of those planes?

I finally identified the company I had hired and, as if I had never heard of them, I asked Daniela to go there with me to get information, "should we ever" decide to do that sacrilegious act. As soon as the lady in a funny suit came up to us, I said: "Hi, I am Daniel Mazzeu, I scheduled a jump for my girlfriend and I". Daniela looked at me in total shock, "Come on? Are you serious?" "Are you going to jump as well or you bought it just for me?" I recovered a little bit of my composure and, although frightened, I took a deep breath and responded as suavely as George Clooney in one of those Nespresso commercials: "Sure honey! I am going with you." Daniela was jumping up and down; not realizing the big surprise was yet to come. At that moment my fears PARTIALLY vanished, for I knew I had wisely chosen the surprise for the wonderful woman I was going to marry.

The lady from the parachuting company pulled me to the side before the short training and said: "Daniel, give me your car keys so I can get the champagne and the ring." I handed it to her so she could have it all prepared when I landed. We got on that tiny toy-like airplane with 6 other people, all facing the nose of the airplane. The plane took off and went around in circles to gain altitude. The noise of that plane reminded me of World War II planes; incredibly loud and nerve wrecking. The only difference is that we were in 2008, so how could a plane still sound like that? It did...

We finally reached the altitude for jumping and the main instructor opened the door of the airplane and started calling one by one: "Daniel, stand up and slowly come up to the door." I wanted to look good for my future wife, but that was too much. Daniela looked at me and said: "Have fun, honey". Have fun?! You have to be kidding, I thought. She was glowing with happiness and excitement, much like those fearless kids who finally reach the acceptable height to go on the toughest roller coaster at Disney World.

As I walked to the door, I looked out onto the horizon and screamed "Holy F* Shit!" before stepping into the air. Trust me,

61

"Geronimo" is the last thing you are going to say when you are jumping out of an airplane. I was free falling for a few minutes, but it seemed like a lifetime. The parachute finally opened and shot me upwards. It was a unique feeling I must say. Would I do it again?! NOPE, once is plenty!! When I realized I was gonna make it alive – a great feeling - I finally started enjoying the "ride". The landing was clumsy as I practically landed on my face. I knew that jump was very symbolic and I had moved mountains within me. Facing the parachute jump would transmute my fear of commitment into courage, so that I could fully embrace a life of love with my beautiful Daniela.

The Proposal

I was still trying to recover my senses after the "stylish" landing, when 2 guys from the parachuting company came up to me and said in rushed voices: "Come on, dude, get ready! Daniela will land in two minutes, get yourself together." They handed me a velvet red box with the ring and said the champagne and glasses would be with them. In less than 2 minutes Daniela landed. She was cheerfully smiling as if jumping off an airplane was as easy as getting off a bicycle. She was happy and, best of all, totally clueless as to what was going to happen. When I realized she had stood up and cleaned off the grass from her jumpsuit, I made the move. I slowly walked up to her, my right hand behind my back with the ring and a smile overflowing with love. I got on my knees and said: "Amor, I´ve got another surprise for you..... Will you marry me?" She looked at me in complete disbelief and in a gasping voice responded: "YES!" All the parachuting instructors that had been watching 20 feet away from us, started clapping and whistling for the new couple that were officially engaged.

I had done it. I had crossed the bridge in a quantic manner. I had jumped the abyss and there was no looking back. I had finished healing wounds I had since my childhood. My parents had a very unstable marriage, to put it lightly, so the emotional blocks I had were as high as the great walls of China. "Good bye, drama. Hello love and peace!"

The next day was a normal workday and I drove to work feeling blessed for being engaged with Daniela. The dream of opening my own business in João Pessoa kept growing on me. We spent the following weeks visiting friends and family to let them know about our engagement. We did not plan a real wedding, but instead, we felt it would be best to have a ceremony in a non-denominational shrine. Family members were excited for us and in less than 4 months we were officially married.

The Total Full Maximum Package

A couple months later, with Daniela´s blessing, I finally decided we were going to move to João Pessoa. I could not stand having such a burning desire and not doing a thing about it. I had Daniela´s support on the decision and that was enough for me. Many people said what I was doing was nonsense. After all, I had a good job, a good house, traveled abroad for work and vacation and had just gotten married. But, as the philosopher Napoleon Hill stated, you may seek for specialized counsel, but it is your responsibility to evaluate the facts and make your own decision. The right answer is always within us, it yells at us but the ego is very powerful and sneaky and gets in the way. Learning to silence one´s mind before making decisions is more valuable than asking others to validate your decision.

I had already registered the name of the company, built a great website, bought an ERP and I had developed a few suppliers for the company. Just as important, I had found a great 5-car garage house for Daniela and I, just 6 blocks from the beach. It also had a nice garden, which was the cherry on the cake. It´s Showtime!!!

The first couple of months running the business would be really draining and we both agreed that it would be best for Daniela to keep her job and stay in São Paulo while I got the house furnished and the business going.

A Tiny Little Detour

We took a 3-day trip to Rio de Janeiro and on the way back, Daniela complained about feeling sick. It was unusual since she never complains about a single headache. I said in joking way: "You´re pregnant, you wanna bet?" I don´t really know where the heck that comment came from, it just did. She laughed and with a concerned smile said: "I doubt it since I regularly take the pill. But what If I were?" I sensed she needed my love and reassurance and I playfully responded: "Hey, that would be the Total Full Maximum Package: Newly Wed, new business, new house, new city and a wonderful baby girl." She said I was crazy, then went on to inquire: "Where did you get the 'baby girl' from?!" I told her that was the first image that came to my mind, and that it was just a feeling. I saw her facial expression grow sad and I told her not to worry and that she was probably getting the flu. Still, I suggested we go to a pharmacy nearby to get one of those pregnancy tests, so she would stop worrying. We bought it and as soon as we walked into our apartment, she ran into the bathroom. Those were some of the longest minutes of my life and when 10 minutes had gone by, I opened the bathroom door to check on her: "Are you okay, amor?!" She looked as if she had seen a ghost! She was shocked and in a sobbing voice she said: "It´s positive". I opened up a huge smile and started kissing her, "Yesssss, Amor!! Our baby girl is on her way!! That´s awesome, it is an absolute blessing!". It was indeed the Total Full Maximum package as I´d joked about earlier. I kept joking around and comforting Daniela as I realized she was happy, yet very concerned. Although it caught me by surprise, I knew we could pull it off, especially powered by our baby girl.

I delayed the departure to João Pessoa so I could go with Daniela to the first prenatal exams. Daniela was finally cheerful about the baby and when I realized the baby and her were well, I started packing. I filled my truck with suitcases, tied my motorcycle to the back and had my copilot Dino join me on the passenger seat. Dino is a Persian cat that had been with me for a couple of years and is still alive today. He is quite a guy! I drove 2.000km heading north, towards the city where my family would settle and my dreams would come true. It had become my promised land.

I moved into the house, and finished all the remodeling and redid the garden for my son or daughter. My business was going well, the employees were cooperative and things looked really promising. Life was incredible and I was enjoying my Sundays riding my motorcycle along the coast from João Pessoa to Pipa Beach. But, there were two people I loved missing, before I could truly be happy. In one of the several Skype calls, Daniela told me: "Amor, you won´t believe it, the doctor was able to see it.... it´s a girl.". How cool! It would be a blessing either way, but to have a small version of Daniela running around the house would blow me away. Daniela finally gave me the date she´d be flying into João Pessoa and we made our daughter´s name official: Giovanna. La Vitta è Bella, Sempre!!

When Daniela arrived it gave color and joy to the house and to my life. Daniela didn´t bring life to the house by decorating the walls, or by redesigning the garden, much less by cranking out some great homemade dishes - that´s not her thing. Daniela embellishes and colors the environment with her presence alone. I secretly hope that she will eventually fall in love with gourmet cooking after watching one of the MasterChef programs. But, honestly, chances of that happening are as slim as me becoming a skydiver.

Road Blocks Ahead

Daniela was going for her 7th or 8th ultrasound when the doctor witnessed some irregularity with Giovanna's heart beat pattern. On the following day we went for another ultrasound and the doctor recommended 3 ultrasounds a week, rest and lots of hearty food since Giovanna was below the expected weight. The business was not running on its own yet, but I had to find time to be with Daniela and go to the doctors with her. I decreased my working hours from 15-hour days to 7-8 hour days and focused on Daniela's diet. Despite the efforts, Giovanna was not gaining weight fast enough and the doctor set her birth date for March 2nd, the 36th week, instead of the 42h.

On the evening of March 2nd, we were all there ready for Giovanna to arrive. By then, we had already changed the baby's name to Giovanna Vittoria. The nurse asked me if I was going to be in the delivery room and I said: "NOPE!!". As I looked at Daniela's disappointment I quickly changed my mind, "Hey, why not, sign me up!". The smells and the terrible green tones of the delivery room were making me sick. I hung in there and just when I was about to faint, I heard a loud cry, "Waaa Waaa Waaaa". Giovanna Vittoria had arrived. That loud, fierce and outraged scream would become Giovanna's signature for her God-given right to fight for life, regardless of the odds. As I looked at that tiny little thing (2.1kg), I knew my life had changed forever. I just had no idea how much.

My in-laws and I sat with Daniela at the hospital room, hoping to see Giovanna at any moment. Two hours had gone by and I finally decided to go and ask the doctors why it was taking so long. I met with one of the doctors who told me they were doing routine exams and that Giovanna would join Daniela soon. Another 2 hours went by and Giovanna was still not in the room. Once again I marched over those cold and awfully green corridors to find out about my daughter. I had run out of stories to entertain my wife and, most of all, I had run out of patience about the lack of information. I talked to one of the doctors who delivered Giovanna, Dr. Marisa. As I approached her she cut me off before I said a word, "I can´t talk to you right now, but I will go to Daniela´s room soon". Another hour went by and only nurses had come by the room. I finally got up and went after Dr. Marisa. As she saw me, she quickly said: "I am gonna to go there," hoping I would go away. I was furious and I replied, "No, you are going to talk to me right now! I want to know exactly what is going on with my daughter and why she has not joined my wife and I yet." She wanted to get away, but with the anger stamped on my face, she chose to respond: "Well, the baby has some respiratory issues and we feel it is best for her to stay in the incubator. But she is okay." I looked her straight in the eye and I said, "Why on Earth would you not tell that to the mother? What is wrong with you? A few weeks later, after other miscommunication issues, lack of empathy and pure incompetency, I had the pleasure of telling Dr. Marisa to her face: "In all honesty, you are an absolutely terrible doctor, you should have been a veterinarian". But, frankly, I deeply regret saying that, after all, not even animals deserve to be treated by that bonehead.

Giovanna Vittoria stayed at the hospital for 17 days due to respiratory issues and for being premature. When Giovanna Vittoria finally went home, we were extremely happy. Daniela, my father-in-law Paulo, my mother-in-law Fatima and I celebrated this triumphant moment. The worse was over. Giovanna finally slept in her beautifully decorated room, listening to lullabies from Daniela and grandma Fátima, whose presence was not only comforting to Daniela, but to me as well. I have always enjoyed watching the interaction of grandma, mom and daughter, 3 generations immersed in love and affection. My father-in-law Paulo was amazing. He was always willing to help and always had an extremely friendly and cooperative attitude.

The Storm Strikes Back

Daniela was playing with Giovanna Vittoria when all of a sudden I heard Daniela screaming for help from the top of her lungs. I ran to the room like lightning to see the most horrifying scene ever. Giovanna had stopped breathing and was turning blue. I shook her up but no immediate response, so I started yelling at Daniela, "Take Gigi to the car NOW, we are going to the hospital". I drove like a madman to a hospital that was 5 minutes away and by the time the doctor started examining Giovanna, she had already started breathing and gaining back some of her color. It was a nightmare, a horror movie, except it was not a movie... it was real life. Worst yet, it was my family. I hugged Daniela out of despair. This was not just a hug, it was a clinch after a horrifying first round. Daniela was as pale as a ghost, apparently fragile and in deep pain. But seeing how Daniela would face other challenges to come, I quickly realized I had married a gladiator, a warrior, a wounded lion that would fight a buffalo herd to save her cub. I was also growing emotionally as well, becoming a better man and building what I call "spiritual muscles".

The next morning, we started researching who was the top pediatrician in town and we ran into the name of Dr. João. I called up Dr. João´s assistant and explained it was an emergency and she was able to pencil us in 3 days later. The routine at home had changed, Giovanna had to be watched 24/7, and grandma Fátima would take turns with Daniela. Business was going ok, but my absence started causing some problems. We had 2 large customers that were running late on their payments and I only found out 15 days after the due date. There were weak links in the foundation of the business and my being absent only made things worse. The savings account was getting smaller by the day. Expenses had tripled and customers not paying were not planned into the equation.

The appointment day came and Daniela, Giovanna Vittoria and I drove there hoping to get some answers. The clinic was not that impressive but I had a good feeling about the doctor. He examined Giovanna thoroughly without saying a word and paid special attention to her fingers and toes, which intrigued Daniela and I. Since he did not say a word, I finally broke the silence and asked, "What is your opinion in regards to her overall health?" He moved his glasses around and thought for 30 long seconds, as if thinking what to say. Finally he said, "Well, she looks okay and her breathing is normal. I noticed her muscle tone is weak and there are a couple of traits that remind me of a particular syndrome, but overall she is well. Let´s do some blood exams, heart scan, karyotype and have you come back in a few weeks." Dr. João came across as a responsible and meticulous doctor, which brought peace to Daniela and I. As we were preparing to get up, little Giovanna stopped breathing again. As she was turning blue, the doctor shook her up and gave her a chest massage and after what appeared to be hours, she was back again. I did not think I would ever see that again! Daniela and I immediately asked the doctor if it would be advisable for Giovanna to stay in the hospital while waiting for the results of the exams and he agreed.

A few weeks later Dr. João came to the hospital room to share the results. He tried as nicely as he could to deliver the awful news: "Giovanna has Edwards Syndrome. It is an extremely invasive syndrome that affects the nervous system, heart, kidneys and other organs." Daniela and I were speechless… absolutely petrified. He went on to say Giovanna had little chance and that we should stay hopeful. As he left, I went after him and asked him to bluntly say what her chances were. He responded: "Practically zero, she will not make it to a year." I asked if he recommended going to a better hospital in a big city like São Paulo and he said it would not make a difference.

I went home to shower and think about our options, if any. When I came back to the hospital, Daniela and I had arrived at the same decision. We would take Giovanna to a major a hospital in São Paulo as soon as she was more stable. Daniela asked me about my business and the house in João Pessoa and I quickly responded: "Screw it! I am dropping it all so we can chase Giovanna´s recovery".

The details of this story is much longer and may end up becoming a book in the future, but the summary is: After hundreds of exams, 2 years in and out of hospitals, 10+ doctors saying "sorry, nothing to be done" and hitting rock bottom financially, Giovanna made it and is doing absolutely great.

The strength of this little girl to reach her goal of staying alive is inspiring and has profoundly touched our lives. We thank God for the teachings and the blessing of still having Giovanna with us – Our Little Guru of Love. For those who have "lost" someone in a battle similar to ours, I honestly feel you have not lost the battle, for love remains and it is eternal. Antoine Lavoisier, father of modern chemistry, said: "In nature nothing is created, nothing is lost, everything is transformed." Wouldn´t it apply to our lives as well? An idea to contemplate.

Were my Dreams Shattered to Pieces?!

My definite major purposes took a marvelous detour so I could strengthen my faith, learn to let go and could better understand myself. As I was absolutely penniless at the end of 2010, I got hired by Mitsubishi Imaging, part of a $42 billion group. In the last 3 years I have spoken in China and other countries about the printing industry. I also gave talks about Napoleon Hill´s philosophy in Brazil, Uruguay and Argentina. Finally, my friend Judy Williamson kindly invited me to lecture at the certification classes in Italy and in the Caribbean, quite an honor. Despite enjoying a great income and lifestyle, in July of 2014 I resigned from Mitsubishi and opened a new company called DMZ Connection. DMZ is doing great and we had a booth at an Expo in Shanghai last year and we will have a booth at an Expo in Mexico this year, where I will also be a speaker. How about that for turning things around?

Dear reader, you too can turn things around. It may be related to your finances, relationships, health or anything else. I am just a 1st grade student in life, but I did learn that great blessings are within our reach if we REALLY go after them with love and passion.

A Definite Major Purpose can take detours or be changed slightly, but it cannot ever be taken away from you. Make it happen!!

GRATITUDE ALWAYS

All my love and admiration for my extraordinary wife and mastermind partner, Daniela Castro, who went through hell in the front seat and did not stop believing and loving for a second. A HUGE thanks to my in-laws Paulo and Fátima Castro, whose love and commitment were a blessing all along.

I cannot thank enough Dr. Roberto Tozze, who believed in Giovanna while another 10+ doctors repeated the prognosis as a death sentence. I thank Luzia Gonçalves for being a great nanny and friend. My gratitude to the spiritual healing places we attended, GAFA in São Paulo and João de Deus in Abadiania. I thank my father for teaching me courage, my mom for teaching me love for humanity and my sister Priscila for teaching me partnership. Big thanks to my cousins Alexandre Almeida Prado and Estevam, who helped with cash when it was desperately needed. My appreciation to Napoleon Hill and The Napoleon Hill Foundation. Thanks Judy Williamson, Uriel Martinez and Alan Chen for the friendship and support. Tom Cunningham, thanks for the invitation to be a co-author for this book.

BIO

Daniel Mazzeu was born and raised in Brazil and lived for 12 years in the United States, where he graduated from California State University of Long Beach.

Daniel developed a successful career in sales working for companies such as Chrysler, Hughes Aircraft, Uninet Imaging and Mitsusbishi Imaging. During his work experience Daniel had the opportunity to do business in the US, Latin America, Germany, Japan and China.

Daniel is also a Certified Instructor at the Napoleon Hill Foundation and gave talks about the philosophy at The World Trade Center in Uruguay and at other events in Argentina and Brazil. More recently, Daniel Mazzeu lectured at the Napoleon Hill Certification Classes in Italy and in the Caribbean.

Daniel Mazzeu owns a company called DMZ Connection, which imports and distributes RFID solutions for the Latin American market. He is currently starting up "Instituto High Performance", a company that will teach leadership, sales and communication skills to executives. The course is based on Hill´s life changing philosophy, management skills and public speaking.

Connect with Daniel Mazzeu:

Daniel@dmzconnection.com or Daniel@institutohp.com.br

Telefone: +55-11-97700-0088

HOW I DISCOVERED MY LIFE'S PURPOSE

By: Mani Maran

I was born in a small village in the Southern region of India. In those places, the entire neighborhood is like one big community, almost a family to each other. I still remember an incident that happened when I was 9 years old, which changed my life forever. When my next-door neighbor, aged around 50, became suddenly ill, his family took him to a government run hospital. Government run hospitals are free but offer only basic services. I was surprised when they brought him back the same day, and so I walked over and asked his family how he was doing. They looked sad, and told me that the doctor told him that he would only live for a couple of days unless he gets further treatment in a private hospital. They did not have money to take him to a private hospital, so they brought him back home to die - which he did a few days later. That was the biggest shock in my young life - for the poor, money can make the difference between life and death. I decided in that moment that I had to do something about it, and that thought is still shaping my life.

Indian parents want to see their child become a doctor or an engineer. Students were score based on class ranks, not on individual grades. I did very well until middle school and was the top student in my school until the 8th grade. When I went to high school, competition was tough and I was not able to maintain my top ranking. I was frustrated. We had state level public exams in 10th grade. I took the final exams very seriously and worked very hard. When the results came in, I was proud to learn that I scored the second best grades at my high school. After failing to do well in 9th grade then reaching a major milestone at 10th grade, my confidence soared. I was jumping for joy, which was a proud moment of my life.

For my 11th grade, I changed courses and all subjects were taught through my second language, English. The 11th grade was very challenging for me, and I began to fall behind. My 12th grade exams were again scored on the state level. I worked hard but did not score enough marks to go to engineering or medical college. I was frustrated that I could not make my parents proud. This was one of the saddest moments of my life.

Since I always did well in math, I chose it as my major in college. I did not get admission into the top colleges, and so I studied at a local college. I worked hard and did well enough to earn my Bachelor degree. After graduating, I applied to three graduate colleges and was accepted by my least favorite choice first. Since I had not heard from my other two choices yet, I was forced to go to my least preferred college. On my way to enroll, I took a detour and went to visit my uncle. After spending a few days there, I reluctantly went to that college to start my Master's degree. I met a friend on the way and learned from him that I got accepted to my favorite college, and my father had already completed the admission process for that college. My joy knew no bounds. This was one of the happiest moments of my life.

After I completed my Master's degree, I gained a lot of confidence. I wanted to become a District Collector; the highest civilian official position in India. District collectors in India are selected at the national level through a grueling three part exam process. People train for this for years. Since I had high confidence, I thought I could face the exams with less preparation. I did not have a training facility in my neighborhood, and so I went to India's capital, enrolled in few courses and studied for six months. I appeared for the preliminary exam and I failed to pass it. I felt so bad. This was one of the gloomiest times of my life.

I did not know what to pursue after that. Since my parents were teachers, they asked me to complete a PhD and become a college professor. I did not want to become a teacher and so I started looking for something new and found an institution that teaches software in a distant city. I moved there and was hired to teach math at a private school. I studied for my software diploma in the evening. That was one of the luckiest moments of my life. I did very well with the software course. I became a top student again. I got a lucky break after completing that diploma course when I got a job with a leading Tire Company. I even got to work on a new UNIX platform and learned new RDMS software as part of my job. I worked very hard for the next few years and spent sleepless nights delivering software projects on time. Then I switched to HP, a US company based in Chennai. This time I had more exposure to the UNIX operating system and different RDMS packages. Life was good and challenging. I set up a goal to come to the US.

I got married in 1993 and was transferred to HP India office in Bangalore, the Silicon Valley of India. My wife and I both worked in Bangalore. After working for a year at the Bangalore office, I received a lucky break and was able to go to the US. I landed in Philadelphia in 1994 and started working as an Oracle database administrator trainer. I ate, lived and breathed Oracle and doubled my income in 4 years.

In those days, I used to go to the Borders bookstore to read and buy books about software technology. During one of those trips, I stumbled upon the personal development section in the store. Until that time, I had vague ideas of what I wanted to accomplish in my life and had never sat down and thought about what exactly I wanted to achieve. After reading the personal development books, attending seminars and listening to audios and watching videos, I started developing more confidence. I tripled my income in 8 years after coming to the US.

After I received green card in 2002, I quit my corporate job and started a web development franchise. I attended networking events and groups like BNI and multiple Chambers of Commerce to develop relationships and create new leads. After 2 years of hard work I started generating revenue from my web development business and then I had an opportunity to start a restaurant. I started a South Indian Restaurant in 2004. It became popular and got reviewed in The New York Times newspaper. I also started investing in real estate in order to have multiple streams of income. Everything went well for the next few years and then; when the recession came in 2008 my business went south. I could not continue with my restaurant and I was at the lowest point of my financial life. I got out of the restaurant business and went back to work.

I was forced to file Chapter 11 Bankruptcy and worked out a 10 year payment plan with the creditors which I have been paying every month for the last 6 years. I lost a lot of money with my business ventures, and at the same time learned from the experiences. This experience made humble. I understood the problems of blue-collar workers because I experienced the feeling of not having enough money to pay the bills. Every week, during the off day at the restaurant, I used to sit in front of a pile of bills and wonder how to pay them.

Once I went back to work, I started breathing again financially but I had lost confidence in myself. I felt like a failure. I did not attend any seminars, read books or listen to audio books or videos for the next few years. I completely stayed away from personal development and growth for a while. Once my wounds were healed, I started playing tennis to focus on my health. Then I started attending coaching programs on personal development. One of my coaches helped me clear my negative beliefs about me and then things started to shift in the right direction for me.

By 2012, I returned to the Information business for personal development. I learned how to develop a huge Facebook fan base for the business. I ventured into writing a personal development book that took me almost one year to complete. My first book on personal development is, "The Magic of Attracting Money." I loved the process of writing the book and learned the system and methods of how to write a book. The book was launched by Jack Canfield and Raymond Aaron at an event in Toronto, Canada. The book launch, and having the book available on Amazon was one of the proudest moments of my life.

Since my favorite leader Bob Proctor always talks about Napoleon Hill and the book Think and Grow Rich, I began to get interested in, and became a huge fan of, Napoleon Hill's work. I have a collection of 20+ Napoleon Hill books and many audios in my library. I wanted to learn some of the concepts in detail by becoming a Napoleon Hill Foundation Certified Instructor. I had a great time participating in the PMA distance-learning course and was able to connect with some great people. The Leader Certification classes were truly life changing. I had attended many seminars in my life and had always observed back of the room sales and how to move a person to the next big ticket item of the organizers. The leadership team from The Napoleon Hill Foundation was truly exceptional. They gave, gave and gave all week long and shared books, ideas, assignments and projects to apply the 17 Success Principles in day-to-day life. I came back from the leadership certification event with lots of friends and tons of ideas. My wife, who accompanied me to this course, had some life changing moments as well. After the leadership training, I did two more projects to earn the Certified Instructor designation. This was one of the proudest moments of my life. I will always cherish the PMA Science of Success book that is only given to students of the leadership certification course.

One of my goals is to become a speaker and so I joined a local Toastmasters group and gave speeches. Bob Proctor always talks about the Bill Gove speech workshop. I enrolled in the Bill Gove speech workshop and attended a 3-day event in LA at the beginning of 2015 and met Steve Siebold and Dawn Andrews there. Unlike many seminars, this was a closed seminar with only 10 or 12 participants. The method they taught was totally different than what was taught at Toastmasters. Steve and Dawn were completely open and they gave everything they had without hiding anything. That was another life changing event for me. At that time, I was in the middle of completing my book, building my information business, and developing a real estate investment business, in addition to my full time job in IT. The idea of multiple streams of Income is totally ingrained in my thinking, but I did not have the bandwidth to do all of them. I started focusing on completing book as the number one priority. By the first quarter of 2015, my book was ready and I slowly put a stop to the information business.

I joined Steve's million-dollar speakers club. I started writing vignettes and testing those vignettes at my local Toastmasters club. While all these things are going on, I also understood the importance of health and so I started training for long distance running. I started with a 5K at the end of 2013 then completed my first Rutgers half marathon in April 2014. I went on to complete in my first Philadelphia Marathon in November 2014 and then completed two more marathons, the NJ Marathon and the NYC Marathon. By the end of 2015, I had completed 3 marathons and had the pride of being a published author. These accomplishments added more and more confidence, which helped me to do everything a little better.

With all this experience, I understand the importance of keeping healthy as the number one priority to accomplish bigger and better goals. When 2016 rolled around, I had chosen even higher goals for my health and career. I decided to lose 20 lbs. and have a 25 BMI (Body Mass Index). I also decided to work only with Steve Siebold in order to become a world-class speaker and develop my speaking business. I always loved playing tennis, and I want to move to the next level at the USTA (United States Tennis Association) level. I have been a captain of the USTA tennis team for several years. From my tennis team experience, I can relate to the Napoleon Hill quote, "The climb upwards will be easier if you take others along with you."

I am turning 50 this year and I feel like it will be my best year ever. I have a definite purpose for my life, to become a world-class keynote speaker. I am working with the right mentor, one of the top keynote speakers in the country. I got over the concept of multiple streams of income and now am focused on one career objective. I know it is a long road to make it in the speaking business and I am ready for the challenge. I understand that health plays the major role in accomplishing big things and so I force myself to prepare for marathons and triathlons. Preparing for these races keeps me in good health. I also love tennis and my fun goal is to move to the next level in the USTA rankings this year.

In the speaking business, Steve talks about ABC. A is the art, B is the business and C is the content. A part of the business is writing vignettes creatively. This is one of the hardest parts of a speaker's life in my opinion. These cute personal stories have to be written in a way that entertains a live audience. The business part is developing relationships with the key contacts in the target market. As of now, I do not have content for the corporate market and so I partnered with Steve and his Mental Toughness content. I love this concept of mental toughness. Professional athletes use mental toughness secrets for peak performance. Steve devised a way to teach sales people to perform like professional athletes in a tough sales environment. Mental toughness is a process of teaching sales teams or leadership teams psychological performance. I am so excited to be working with Steve and learning the mental toughness content so I can make a positive difference in people's lives.

I had had ups and downs, confusions, and lack of focus in my life. Now, at 50 years old, I have clarity and purpose in my life. You may run into the right mentor or decide on your career much earlier in your life. For me it took lot of time to figure out what I wanted to do for the rest of my life. Even today, it is not easy to stay focused and do the right things to march forward with my goals. Some days I lose interest or focus when things do not turn out the way I wanted. It is not the instant gratification, but the delayed gratification that works. It is all about leaving a legacy. It boils down to learning the skills and gaining the experience, and preparing to become the best at what you do. My advice to you is to choose the profession that you love and try to find a way to make money from that. It is not easy to make big bucks; you have to be in the top 5% of your field to do it. Once you put the effort in to become the top 5% in any field, money will follow.

My life's purpose is to make lots of money and give it away to people in need. There are people from some parts of the world who do not know how to earn money, just like my neighbor in India who died young due to a lack of money. I want to help those types of people. The root cause of their problem is lack of education. I want to fund schools and colleges in third world countries so that kids from poor families can go to school and become self-sufficient. This is the vision for my life. I wish a wonderful career, health, wealth and peace of mind.

BIO

Mani Maran's real-life story starts from a humble beginning. He was born in a small village at the interior part of South India. Through his hard work and efforts, he came to the US in 1994 to work as a software consultant. Though he was successful at his corporate work, when he ventured into business world, he was not so successful at it.

He owned and operated restaurants, apartment complexes, real estate investments and a web development business. He was forced out of all these businesses during the economic recession in 2009, and reached the lowest point of his financial life. But these failures taught him great lessons.

He searched for answers as to how to develop success. He reached out to business coaches and studied self-revealing books and became Napoleon Hill Certified Instructor. These efforts helped him realize that success comes from within you.

Mani can be reached at 1-609-799-7840 and email srmmaran@gmail.com

MY MISSION: NOT JUST TO EXIST

By: Makiko Watanabe

"Definiteness of purpose is the starting point of all achievement. Without a purpose and a plan, people drift aimlessly through life. "
- Napoleon Hill

Have you ever thought about the reason why you were born? Of course you have because it is a natural desire for all of us to search for our purpose in life. We start by asking ourselves; what is my dream? What makes me happy? But this is only the beginning. You must listen to your inner voice about what you really want to do with your life. Have you taken action toward your purpose?

MY MAJOR PURPOSE IS TO HELP PEOPLE TO RECALL THEIR MISSIONS AND CREATE PEACEFUL MINDS IN ADDITION TO SPREADING THE JAPANESE CULTURE AND JAPANESE SPIRIT ALL OVER THE WORLD.

Everyone has a mission to not just exist in the world. It is important to know that the answer you have been looking for is in your own mind. The idea of what you really want to live for does not come from outside of yourself. It has taken me a lot of time to come to understand this secret. In the past I was looking for answers outside of myself. I believed I could discover them someday if I always did my best. I had come to realize that there were no answers that I really wanted to know about myself from the outside world. The point is many people don't focus on their inner voice, which helps them to reveal their own mission for life. The word "mission (使命(shi mei))" means "using our life" in Japanese.

A strong will to charge for my dream

Life is a precious journey to know oneself. While seeking importance externally, people may not notice that they already have it internally. Through the decisions I have made I gained wonderful experiences, which directed me to become who I am today. When I think of my life, there are several turning points that come to mind. The first one was my decision to go abroad in order to study psychology at a university in USA. When I was a high school student, I was interested in learning more about our heart and mind. So I decided to take the exam to be a psychology major. However, I failed to pass all of the entrance examinations for the national universities and famous private universities in Japan. I wanted to study psychology because I wanted to become a counselor and help people to solve their hardships and difficulties. On the other hand, I had developed a deep inferiority complex about myself because of failing the exam. I was in a situation where I felt such a big gap between my ideal life and my current reality.

Then one fateful day I received a postcard that was written about state universities abroad. I never thought about attending a university abroad before. I still remember the exciting feeling I felt in my heart that special day. When I received the postcard, it was like a bright ray of hope that released me from my despair. I couldn't help thinking about it and I believed firmly that it was the only way that I could satisfy my empty heart. My father was very strict with my sister, brother and I during my childhood. I am the middle child in my family. My siblings and I believed we would go to college, but it meant it would cost a lot of money. So I needed to be strong courageous to tell my parents about my thoughts. So I talked with my grandmother about my desire and she listened to me very carefully and encouraged me. However, when I asked my father to support my desire to go abroad to study psychology, he refused my proposal. But I didn't give up on it and talked to my mother. She understood me and she also took sides with me. My mother was there with me when I tried asking my father again. He looked straight into my eyes and finally agreed to support me to go abroad. He said there was no choice except to say "yes" when he saw the determination in my eyes.

I later understood why it was very tough and difficult for my parents to support my desire. It was not only the financial aspect but also the mental aspect that was tough for them. Thanks to a lot of support from my family and relatives, I was able to spend a wonderful time in the United States. I received several scholarships from the psychology department and international office. I was able to graduate from the university in three and half years. Because of my father's foresight and approval, and my mother's deep understanding and support, I developed a strong will to charge ahead for my dream. The decision I made for my dream taught me how powerful having a definite purpose can be. Without my definite purpose, I would have taken a completely different path for my life. The knowledge I gained gave me the power to move toward greater opportunities, which established the fundamental foundation for my life.

Listening to my inner voice

My next turning point was during the Great East Japan Earthquake in March 11, 2011. On that day I was in Sendai, which was one of the main areas that received damage from the tsunami.

After returning to my country, I worked for a consulting company in Japan. I helped people who had worries and wanted to live a happier life. I acquired enthusiasm and a sense of mission in those days. Because the work was so rewarding and enjoyable to me, I worked all day long without taking a lot of time off. I strongly believed that I had a vocation for this work. One day, I cleaned up at the workplace in the morning, consulted with clients and had lunch as usual. I had a meeting with a client at three, so I was preparing for that appointment. The bell rang at two forty and I went to the door to greet her. A few minutes later, at the moment she sat down on the sofa, I suddenly felt the rumbling of the ground. The building around me was shaking which caused a sudden power outage. After a brief conversation, we decided to wait for it to finish because I thought it would stop soon and the electricity would come back on. However, we felt the shaking was taking longer than usual, so I opened the door to look outside. I saw many cars shaking in the parking area and all the traffic lights went out. I told her to leave for her home soon and called for a taxi to pick her up at the front of the building because we didn't think trains would be in service. Then she told me about the heavy traffic jam and that it would take her more than twice the normal time to arrive home.

The earthquake was followed by many aftershocks. I tried to talk on the cell phone, but there was no cellular connection and public telephones were also not working. I looked outside and saw strong winds blowing the snow. There was a blizzard during what was supposed to be a sunny day. The situation was bizarre because it didn't snow in March. At the night I walked around our neighborhood to see what was going on. I walked in the darkest night and I saw only the light from many stars glittering beautifully in the silent night. I felt as if I had been in a disaster movie. The blackout lasted three days in my area and many aftershocks still continued to occur.

I started to think about what to do after the earthquake, but when I tried to focus on my decisions, the earthquake experience gave me an opportunity to think about myself. As the sun went down, I went to bed earlier than usual and thought I could sleep forever. During that time I found myself exhausted. I tried to believe in myself and that everything would be all right. On the other hand, there were aftershocks one after another, so I was becoming consumed by fear. At the darkest hour of the night I asked myself how I used my life to exist and I tried to listen to my inner voice. I found there were some concerns in my mind since I started working the consulting job. One of my concerns was a custom of speaking English because I seldom spoke English in those days. Another one was to understand Japanese culture deeply so that I could explain about Japanese culture and Japanese spirit.

As I continued to work, I started volunteer activities in the damaged area. After a year, I decided to quit my job and went back to my hometown. I started to work as an English teacher for kids and a translator in an agricultural company because I believed that teaching was a great way to improve my English skills, and the Japanese agriculture technology is the best in the world. I had gained many experiences and increased my skills for two years. Listening to my inner voice has helped me to strengthen my definite purpose in life.

The Achievus experience

After two years, I got married and I moved to Yamanashi prefecture where Mt. Fuji is located. During this time my husband, Keisuke, showed me how to play Achievus. He was so excited about it and told me how wonderful it was. "Achievus" is a cooperative board game, which is based on Dr. Napoleon Hill's 17 Success Principles. The inspiration for inventing the Achievus game came from Jeremy Rayzor's study of Dr. Napoleon Hill's 17 Principles and his desire to create games that educate through the value of play. My understanding of playing "Achievus" is that it provides us with a fun way to learn the 17 Principles of Success through face to face communication, creating profound harmony among the players. My husband is No. 8 of the Achievus trainers in Japan. He has held a lot of Achievus Events all over the prefecture. He has introduced Achievus to many people, families, groups and schools. He says it is a powerful tool to use for developing strong relationships, and bonding with people of different ages. Because he has played Achievus many times, his pleasing personality has increased.

There are particularly two positive outcomes of playing Achievus with families that I would like to share with you. One family played Achievus with their 6-year-old daughter many times. Because of the parent's initiative to play Achievus with their daughter she was able to memorize all of the 17 principles by discussing them with her parents. Then one snowy day her parents were shoveling snow and their daughter decided to take "Personal Initiative!" She started to help her parents shovel snow without being asked. The parents were very impressed with her because she had never taken personal action to help them like this before. As the family continued to play Achievus, the 17 principles became a common language used by the family. One of Mr. Rayzor's hopes for inventing the game was that children and parents would build harmony together while becoming familiar with the 17's principles through playing Achievus as a family.

Another wonderful experience was between a husband and wife. When they played Achievus, the husband showed hesitation for playing the game at first. As time passed, he started to enjoy it and became very excited during the game. The husband told me that he couldn't look at his wife's eyes at first, but at the end of the game, his actions and feelings changed. He was able to look into her eyes again. Through the game Achievus, they were able to interact positively and his attitude about her was changed into a positive mental attitude. After playing, he shared with us "Achievus showed me how important family is and the way I ought to be." Then he said "I remember the way I felt before about my family."

A unified dream

By playing Achievus, I can learn the 17 principles and feel a sense of unity with the group even though it is only for a short time. Back in

2014, an Achievus convention was held in Japan. Mr. Rayzor came to Japan and I supported him as a translator for two weeks. We all had fun time during his visit. He shared with us how he came up with the idea to create Achievus and what he has learned about Dr. Napoleon Hill's 17 Principles of Success. He showed us how to play his new educational game called "Ticket to Wealth" 100% Pure Mental Gold, which provides multiple choice challenges to help understand the 17 principles more deeply. After a successful Achievus convention, we came up with the idea for an Achievus English Project. This project is a "Dream Camp": a unified dream for Achievus English Program members.

"Cherish your vision and your dreams as they are the children of your soul, the blueprints of your ultimate achievements. "
-Napoleon Hill

When I was studying at the university, I had a dream about traveling to many countries and understanding their cultures as well as eating delicious foods, watching beautiful scenery, and seeing wonderful people beyond the border. I attended cultural events of foreign countries several times at the university. These opportunities were really wonderful for me to understand other cultures. However, I noticed I couldn't talk about deepness of Japanese culture at the time. Because I understood the importance of cultural diversity in addition to respect for individuals from other cultures as being equal, I strongly hoped to establish and develop my identity as Japanese.

On the morning after the Great East Japan Earthquake, I saw people in line waiting to get free food in front of the supermarket. Without any problems and any complaints, they waited for their turn silently, regardless of the difficult circumstances. No one had to order the people to be silent because the Japanese people waited patiently. This is one of the moments that helped me to appreciate the Japanese spirit.

Achievus helps me to meet many wonderful people. In particular, a wonderful married couple brought me many changes, especially the wife Miki. She taught me the essential parts of Japanese spirit that I had been eager to know. Now I had two desires; to teach English, and to provide women with Japanese culture and Japanese spirit so they understand their mission and their roles. Every experience has a meaning. When a point is connected to a point, it becomes a line; one experience is connected to another experience, which creates our life. When I was in Japan and looked for something important from the outside world, I couldn't find it. But now I believe I have found the secret that is in the Japanese culture.

Peace around the world

I'm an Achievus trainer, and I can see some similarities between Achievus and Japanese culture. Because Achievus is a powerful educational game that shows players how to help another person, it creates harmony. Harmony is one of the most important values of the Japanese culture. The more people play Achievus, the more consideration for others they acquire. The players become thoughtful of others, and can put themselves in the place of others because they try to achieve a common goal together. We call such a warm consideration "Omoiyari（思いやり）" in Japanese, and we Japanese people also put value and importance on "Omoiyari". The feelings of "Omoiyari" can increase a peaceful state of mind because people who have the "Omoiyari" cannot be self-centered. They consider other people's feelings as if it were their own. In addition to acquiring "Omoiyari", we can gain knowledge of the 17 Principles of Success by playing Achievus. The principles of success can guide us to become quality global leaders.

For the Achievus English Program, we offer an opportunity to become familiar with speaking English: to break emotional barriers toward speaking English, and to open one's heart by playing Achievus and other activities. The Achievus English Program also aims to encourage Japanese people to define their dreams and make a speech of their dream in English. Then we want to support the people who conduct activities across national boundaries with their strong definite purpose. We hope that it will be one of the powerful tools used to bridge Japan and other countries. And I hope it connects to world peace because the more people that have "Omoiyari", the more peaceful the state of peace in the world becomes.

BIO

MAKIKO WATANABE worked as a counselor for seven years. Since she experienced the Great East Japan Earthquake on March 11 in 2011, she has worked as a translator and an English teacher. She is also an Achievus trainer and she provides opportunities to encourage people to understand the 17's Principles of Success by playing Achievus. During "Dream Camp", which is the Achievus English Program, people looked for their dreams and they give speeches about them in English at the end.

She believes it helps people to take actions toward their dreams and develop human resources as global leaders. In addition, she puts a high value on Japanese culture and the Japanese spirit. She has a course called "Yamatonadeshiko", which stands for the beauty of traditional Japanese woman. The course helps woman to awake their missions and understand their roles. Her mission is to spread the secret of Japanese culture for world peace. Makiko can be reached at taramakiko@gmail.com

BEYOND "WHAT IF"…
By: Dave Doyle

"What if I'm too small, big, slow, fast, smart, dumb, ugly, beautiful?"

"What if I try and it's just not enough?"

"What if make the wrong choice?"

"What if I'm not good enough?"

"What if they don't like me?"

"What if I'm wrong?"

"What if I'm right?"

"What if I can't?"

"What if I FAIL?"

"What if…?"

"What if…?"

"What if I WIN?"

"What if I Can?"

"What if I'm Right?"

"What if I'm Not wrong?"

"What if they LOVE Me?"

"What if I Am good enough?'

"What if I make the Right choice?"

"What if I try and it works and I Succeed?"

"What if I AM small, big, slow, fast, smart, and beautiful enough?"

"What if...?" is a very powerful question. The challenge is to decide what words or thoughts we will use right after it. As I've illustrated above, we can decide to follow the downward, spiraling path of doubt or we can decide to follow the path of Possibilities and Rise to the top.

A Story of Purpose and Moving Beyond What If...

Long before I ever heard of Napoleon Hill and his 17 Principles of Success, I was putting out to the universe my personal Definite Major Purpose. I remember that as a teenager when people would ask me the question "what do you want to be when you grow up?" I always had my answer. In fact I vividly remember a time standing in the kitchen, when my amazing, supporting Mom asked me that very question and I answered her with "I'm going to be a business owner. I'm going to be my own boss." She looked at me and asked, "what kind of business?" and I replied, "I have no idea, it doesn't really matter...I just know I'm going to own my own business."

That is the first specific memory that I have of the evidence of my entrepreneurial spirit. I don't know where it came from; it was just there and it wasn't going away.

I started working at 13 years old with a newspaper delivery route and was hired for my first 'real job' bussing tables at Pizza Hut at 15. I always had a job after that and developed a strong work ethic, performing well for my employers but never staying too long at any position. I found that I got restless once I was comfortable at a job, so if I didn't see something new or better on the horizon, I started looking elsewhere until I found something fresh to try.

Looking back, I still feel that I was a decent employee for the time that I spent at any one job, but I also understand that my DNA is set up for me to be an entrepreneur. The jumping around from job to job over the years was actually my education system and playground for learning the many things that would prepare me for what I really wanted to do. I learned different company cultures, management styles, operation systems, sales systems and techniques, I learned what I liked about some bosses and what I didn't like about others and so on and so on. I also distinctly remember paying attention to what my supervisors, managers, and employers were doing. I was always curious and poking my head into wherever the bosses were, eavesdropping on their conversations and trying to hear the inner circle talk of the people at the top. I learned how they interacted with each other which was often much different than how they interacted with staff. I learned how they thought and how they talked about the staff they were in charge of and this enabled me to position myself in the best light – I had the inside edge, the inside Intel to give them what they wanted.

I was never consciously aware and thinking about these things. It wasn't a thought out plan or strategy. It's only in hindsight that I now see exactly what it was that I was doing. I was simply acting from my own DNA and instinct to fulfill my Definite Purpose of 'being my own boss and owning my own business'. It wasn't defined, written down or planned, but it was ingrained through a burning desire to have it.

This back-story is a simple example of how the 1st of Napoleon Hill's 17 Principles of Success works. The principle is called Definiteness of Purpose and it basically says that when you have a burning desire to obtain or achieve something to the point that it becomes an all consuming purpose in your life, you will continue to think about that thing all of the time, and if you are constantly thinking about it you will automatically start acting in ways that will put the pieces of the puzzle together for you to eventually get that thing that you desire.

Now that I know of this principle, it's easy for me to look back and see how it worked. In fact, I would bet that you who are reading these words now, may already have been thinking of times in your past when you have done the same towards a Definite Purpose of your own.

After attending College and receiving a Diploma in Criminology, I continued to work at different jobs and continued to learn and grow. At the same time, I was always open to opportunity and anytime I heard someone talking about business or when someone approached me about something new, I was all ears and digging deep into whatever was presented wondering if this would be my break into business. I also had many ideas of my own, some of which were ok and I attempted but never got anywhere with. The experiences that I took away from each attempt however, was huge. Those were the baby steps and trial & error lessons that started it all.

Life was also happening throughout all of this; loves found and lost, family dramas and reconciliations, death and taxes...all of the realities of life that can easily derail or delay the achievement of the dreams and goals that we are after. And so it was that I found myself living a life where things felt blurry and out of focus. My marriage was slowly falling apart, there were concerns with family and I was working at a job that I was comfortable in and doing well at but knew deep down that I would never be truly happy there even though I was being groomed for promotions and management.

It's often in these times that we are defined. I could have succumbed to the numb and drifted, but my burning desire to be in business was still there, just below the surface, and when opportunity presented itself the chills and shivers of excitement came instantly. It was game on. Again, it's a simple story but it illustrates the concept of Purpose and choosing one path over the other in regards to the question of 'What If'. Here's how it happened…

I was working 2 jobs to make ends meet for my wife and I as she finished her University Degree. The first was a newspaper bundle drop-route that I did from 3:30am - 6am, 7 days a week. I was then commuting 30 minutes across the city to get to my main job every day, working 7am – 3pm; a pretty good gig. It was a good job in a big company that treated its team well, offering training and learning with room for promotion. Things were looking up for me there, but I knew that it was not something I was passionate or even excited about doing long term.

It was February of 2000 when I heard that a friend of a friend opened up a new sandwich shop just 2 blocks from my apartment and a few days later I decided to check it out. The moment I walked in I was impressed on many levels. It was a tiny shop, painted super bright in red and green with crazy cartoon meats and vegetables painted all over the walls. I'd never seen anything like it…and I loved it! The place was called Pita Pit and I ordered a Pita sandwich from the kooky menu. I looked around and took in all the details and when I saw the flat-top grill with meat and veggies sizzling on it then arrived at the sandwich station where they made the Pita to order right in front of me thoughts began racing through my mind; "this concept is brilliant!" "Look at how fresh and delicious and healthy it all looks!" "This is totally the trend for the future, a healthier fast food that's still cool and fun and tasty!".

I sat down and bit into my very first Pita Pit Pita and it was absolutely everything I had hoped it would be - X10. My entrepreneur DNA took over and I watched what was going on as I finished my Pita. I had already noticed that the tall guy making the Pitas and hustling just had to be the owner. As he cleaned up between customers I went to the counter and started asking questions and learned that he had been open for just over a week and was struggling to keep up. The sales were way higher than projected and he had not hired enough staff to keep up to the demand and could not even find the time to hire more. Meantime, he still had a full-time sales job that was being neglected and his bosses' patience was wearing thin.

"Listen Jeff," I said, "I could use a few extra bucks, could you use my help part-time in the evenings until you get staffed up?"

"Really?" he said. "Can you start tomorrow?"

I did start the next day and gave up the newspaper deliveries by the end of the week. I helped him train a few more staff (even though I was a rookie myself) and 3 weeks later he was spending less and less time at the Pita Pit and called me up for a meeting.

"Dave, I talked to my partner and he's onboard. I need to get back to my full-time job and I don't really want to be that hands on in this business. I've seen what you can do and we want to make you an offer. You come work full-time for us and you can have full reign of this store. You will be the manager and run the operation, reporting directly to me." We discussed salary and bonuses and it was more than I was making at the other job. I knew what I was going to do before the conversation even got rolling. This was my opportunity to really learn about running a business and getting my foot in the door. The fact that it was 2 blocks from home and more money was secondary. I was already seeing the future where I would own a Pita Pit. 4 weeks earlier I had never even heard of them.

For the next year I kicked ass! I started to learn the art of marketing and networking B2B (business to business), sales continued to increase and I found that I was loving everything that I was doing. I hired and fired, discovered a passion for building a team and for serving others, creating raving fans in my customers. I'm proud to say that I have developed relationships with customers and Team members (staff) that I still maintain over 16 years later. I kept a private journal, which I filled with business notes about the things I learned and ideas for the future. I went through the process of applying for a franchise with a couple of friends and learned what it was going to take to get it done. I was on a roll and I could start to taste it...the taste of the Pitas in my very own location.

A speed bump turned up after one year when Jeff and his partner sold the store and the new owner sent in a new manager. I was caught complete unaware, was paid 2 weeks severance and pushed out of what I felt was 'my' Pita Pit within a matter of hours. Ouch.

I took a seasonal promotional job at a radio station for the summer (a contact made through marketing for Pita Pit) and maintained the relationships that I had made over the last year. Another Pita Pit location had just opened up in another part of the city and I had good relations with the owners there as they had come into the store I managed to do some research 6 months earlier. I had been accommodating and helpful and it paid off. I went into their new store to say hello and let them I was no longer working at the other location. There were 4 partners and they already had 3 stores and were looking to expand. They quickly offered me a position to come help manage the new location as they worked to expand their Pita Empire.

I got to work but it really wasn't ideal for me. I didn't have the control I had at the other store and didn't see an opportunity yet in their bigger operation. I kept at it, staying open and ready for something to pop. Now we get to the punch line, the part of the story where it all comes together.

My wife and I were just separated. We were on good terms and owned a house together which had little equity and that was about it. I had nothing else and my personal life and finances were in the lurch. I had become friends with my employers, Neil, Jason and Wayne and one normal morning, Neil asked me the simple question, "Hey Dave, aren't you from Grande Prairie?"

I said, "no, but my in-laws are there and I have lots of family there and in that area, why?"

He said, "There's a Pita Pit opening up there."

"Wow" I said, "That location is going to absolutely kill it! They are about to go into a boom period up there and this concept is perfect. Great move by that owner..."

Then Neil said something that changed everything. This next moment was literally a defining moment for my entire life and I remember it like it just happened 5 minutes ago. Neil said, "Actually, they don't have a franchisee yet, just a location."

My brain worked through more raw data and processed more thought, imagination, planning and excitement in those next 2 seconds than in the last year! In those 2 seconds my future was decided upon, planned and executed. I don't know what happened after that, the rest of the day is a total blank. I do remember getting no sleep that night and working my brain to overload and I remember arriving at work the next day and asking Neil and Wayne into the office for a word.

"Hey guys. Something has come up and I need to let you know that I have to give you my notice that I will not be able to work for you for much longer. I'm not sure exactly when my last week will be, but I have to give you fair warning." They looked at me and asked what was up? Was everything ok? Did I find another job? I said, "No, everything is great. It's just that I'll be opening up the Grande Prairie Pita Pit soon so I won't be able to work here any longer."

Now these guys knew my personal situation and knew that my resources were limited to say the least. So they asked me straight out, "How the heck are you gonna do that?"

"I have no idea. All I know is, that location is mine. I don't know how yet, but I already know it's my store. I'm getting a hold of the franchise today to let them know and start the process."

For the next two days, I made phone calls to family, friends and contacts that I thought had the resources to help me make this happen. I painted the picture for them, selling the dream and opportunity that I knew to my core was a great one. I told them they could put the money up to finance the whole deal, I would do all of the work and I would give them 49% ownership. With my experience over the last 18 months running two locations it was a slam-dunk. I had a few people on the hook and thinking about it when I got to work a few days later to see that all 3 of my employers were at the store together. This was a rare event. They called me into the office for a meeting.

"Dave, did you find what you needed to get the deal done?"

"Not yet," I said, "but I have people looking into it."

"Ok, well we need to talk then. How sure are you that this location in Grande Prairie will be a good one?"

"100% sure," I said. "I would bet that it will be one of the top locations in the franchise."

"Well in that case, here's the plan," they said. "We've talked over the last few days and we've decided that we're going to buy that location. We are set with the franchise and have the resources to do it. Our challenge is that none of us want to move up there. So the plan is that we set you up and move you there. You become our Managing Partner and earn shares in our company and you can buy us out in a year or two. We'll get you a new vehicle, pay you a manager salary and you'll earn the shares. What do you think?"

After 5 more minutes of discussion to go over a few details and to make sure I was getting what I wanted, we made a deal with a handshake and the rest as they say is history. I signed the house over to my ex-wife and moved to Grande Prairie a few months later to oversee the final build out of the store and we opened Jan 2, 2002. For that year, the sales at my new location were 2nd highest in the franchise. Just over two years later, I had 25% ownership in earned shares and bought the franchise, partnering with my parents. Fifteen months after that we opened a second location in the same city. I still own and operate both high performing locations today.

The future that I saw flash in my mind in that moment of my core decision when Neil made that statement had now come to pass.

What if?

What if, when Neil made that statement I had said things like:

What if it's a bad idea for that city and location?

What if I can't really run a store on my own?

What if I can't find all the money?

What if the economy crashes?

What if I'm not good enough?

What if I can't find a partner?

What if it's too hard?

What if I fail?

What if…

If I had entertained even a thought of asking questions like these, I would not be where I am today. I would not have moved to a new city, I would not have met Amanda, the Love of my life and we would not have had our two amazing boys, Ashton and Rhys who are now almost 12 and 13 years old.

My life is amazing and I am so very grateful that as someone with a positive outlook on life and having a definite purpose, my mind rarely thought in terms of 'what if' and usually thought more in terms of 'I will' or 'When I'.

One of Albert Einstein's quotes regarding imagination is that "Imagination is more important than knowledge. For knowledge is limited to all we now know and understand, while imagination embraces the entire world, and all there ever will be to know and understand."

When we look to our own futures and can vividly imagine ourselves learning and growing, becoming better and better and more successful, we are on a path to making it happen. When this is backed with a driving and burning desire to achieve a definite purpose in life, we are surely in a state of achieving, moving beyond the question of 'What if' and turning dreams into reality.

> *"All our dreams can come true if we have the courage to pursue them."*
> – Walt Disney

What if it were true?

What if we all have the power to go and Do?

What if all we need is the courage to pursue?

What if...

BIO

Dave Doyle grew up training to be an entrepreneur.

He still owns and operates two top performing restaurants in the Pita Pit franchise and he served for 4 years on Pita Pit Canada's Marketing Advisory Committee.

He has been a top performer since 2009 in his current business as an Independent Consultant with ORGANO International.

He was a founding member for three and a half years at the first BNI Chapter in his city and served as President in its second year.

Dave has been a student of personal development for almost 20 years. Since studying the 17 Success Principles of Napoleon Hill and taking the Leadership Certification Course through the Napoleon Hill Foundation, he is driven to increase PMA around the world and was a contributing Author of the Amazon International Bestselling Book "Refusing To Quit", written by Napoleon Hill Students and Instructors.

He is now sought after as a speaker and trainer and is a co-creator of the Life Mastery Symposium.

Dave's passions are Business and Personal Development for himself and others but his 'Why' is his family. His wife Amanda and his two sons Ashton and Rhys fuel his passions and bring him home every day.

Please send a virtual Hi-5 to Dave at:

LinkedIn: https://ca.linkedin.com/pub/dave-doyle/12/646/987

FB: https://www.facebook.com/pmadave/

Twitter: https://twitter.com/DaveDoylePMAPro

SnapChat: the-davedoyle

Instagram – davedoylemrpma

Periscope: @PMAprofessor

ORGANO – www.quidditycoffee.com

MY GREATEST FAILURE

By: John Westley Clayton

A Tragic Beginning

During my birth mother's engagement to my father, she received a letter from one of his co-workers. In the blink of an eye, the father of her unborn child—my father—was gone, having fallen from a cargo ship while at sea. Her dreams of a new beginning blurred in her tears.

Already parenting two children, her belief that she could not raise a third led her to a wonderful woman named Berta. The one thing Berta wanted more than anything in life was a child. She'd previously lost a child at birth, and had been told she'd never have another. The two women worked out the details through love instead of legalities.

When I was born, my Mom, Berta, went through the profound changes that only love can bring. Her affection for me opened new doors to more lives: she became pregnant and gave birth to a son she called Jimmy. Although she came to divorce her husband, she remarried and had two more healthy babies.

Though Berta's love was large, we grew up poor. I felt enriched and privileged—she seemed to credit my arrival as paving the way to her happiness, therefore the reason she could have more children—but that did not provide financial stability.

"I had all the disadvantages to be a success."
-Larry Ellison

As a child I'd look up at people who lived in big houses, drove luxury cars, and wore nice clothes, and I'd ask myself, 'What do I have to do to be like them and have what they have?' The innocence of childhood did not take into account the hows, or if each 'wealthy' individual was truly happy. Success equated to images of luxury goods.

I even considered going to an upscale neighborhood to knock on every door and ask each person for their secret to achieving the wealth they'd acquired; a mere child thinking of doing a survey.

At that time I did not have a successful role model in my life—no mentor extraordinaire, no solid leader from whom I could take notes. I had the love of a wonderful mother who lived in poverty, with a husband who parented the best he could with what he'd learned from his father.

Despite the chaos at home, I remained a 'white sheep' and received good grades; never got into trouble. I always looked at my situation with an inner knowledge that I would rise above my poverty-stricken childhood.

> *"He's got to make his own mistakes*
> *And learn to mend the mess he makes."*
> (Band: Rush, Song: New World Man,
> Album: Signals)

The Big Mistake

The word mistake has many definitions, from typo to goofy-blunder, from carelessness to downright stupidity; it's called a boo-boo, a brain freeze, a screw up, as well as being labeled with a few expletives. But beyond the slapstick, harmless, and ridiculous, it has a serious meaning in that it is a result of poor judgment; even the disregarding of rules and principles.

I longed to be 'rich'. I looked to those with extravagant lifestyles and wanted to know how they'd attained their status: the cars, the clothes, the houses. The first person I found to model my success after was Donald Trump. I saw him on TV, and I read his book. I wanted to be him. I was searching for a mentor without defining what 'rich' meant; I only knew what it looked like.

Full throttle, I headed toward 'rich'. It would be easier to leave this out of my story, but then it wouldn't show the distortion of my path at that time, nor would it reflect the record. And, in short, there simply wouldn't be a story—at least not this one.

Yes, I told myself, I would be a real estate mogul, and then I would be rich.

Though there's nothing wrong with having one's eye on the prize,

it's important to understand the entire package:

wrapping, tape, ribbons, box, as well as the contents.

I signed up for classes, arranged to be licensed under a broker, and obtained that license. Mogul-dom was just a step away...so it seemed...so I thought.

My real estate career ended before it ever got started: the broker closed up shop for residential sales. Bad luck. Hang head. Next dream?

I persevered. Something inside burned. And I truly believed that the solution was to work harder—not necessarily consider what it was I wanted to do to get to that vision of 'successful', rather a tunnel vision with excess wealth as the light of success at the end.

I grew up in a blue-collar family where all work was regarded as hard work. There was no passion in that toil: it was simply task-driven and chore-oriented. No joy was anticipated from the onset. No pleasure was attached to the outcome. It's safe to say that the 'mind' was not a part of it. And neither was the soul. Basically, hard work in my past was regarded as soulless, heartless, and mindless.

And yet I had a drive inside me, and a good work ethic, from learning that when there's a job to do, you do it. I had the mechanics of doing hard work. That part of the work ethic—get stuck in—was instilled in me, but it was not magnified until much later when I made a key connection.

With the real estate non-career behind me, I continued to pursue 'getting rich'. I read and researched ways to make money. I lost money— at least it seemed like a lot back then—working on 'get rich quick' schemes. I hated every one of them. I only did it because of the promise of riches. Eye on the prize, without understanding the prize.

At that time, if someone would have offered me 'any' prize on the shelf, I would have snatched it up, coveting it only because it was labeled as such. I have deep gratitude that such a gift was not offered to me, else I likely wouldn't be where I am now.

And that's where the two roads—of life—diverge. Once certain principles are understood, the path is clear for 'a-ha' moments, and stretches of learning open up and let the light flood in. And when it does, you are never left in the dark.

"Every day is a new day
I'm thankful for every breath I take
I won't take it for granted
So I learn from my mistakes. "
(Band P.O.D., Song: Alive, Album:
Satellite)

A Great Discovery

During my search to become 'rich' I came across the book "Think and Grow Rich" by Napoleon Hill.

"Wow, that sounds simple enough," I said.

I dived in. I loved it, even though I didn't completely understand it. So, I read it again. Funny how we repeat things until we learn them, isn't it?

I became super-charged from Dr. Hill's philosophy. I began following the principles he spoke of, and they lifted me to new levels. I began to achieve more. My hard-work ethic, combined with his principles of positivity, advanced me in all areas. When I adapted his principles, I found I excelled at everything I did.

And the principles were easy to apply. It felt good to engage in 'Going The Extra Mile'. Focusing on a 'Positive Mental Attitude' generated more positives. His other principles, including Enthusiasm and Teamwork, yielded positive results and gave me confidence.

I thought: 'This is what I've been waiting for to match my work ethic.'

I thought: 'Anybody can do the things that are suggested because they are not difficult.'

But, I also knew that these principles alone wouldn't make a person "rich".

I went into the sales business because I read somewhere that a good salesman will always make good money and will rarely be out of work. I studied the art of sales from greats like Zig Zigler and Tom Hopkins. I excelled. The pay was fantastic, but there was still something missing. I wasn't 'getting rich'.

"I'm convinced that about half of what separates successful entrepreneurs from non-successful ones is pure perseverance."
-Steve Jobs

I returned to Dr. Hill's book. I reflected on what he'd done and then written. He'd performed the same research I'd thought about doing as a kid—surveying the 'rich'. He'd interviewed 500 of the richest people who were living at that time: Henry Ford, Thomas Edison, Andrew Carnegie, John D Rockefeller, Charles Schwab, and others. I knew that there was an answer in that book. I'd read it TWICE, yet I could not figure out what I was missing. But I did not give up searching. I worked hard. I applied the principles. I was rewarded for the combination of both. But I was not satisfied.

The Greatest Failure

Hard work is drudgery when it has no meaning behind it. Ask anyone sentenced to labor how they feel about breaking rocks and hammering railway ties. Poll any group of people forced to do something they didn't choose. Hard work only pays when one understands the key ingredients needed for change.

The first ingredients of the recipe for 'the answer' came years later.

PURPOSE

and

PASSION.

Refer to it as purposeful passion or passionate purpose;

the combination is interchangeable, and dramatically life altering.

"Passion will always trump logic."
-John Westley Clayton

I was missing the first and most important principle of all. I was missing A DEFINITE MAJOR PURPOSE. And all three of these words are essential to becoming successful.

Definite Major Purpose is to Success what Air is to Breathing.

CLICK, CLICK, CLICK—like the tumblers in a safe lining up to open and reveal a philosopher's stone, a jewel filled treasure chest, with the bonus of the elixir of life. I had the combination. Kid in a candy shop? I was in the factory!

I realized that, when I added the component of 'passion' to the hard work and Dr. Hill's principles, it didn't feel like work. It felt like purpose. It felt like something had chosen me, and it became a privilege to perform, dance, entertain, sweat, cry, create, and innovate in every interaction with my passion. It was no longer work. As if magical, as I threw myself into that which I was passionate about—fulfilling my purpose—I thrived emotionally and financially. Who knew? Money could come as well as total happiness. Work didn't feel like work. Work felt like living life to its fullest.

The Three Words

DEFINITE: this means without a doubt—total confidence, sure, and with conviction that your PURPOSE is certain.

MAJOR: as in chief and foremost. The main reason. (Yes, you can have many minor purposes—and you should—but only one major PURPOSE).

PURPOSE: your reason for living. The object of your existence. Your cause. That which you are the poster child for. That which you're loyal to and would die for—and will die for.

"If you don't create your life purpose
and live your own dream,
you'll end up a roll-player in someone
else's. "
-John Westley Clayton

Many people live without purpose their whole lives. Others default to a sort-of-purpose. They experience ups and downs, but mostly the path is unexciting. They might look for stimuli to spice up life, not realizing they are missing a purpose; they are only filling a void. They survive. They manage. They get by.

Lack of purpose does not discriminate. Those who are financially secure, have wealth beyond the norm, and those who have talent but do not direct it, are not immune to lack of purpose. In many cases, happier is the volunteer who passionately works at his or her purpose in a homeless shelter, than an industry CEO. Purpose is available to all, yet few fully investigate, define, or exercise it.

"…falling is easy, it's getting back up that becomes the problem.
If you don't believe you can find a way out,
you become the problem…
if you believe you can find a way out, then you solve the problem."
(Band: Staind, Song: Falling, Album: Chapter V)

The Not so Obvious, Obvious.

Question: How does a person figure out their life purpose?

Answer: DO WHAT YOU LOVE!

And doing what you love means identifying and classifying all that you have not loved. It means engaging in some soul searching. Some would say taking a risk—but what risk? What could be more important than total happiness? I say it's taking a step. One step at a time, guided if you like, to finding the path to your PURPOSE.

When you do what you love—labor at something you are passionate about, something that is more important than anything else in the world—it will never feel like work.

You can go do something that makes you very wealthy, and live a miserable life. Or you can live your Life's Purpose and live in extreme bliss every day of your life AND still have an opportunity to become financially wealthy.

'Getting rich' isn't about having a lot of money. 'Being rich' is more about being happy than having luxury goods which you cannot appreciate because you have not found what makes you happy. Being financially wealthy is about having a lot of money.

"You are who and what you create
yourself to be."
-John Westley Clayton

BIO

Certified Napoleon Hill instructor, John Westley Clayton, motivates individuals, inspires business leaders, and moves mountains. His body of work includes the highly rated published books: Refusing to Quit (Compass Mastermind), and Journeys To Success. A forthcoming book titled Beyond "What If?" will continue the ripple effect of success. His personal brand of inspiration, Rock Star 4 life, is delivered from various platforms and presented with candid honesty and a genuine enthusiasm toward everyone's dreams. His active involvement and solution-oriented vision are backed by solid experience in business and sales. His extraordinary life story is worth the backstage pass. Clayton does not simply perform; he is the concert.

Got a dream? John Westley Clayton will put you center stage.

Got a pulse? John Westley Clayton will get you dancing to it.

Got a heartbeat? John Westley Clayton will get you rockin' to it.

Visit his website at www.johnwestley.com

or drop him a line at info@johnwestley.com

IS YOUR LIFE ON AUTO PILOT?

By: Ana C Fontes

Turn your life into a life that has meaning

Our negative thoughts and false beliefs distract us, and we lose control of our lives. Sometimes, we push the autopilot button to avoid facing reality. Life is simple, but we do a great job complicating it. When was the last time you dedicated a few hours of your day to evaluate your life? Have you ever boarded an airplane without knowing its destination? An airplane doesn't leave the airport without a "flight plan." It's the same with your life. You are the pilot of your own airplane. Living without a plan is like leaving without knowing your destination!

I am sure you plan a birthday party, a weekend trip, or a vacation, right? Of course! We all do. That is always exciting, and we want to make sure everything happens the way we planned. The first thing we do when we build a house is draw the blueprint. Then, we follow that blueprint in every step of the construction to make sure we get the house we planned. Why don't we do the same with our lives? Have you done your flight plan, or are you one of those people who wait to see what life will bring them, as if they have no control?

> *"Most people don't live their life; they accept their life."*
> -John C. Maxwell

Most people wake up in the morning without a target. They just HOPE good things will happen. If this sounds familiar to you, WAKE

UP! Change your life. To change your life, you have to change first! I will tell you a few stories of my life that made me who I am. I hope they will inspire you as they did me.

Learnings from my HERO: My Father

I was born and raised in Uberaba City, southeast of Brazil. I had a "normal" life, until I had my first loss experience when I was fifteen. My father passed away at 46, leaving my mother with three kids (16, 15 and 10 years old). My father was a very respected doctor, smart, and very dedicated. He went to the big city of São Paulo for college, and after long years of college and medical residency, he came back to his hometown with one goal in mind: to build something to improve the community's health. He founded a Pathology Laboratory in the city and later he also founded a Hematology Center. He implemented new blood exams and the latest technology, and after a while his company was ranked number one in the state, which made the city attractive for other companies in the field to come. He was loved and admired by the city. When we were walking on the streets, people would stop us all the time to talk to him and ask many questions, personal, and career advice, or they simply wanted to receive the positive energy he transmitted through his calm and peaceful smile. I never saw my father speaking loudly or yelling at anybody. He used to solve all problems talking with tranquility and common sense. The one thing he gave the most to his patients was love. People used to say he had such a great heart and energy that his patients would feel better, just by looking at him during their hospital visits. There was one thing that he could not do; separate his work life from his personal life. I remember like it was yesterday when my dad came home after spending several days at the hospital after his first heart attack. He was lying in bed and holding my hands. He said: Sweetheart, I love you so much. I recognize that I've devoted too much of my life to working. I knew that Mom was handling everything at home and so I put all my energy into my career, which I also love very much. My goal was always to give the best to my family. My big mistake was to think I had to work like crazy to accomplish it. That wasn't hard for me, because I really love what I do. I was taking care of my patients, devoting all my time to them, when the sickest one was myself. You are 15, and I'm finally spending time at home with my family, but I am sick and not able to have fun with my kids. I promise, when I recover, I will not work as much, and we will go on vacation more often. I want to enjoy life with my family, and I want to make up for lost time. Everything will be different. I promise!

I should have felt happy with my Dad's promise, but I felt so sorry and sad for him. I could feel by the tone of his voice how much regret he felt. Nowadays, when I think of that moment, I know his tone was so sad because, as a doctor, he knew he would not live much longer due to his heart condition. Unfortunately, he was right, and it was too late to accomplish his new life plan. He passed away 5 months later from a second heart attack. We felt we had lost our ground, and life made no sense. My Dad taught me the values I carry and, with his loss, I learned something I consider a key of life: BALANCE! We need to find balance in all we do. I teach this to my kids every day!

The most important lessons learned from my Dad:

"Respect others. Be always available to serve.
Do what you love. Never lose focus of your goals.
Have determination. Add love to everything you do."

Learnings from my role model: My Mother

It is a big challenge to find words to describe a person as special as my mother. My mother is my role model. She has always been ahead of her time. She bought her first car when the streets were dominated by men. She went to Law School when women were supposed to stay home. She was the chosen speaker to represent her graduation class. And you will not believe this one; when she graduated from Law School, João (Jango) Goulart was Brazil's president. Jango and Leonel Brizola, the state governor, attended the class graduation dinner. During his speech, Jango, Brazil's president, surprised the graduates, offering a trip to South America with all expenses covered. While the graduates were very excited with the gift, my mom did something that surprised everybody. As soon as the president finished his speech, my mom, on behalf of her class, stood up and with a classy, formal, and short speech, she thanked the president, but she also asked him to write down what he was promising and to sign it so there would be no questions asked when they claimed the gift. And so he did. While everybody was still perplexed with her speech, the president whispered in her year: "Congratulations! You just showed us that you will be a successful lawyer. Success is in your destiny."

My Mom is 84 years old as of this writing in 2016, and she still teaches us life lessons every day. When I am about to make a big decision, I always ask myself what my mom would do. Giving up was never an option for her. She faced a lot of adversities in life, but she never stopped chasing her dreams. She lost her mom when she was a teenager, and Grandpa was left with six kids. My mom supported Grandpa the most. She worked with him, and she was always with him, trying to alleviate his pain. Her support was very important to Grandpa, and she knew the experience would be very important to her later in life. She did not know the Universe was preparing her for what she would face later in life: the premature loss of her husband, leaving her with three young kids.

She got married later than usual, at 31 years old. She always believed it would happen when she met the right person. When she met my Dad, she knew he was "the one" in the first five minutes of their conversation and he had the same feeling about her. They got married a year later and had three kids. Seventeen years later my Dad passed away at age 46. I remember like it was yesterday, when we were in our beautiful backyard (Mom was known for her green thumb) a few days after this tragic loss, for our first family meeting, and this was my Mom's speech:

"We are experiencing the toughest time in our lives. Everything looks dark and sad now but that is not the end of the world. There are a lot of kids out there who faced the same thing. Some of them recovered from the tragedy and grew with it. They discovered an inner power that made them stronger. Others went down a wrong path. They went to the world of drugs and other addictions, using the tragedy as an excuse." Then she continued: "Listen: there's always a bright side in a dark situation. The Sun rises every day for everybody. You are smart and powerful enough to see it. We will learn from this loss experience, and we will grow together. We will be a good example to other families that will face the same pain. Count on me, and I will count on you. I am your best friend, and I will always be. Let's thank God for giving you the privilege of having a wonderful and unforgettable Dad. Dad did a great job here. You will show him that you learned from him, and you will be a dedicated and respected professional like he was. He will always be with us. Thanks for being such great kids. I love you!"

That moment was fundamental to us. We understood there are always two paths to choose in life. We felt committed to our family's destiny. We understood that each one of us had an important role in our family, and we had to support each other. We felt how much we loved each other and the power that a family has together. She could not have done a better job teaching, guiding, and preparing us to face the world. We learned there is no limit where there is love, faith, and belief!

"It's not what happens to you, it's what happens in you."
-John C. Maxwell

The four most important lessons learned from my mom:

"Set goals for your life and do something every day to reach them.
There's always a bright side in a dark situation.
In doubt, always follow your heart and intuition.
The best team in the world: Family."

Stop... Think... Plan... Action!

It is time to stop and review your life goals and plans. Do you like your life? Are you happy with the results you are getting? Do you have a family and career you always dreamed of? Listen, you can change your life just as a pilot can change an airplane's destination!

Do it, right now, because now is the only NOW you have! I consider myself a "lucky" person because, since I was born, I have been surrounded by very positive people, especially my parents. I learned from my mother the importance of having positive thoughts. I realized early in life the amazing power of the mind. I studied to learn more about the mind when I was only 15. My first training was the Silva Mind Control course and it propelled me to explore it even more. Then, many years later, I learned about Napoleon Hill's philosophy, and it made complete sense. We need to know where we want to go and what we want to be in life. The difference between you and successful people is not the money they have in their bank accounts, but their ability to plan their lives, chase their goals, and take ACTION. Successful people make things happen. They know they can create their own destiny. Making a PLAN means setting GOALS. Believe you will reach them. Once you have clear and well-defined goals, make a list of ACTIONS to reach them. What you make of your life is entirely up to you. Like coach Wooden used to say: "Make everyday a masterpiece."

"10% of your attitude is determined by what life hands to you and 90% is how you choose to respond."
-Charles R. Swindoll

I want to share with you a short story that happened some time ago. I was in San José, CA, attending an aviation convention. The first day was over, and I went back to my hotel room. I was planning to take some time to write. I was writing my first book, and I was very excited about this new challenge. I laid in bed, turned on my laptop, and spent a few minutes thinking about the chapter I was about to start. I was so tired after standing up all day at the convention center that it was hard to get inspired so I decided it was time to rest and watch television instead. It was November 6, 2008, a very important day in America. Barack Obama had just been elected president. Most TV channels were talking about the election. Suddenly, the election news was interrupted by other news, and it caught my attention as much or more than this historical election.

The news was about a pilot, flying by himself, on a small, two-seat piston airplane. He was flying at 15,000 ft. altitude when he felt something was wrong with him. He took a few minutes to realize he was having a stroke in the air. As if that was not enough, he suddenly became temporarily blind. He contacted the air traffic controller for directions. He stayed focused, followed the directions precisely and made a perfect landing! Even the air traffic controller did not believe he could make it. Can you imagine the situation? Literally, he was the pilot of his own life, and dying, at that moment, was not part of his "Flight Plan." He fought hard to survive. This story proves the power of a Positive Mental Attitude (PMA). I would love to know what came to his mind when he experienced this almost unsolvable situation. His faith and belief was so strong, he made it happen. He shifted all his focus and strength to only one thing: his survival. Nothing else mattered. He would never know how powerful he was if he had not had this tragic experience. And that is key in life! We all have that same power, and we need not experience a situation like that to believe it. Once we BELIEVE in it, we will make things happen! This pilot changed his life from tragic to magic, and we all have the same power.

That is all I needed to get inspired and so I turned on my laptop and wrote. I hope this pilot's story inspires you as it did me. He saved his own life when nobody thought it was possible. Like a hero, he changed his destiny when everything seemed to be against him. We need to find the HERO that resides inside of us. That pilot had a burning desire to live, and that was key for his successful landing. You must be thinking of other inspiring stories you have heard or experienced in your own life. Usually, we recognize these as "miracles." Do you agree with the air traffic controller, when he said it was a miracle? Or do you think it was the pilot's positive thinking that made it happen? The answer is: it doesn't matter! The RESULT matters! I'm sure you have had situations when you were pushed to do something out of your comfort zone and then discovered you had a hidden power. It need not be tough situations, like this one. Maybe a dog chased you when you were little. You were so scared of the dog that you could jump a fence twice as tall as you. Then after you did it, you looked at the fence and said: I can't believe I jumped over it! Yes, you did! That is the inner power we need to find in ourselves and use it to reach our goals.

"Do not ask yourself how long it will take to change, ask yourself how far you can go."
-John C. Maxwell

When I was teenager, I had no idea what I wanted to do in life. I knew I did not want to be a doctor like my Dad. I never liked the idea of dealing with illness. I was very business oriented ever since I was little. I always believed I would have a "Eureka" moment and would come up with a business idea that would change my life. I was also very fascinated by the world and the differences between cultures, countries, and languages. I had a burning desire to experience and learn about it. All cultures have great things to share. The world would be much better if we could understand them. When I was in my early twenties, I went to France to learn the language and experience the French lifestyle. I visited several countries in Europe, and it reinforced how much I love to learn about the world. Then, I went back to Brazil, got married, and got my Bachelor's in Business Administration degree. In 1999 we moved to the US, and it was a turning point in my life. I have chased my dreams every day since we moved. My first challenge was to learn the language. At that time the Internet was booming and thousands of "dot coms" were created daily. I felt it was important to understand this new "virtual" way of doing business, and that was my second challenge. I went back to school and learned as much as I could about it. The Word Wide Web fascinates me as cultures do, because it brings together the entire world through one thing: the computer.

After doing a lot of web work for several companies in different industries, I was introduced to the aviation industry. I fell in love with it right away. Working in the aviation industry gave me the opportunity to explore the world, which was always my passion. And even more important, it gave me the opportunity to make wonderful friends worldwide. I feel so fortunate; because I am surrounded by so many successful and inspiring people I can call my friends. I learn from them every day. They naturally follow the Laws of Success taught by Napoleon Hill. I also learned from them that the most successful people are always the most available, and this was a big lesson.

I have another story to share. In April 2012, I went to South Africa for three days of meetings with a few aviation friends and then we flew back to Brazil, straight to my friend's beautiful farm. Besides a 1,450 meters' runway and a control tower, this farm has a zoo, a golf course, and a beautiful, well-maintained aircraft collection. I have been there often and every time I went I would go flying with my friend. He either had a new "toy" to show me, or we would fly just for fun. This time though, something different happened. The day after we returned from South Africa, he went flying in his beautiful T28, and I went for a meeting with his marketing team. They were planning an aviation air show event that would happen a few months later at the farm, and he asked me to help the team with some ideas. I was in the meeting, but could not resist the noise of the T28 landing so I left the meeting to watch it land and take pictures. There was my friend, happier than ever, because he was doing what he loved the most, "flying." When he saw me at the end of the runway taking pictures, he waved and yelled my name. He wanted to take me for a ride in the amazing T28, which sounds like a dream for most people.

On a normal day, I would not think twice and would jump in the plane but there was something different that day. I did not want to disappoint my friend by saying no so, without thinking, I pretended I could not hear him calling my name. I made myself busy, looking down, trying to put the camera in its case, and walked away. Then, one of his employees came running, yelling my name. He told me his boss wanted me to go fly with him. It was my turn to experience that beautiful ride. Then, another strange thing happened. An excuse came to my mind, and without thinking again, I told him I could not go because I had to go to another meeting at the hangar next door. I guess, I was forced by some extra forces to lie, and I walked away to a hangar far away. Then he gave up on me and invited somebody else for the ride, and they took off. As I arrived at the hangar, I heard somebody yelling with a tragic voice: "The plane is coming down!" I got out of the hangar, and I heard a huge noise from an explosion. I could not believe what I was seeing! It was the end of their lives. They never thought that ride would take them to another dimension. I will never forget that day. I was devastated with the loss of my friend, and very thankful at the same time for that "extra force" that saved my life. Was that my intuition, an angel whispering in my ears, or some extra forces telling me not to take that ride? I don't really know the answer, but I know that in tough situations, I always follow my intuition and my heart, and they never disappoint me.

When something goes wrong in business, we review the Business Plan and make adjustments. We should do the same with our lives. This sad story was another turning point of my life. It made me stop and review. I got a second chance that day when I decided not to go flying. I felt it was time to do something, to take control of my life, and to make the best of it. What legacy have I left to my kids? What have they learned from me? Have I made a difference in other people's lives? All these questions were stuck in my mind.

"We cannot solve our problems with the same thinking we used when we created them."
-Albert Einstein

I thank God every day for giving me ears to listen to my intuition, eyes to see the hidden opportunities, a mind that empowers me to face any situation, and a heart that reminds me every day that feelings become thoughts, and thoughts become things. The world is rich with opportunities, and the obstacles are stepping stones, helping us to reach them.

Do not waste time; transform your life, now! Only YOU have the power to transform it! Monitor your thoughts and do not allow negative people to take you down. You are the owner of your life!

"Keep your thoughts positive
Because your thoughts become your
words.
Keep your words positive
Because your words become your
behavior.
Keep your behavior positive,
Because your behavior becomes your
habits
Keep your habits positive
Because your habits become your values
Keep your values positive
Because your values become your
destiny. "
- Mahatma Gandhi

BIO:

Ana C Fontes was born and raised in Brazil. In 1999, she moved to the US with her husband and their two kids. They became American citizens a few years later. Ana's passion to learn about different cultures and countries guided her to do what she does today. Her cross-cultural business expertise spans 27 years in marketing and international business development. She has worked in Latin America, the US, Europe, and China and has held executive leadership positions for multi-national companies.

Ana has been named as "Woman of The Year in Aviation Manufacturing" in 2008 by NAPEW – National Association of Professional & Executive Women. She also has been recognized as one of the newest members to appear in the 2008-2009 edition of the Madison Who's Who Registry of Executives and Professionals, having demonstrated exemplary achievement and distinguished contributions to the business community. In 2008 Ana was also recognized as "Women of Excellence" by NAPEW – National Association of Professional & Executive Women.

Ana lives in Texas, US and considers herself a fortunate person because she does what she loves. She works with people from different cultures and companies around the globe, helping them to find opportunities to expand their businesses. In her personal life, she focuses on helping others learn how to turn obstacles into opportunities. She discovered the Napoleon Hill teachings about 10 years ago, and it was fundamental in her personal and professional life. Ana joined the Napoleon Hill Foundation in 2014.

Ana loves to receive messages from readers with their life learning stories and experiences.

Contact Ana at anafontes@anafontes.com.

Check out Ana's BLOG at www.anafontes.com for more inspiring stories.

Ana's main message:

"See opportunities where others see obstacles."

ARE WE PUSHING THE PRESENT INTO THE FUTURE OR PULLING THE FUTURE INTO THE PRESENT?

By: Valen Vergara

Have you ever asked yourself the universal question: Are we pushing the present into the future or are we pulling the future into the present? We can live out two lives. In the one life, we are who we are in the present tense, an identity we were conditioned to live out up until this point, and a life that we have approved as our reality. The other life is the existence we envision and dream about. A life crafted by candid wonder and curiosity. These lives come from two very different points of view. One of these lives is how you see yourself in the mirror, and the other is who you see you could become in your mind. You have the choice to invite the one you can become.

This chapter is for the change agents, the champions, and only for the brave at heart. Just paying attention to this means that you are the type of person who, for as long as you can remember, has been dragged kicking and screaming against your will, and has known deep down inside that your purpose is to go down in history for the greater good.

Before you begin, let me caution you, that in order to have anything, you must know how to be it first. Most human beings have it backwards; they think they must have things before they can be things. We can be anything we want by choosing it first in the mind, and then we can give permission for what we want to have in our physical environment.

"You will become as small as your controlling desire; as great as your dominant aspiration."
—James Allen

This means making emotional decisions about who we want to become, and defending them logically. Imagine yourself as a caterpillar making the decision to become something new, to weave its own cocoon to prepare the way to have wings. This is likened to you before reading this chapter, and the butterfly is the transformation of your possible identity after reading it. Hidden in plain sight in this chapter are golden nuggets that can only be mined as you increase your level of becoming.

There was a time that my mind did not matter to me. I lived a shell identity. I was living out of sight, out of mind, dormant inside an earthly purgatory. I was a reasonable person that waved a conditional surrender. Life became a required option, something of minor importance. It was about the years in my life and not the life in my years. I was not living on purpose; I was just filling up space. I was constantly worrying about money, and was not making my family and friends proud. It was in my twenties that I intoxicated myself with work and had a heart attack. I relived near-death experiences that I called everyday life. I said to myself at the hospital that day that something needed to change and that change was me.

If you've ever made an action plan to pursue something bigger than you, you may have said to yourself, "that's just not me!" You're right! You must become not you! It's the staying of who we are that stops us from having what we want. Imagine all of the things you can do when you start to become not you! What you could become, have, and do in your world! You were fearfully and wonderfully made to create change on command.

"I want to put a ding in the universe!"
—Steve Jobs

A Quick Disclaimer: as you learn more about knowing how to become someone who can have anything that they want by reading this book, you will have more control to affect a difference in your world. However, if you continue to hunt after having things before you know how to be someone ready to have those things, you will give up your power to anger, greed, laziness, pride, lust, excess and envy. Now, if you choose to discard those due to the fear of change, the chances of you discovering this information on your own is quite unlikely. By not learning this information, your chances of having the leverage that is needed to become a community, city or country leader in your chosen purpose is slim.

"Perceptions are all we have, choose them wisely!"
—Ken Wilber

You will find that, as you learn to become more valuable, you will be able to reach out to people who you never thought would ever want to get to know you. They will recognize that you are someone who is in the process of becoming greater. That greatness, even if you just started to become "not you" for the better, is recognizable by the great ones you admire. Those who have greatness do not value what they have over what they have become. They would not trade it for all the things they could have in the entire world! If you do not know how to become someone who has made the decision to be more valuable, the type of people you would like to resemble will not notice you. This means that the more you know about being someone who can change their thinking, the more you can do and have in your world. The more you can change your world and work toward being remembered in your family tree for doing something special.

I made a root deep decision in 2011 that I would dedicate time, energy and money to becoming someone that deserved more. It was then I started to become more valuable. I felt ten feet tall and bullet proof. I dressed to impress and opened my eyes to opportunities that would increase my success level. I started to break through barriers and push past limitations I had set up in my mind and I finally transcended past my traditional thought patterns. My brain changed itself and I developed strategic partnerships that grew my business, profit and income. I never looked back and I owe it to possibility thinking. Ask yourself this question:

• Are you ready to become more so you can have what you want?

Think about it! It all starts with your point of view. Human beings are just that, Beings. In order for us to understand how to become great we must understand what it means to be. Being can be defined as the state or quality of having existence. To improve the quality of your life, and your world, you must know how to increase your level of being. In order to learn how to enhance your existence, to live out your ideal lifestyle design, right now not later, you must start to define who you are so you can discover how to become greater than you are now!

> *"Have you ever had a dream, Neo, that you were so sure was real? What if you were unable to wake from that dream? How would you know the difference*

between the dream world and the real world?"
—Morpheus, The Matrix.

We humans learn through understanding of words and symbols as we experience the process of taking in and connecting up different viewpoints to form our own perspectives. However, up until now you may never have felt the need to define yourself and what your reason for living and breathing is. Freedom is found through definition. If you fail to define things, you become confined in the fog of confusion. You can casually respond to the environment or become purpose driven. This is the difference between the vital few and the trivial many.

• Why should we define anything anyway?

Can we truly be something without defining it? Impossible. If we do not fully define something we are learning it in part. Not in a deeper, fuller sense. That is why we must state how we perceive our self. This is an action statement.

In Ancient Greece, Aristotle defined the word Praxis as the activity of translating knowledge into a state of action. Or the process by which a theory, lesson, or skill is enacted, practiced, embodied, or realized. Did you know that it is the realization of information and the motion of action that can invite anything you desire?

• Are you ready to begin?

This is a commitment you must make to yourself and it requires you to focus your attention on your 50,000 to 60,000 daily thought, resulting in something known as awareness. Awareness is the ability to perceive, to feel, or to be conscious of events, objects, thoughts, emotions, or sensory patterns. The activity of awareness can be applied to the self. Others call this activity self-reflection. Awareness allows for a human being to better realize and pass through the process of Praxis. Awareness articulates action!

"No amount of reading or memorizing will make you successful in life. It is the understanding and application of wise thought that counts."
—Bob Proctor

• How do we pull the ideal future into the present tense?

We do this by pulling a future manifested in our mind and making it real in the present. Placing importance on the meaning of words and symbols and how they control our state of being helps us reach our knowable goals. When we use understood words that we value and then form a sentence with them, this creates a statement that we can fasten significance to. Since this kind of statement is so concrete, it becomes a time sensitive reality. A dream with a due date. Managing your own perceptions can only be done if you know what you stand for. Decide today and it will determine tomorrow!

"Engage the imagination, then take it where you will. Where the mind has repeatedly journeyed, the body will surely follow. People go only to the places they have already been in their minds."
—Roy H. Williams

• Do you know what you stand for?

That question is seldom asked, but it holds the weight of your world. A query such as that, left unanswered, is perhaps the greatest tragedy of all time. Apply praxis with the right definition and you will go in the right direction you want. Guaranteed!

> *"If you don't stand for something, you'll fall for anything!"*
> —Malcolm X

It is time to become a living and breathing action statement. Venturing out into a not unknowable future turns you into a walking and talking goal with a deadline. Before you can become something greater than you, you will need to declare your own Self-Perception Statement.

This statement is one that you will live by and stand behind. It should promote your principal goals in life. It summarizes not only who you are now but also who you want to become. This statement is passion in action (purpose). Start to view these statements of belief as a business with a bold vision and imagining yourself as the President of this personal service enterprise.

This statement of belief should be so profound you would not hesitate to engrave it on your tombstone! Furthermore, if your Future-Self could read your statements now that self should be able to say proudly, "with you I am well pleased!"

• The action item here is for you do it now by writing it down and documenting it.

When I wrote down my Self-Perception Statement for the first time it was a game changer for my business and life. I put my purpose on paper with my first entrepreneurial mentor in 2012. He secured me to my seat for about six hours and made me do self-improvement exercises. I remember looking down at my statement of belief and pausing to reflect because it was a surreal moment for me. Up until that point I had never made myself meaningful so that I could maximize my potential.

• Below is my Self-Perception Statemen:

> *"Maximize earning ability for the express purpose to fundraise for humanitarian aid and development campaigns!"*
> —Valen Vergara

• What does your point of view look like?

Your statement will change as you become more valuable over time. Remember, your state of being is a process, and not a stationary object. Who you are is not what you do! The express reason of the previous statement is to show you that you are an emergence, not a designation. This is why a statement is a sentence or more; one word does not do your being justice! You must be to have, not have to be. This is why you must change your be-hav-iour; be comes before have.

Before you can be great at something, you're going to be good at it, prior to being good at something you're going to be bad at it, and before being bad at whatever it is you're interested in doing, you have to decide to do it and take immediate action! Become a greater you! Become "not you"!

BIO:

Valen Vergara is an Award Winning Bestselling Author, Social Entrepreneur, Real Estate Investor, Publisher, Humanitarian and Entrepreneur Trainer. Valen is the author of The People, Planet, Profit Entrepreneur, Beyond What If and the brain behind The Thought Authorities.

He is the president of the multi-divisional real estate firm, Team Made Real Estate (TMR) Inc. TMR Inc. is Manitoba's largest real estate education, event and investing platform and the President of Everyday Investors United Manitoba, Winnipeg's number one investor network.

He is the Co-Founder of the Young Entrepreneurs Society International and a mentor to the 3000+ members who span over 70 countries. He is the COO of an international event, marketing and graphic design agency, VA Productions Inc. (Winnipeg, Madrid & Paris) and is changing the world one culture at a time through Culture Card Inc.

Valen Vergara is one of a select few entrepreneurial experts featured in the movie "Game Changer," a documentary about increasing performance in business and life through the delivery of advanced, practical and implementable strategies. As well as a Public Speaker who has been featured on many top radio shows.

Valen is the Founder of The Worldwide Expedition for Peace & Truth Project (WEPT) Inc. The WEPT Project Inc. subscribes to sustainable philanthropy.

Valen's strategic objective is to maximize his earning ability to fundraise for humanitarian campaigns. His life's work is centered on mentoring, empowering and investing in the field of human potential.

Become visible and credible in business and career at www.valenvergara.com.

TENACITY AND CHUTZPAH

By: Dori Narebo

Principle 1 Definiteness of Purpose

*"Definiteness of Purpose is the starting
point of all achievement"*
-Napoleon Hill

The starting point for all achievement is definiteness of purpose. In this chapter, you will learn that you can have many accomplishments throughout your life. The journey to achieve your purpose is just as important as the goal itself. Life's journey is like baking; you have several ingredients that need to be measured and added at a precise time to ensure a perfect end-result. However, sometimes you cannot be bothered sifting the flour with the other dry ingredients three times or creaming the butter and sugar together. Instead, you may decide to take a shortcut and throw all the ingredients in a bowl at the same time without following the directions precisely. The result is less than perfect or a total flop. What do you do? You try again until you succeed, which means you follow the directions. Likewise, "The Principles" are the instructions to success and are designed to work synergistically together.

Some will go through life aimlessly trying to find their true destiny or mission, while others know their lifelong purpose at an early age, and they fulfill their dreams with laser focus and an academic mindset. On the other hand, some people are multi-talented with numerous abilities and have more than one purpose throughout their lives. Why do we have to have only one purpose in life? Why can't we have more than one? For example, Tony Bennett is a singer and is also known as a successful painter. His works of art sell for more than $10,000. Erykah Badu is a singer and songwriter, but she has another passion, and that is helping mothers have their babies. She became a doula and may pursue midwifery.

Finding "the one" true purpose in life can be challenging. Many challenges transform our lives. Think of these difficulties as life's stepping-stones. Each stepping-stone along your journey unlocks another talent or ability. For example, Jimmy Steward a well-known actor for over 50 years did not dream of becoming a movie star. He dreamt of becoming a pilot as a boy and loved aviation, but he became sick with scarlet fever. Steward studied architecture at Princeton and was granted a full scholarship to a graduate school for his thesis on airport design. He joined the University Players for performing arts and during this time, he met Henry Fonda. Fonda convinced Steward to go with him to Hollywood since it was hard to find jobs during the Great Depression.

It's Never Too Late

Equally important to realize is that it is never too late to find your purpose either. Look at Harland Sander's; best known as Colonel Sanders who became the Kentucky Fried Chicken mogul at 65 years old. Ronald Regan, a famous actor, became a two-term President and the oldest in office at 77 years old. Cup of Noodles inventor was 61 years old. Roget's Thesaurus author Peter Roget was 73-years-old. Remember, no matter where you are in life it is never too late.

What is your heart's desire?

Let's say, for example, you pick a profession that you are passionate about and lack the academic requirements. What is the solution? You take the academic requirements. The answer is clear. It just may take you a couple of years longer. Fast-forward to 15 years in the future, you are doing what your heart desires! You will not lament those extra years that enabled you to fulfill your dreams. There are only solutions, not obstacles.

Many people will defer the pursuit of their dreams because of debt or family responsibilities. The debt is insurmountable, there are not enough hours in the day for family life and to make matters worse, you are in a rut loathing your job. In hindsight, you regret that you did not do what you wanted to when you were younger. You stay in a meaningless job to work for someone else's dream just to make the monthly payments and survive. All is not lost; you have just been on a training path and took a detour and it is still not too late.

One reason people have trouble discovering their purpose in life is because they do not know themselves. If you ask someone if you could do anything, be anybody, and money is no object, what would you be? The answer heard most; "I do not know". The next question, "What did you dream of becoming as a child?" "What childhood character did you play?" Most people will say they cannot remember, or do not know. Their mind is closed off. The conscious mind has slammed the door to the subconscious mind. The next problem is that most people just dream about ideas but are not doers; there is no action behind their words.

There are many ways to use Definiteness of Purpose but discovering your true destiny is the ultimate goal. However, the problem with this is that 98% out of 100 people cannot figure it out. Only 2% have a clear direction. Even with the right upbringing and all the positive mentoring, many people still have problems. Let us look at the jobs you have had in the past. Make a list of all things you liked and disliked about your most meaningful jobs. Find the commonalities and you will start to notice a pattern emerge. Think of this as a roadmap, guiding you towards your purpose. Hone in on your talents and abilities to develop more successes. You will start to see that you use Definiteness of Purpose in many areas of your life. As a result, you will gain more confidence and develop courage, instead of self-doubt and fear. Here are two examples of how you can use Definiteness of Purpose.

Example 1

After moving to Norway, one particular question asked frequently was if I liked my job. It seemed like a strange question because I never got asked that question until I moved. In Norway, happiness and job satisfaction are important to the employer and colleagues. Of course making lots of money, and traveling the world is great fun too, but it may not be what your heart and soul yearns for, and you may have a hard time trying to figure it out. Time for a decision, should I pursue medicine or technology and money. I chose the latter and worked for the 3rd largest consulting company and became known as the Renaissance woman with a wagonload of talent. It was an excellent choice, and I loved my job, but it was short-lived. Then, tragically, my mother and brother died four days apart before Christmas and the following year I had my first heart attack. Four traumatic events in less than two years! It was not until my second heart attack, 30 days after the first attack, that I began to have a new definiteness of purpose.

Let us say you are sick, or you have been diagnosed with a condition, and you are determined to get well again. Your definiteness of purpose is to get healthy. What does it take? First you need to have an idea.

For me, this idea occurred after the second heart attack since the doctors did not know the cause of the attacks. They even told me that I would most likely go home and have another! After three consecutive heart attacks and with a fourth looming like a dark cloud, I had to take action and figure out why I was sick. I had to prevent the next heart attack. Numb, depressed, paralyzed with fear, and frustrated with traditional medicine, I started my mission, determined to solve the question that no one seemed to be able to answer for me.

I became fed up and realized I had to save myself because the doctors were only dispensing medicine because it was protocol. The second attack was seven times worse than the first. I was even more determined to get to the root of the problem as to why I had the attacks in the first place.

It was important to get my heart back to normal as soon as possible. I expected my body could and would heal itself as long as it had the right environment. This meant optimizing mind, body, and spirit, working together as one, supported by nutrition and the correct mental programming. Nutrition and the way you think influence the ecosystem of your body.

I became a person on a mission; this idea became a burning passion, my only thought, and primary focus. It became my obsession to get better and heal myself. Having a major purpose is your starting point towards achievement according to Hill. Start with one thing, go ahead, and put all your eggs in one basket so you can focus. Having an A-B- and C-plan only de-focuses you. I used to think that you needed backup plans but in retrospect, my greatest successes were when I had all my eggs in one basket. Develop your one-track mind. Your major purpose right now may be to heal yourself and improve your quality of life.

Next, you need to know where you are going. It is like driving a car. You go from point A to point B and take the quickest route. You do not get in a car and drive aimlessly or take a detour, get lost, and never find your way back.

My goal at this moment in time was to be healthy. I wanted to affect my body chemistry by optimizing the environment, for the body, mind and spirit to work as one. I began journaling every day to find a pattern that would lead me to the answer, and it finally paid off. I found the possible cause of the problem, which led me down another path. One sunny morning, while making breakfast I said to my husband, "Isn't it funny how life has come full circle in my career?" He replied, "What do you mean?" I responded, "Well, because of the attacks I am back in medicine again." Back to my true passion and as a result, I wrote a book,

A Woman's Heart Attack: What Your Doctor May Not Tell You to share my story as a patient advocate to empower and help others. At my last cardiovascular visit, my doctor said, "You've completely healed yourself! I can see no evidence that you have had a heart attack!"

Example 2

Here is another example of Definiteness of Purpose used in a family business. Remember, all achievement starts with an idea. At 22 years old my grandmother offered to send me to veterinarian school at UC Davis, but I got married instead. My husband supported the idea and was willing to go with me, but we felt conflicted and obligated to the family business because they lost all their contracts with Caltrans, a governmental state agency. They supplied all the landscape rental equipment to Caltrans at various locations throughout the State of California. They shifted the business focus from rental to providing a service. It was just an idea at first. They wanted to offer a service for roadside mowing of oleanders down the center mediums of streets and highways. We were the first company to start this type of service in California; there was no market for this service.

My father-in-law had a thick Norwegian accent, and no one understood him so he could not make the sales calls. Since I was the native English speaker, I became the sales manager. I remember my very first sales call; I went to my parents' bedroom for privacy, picked up the Yellow Pages phone book and looked up the phone number for the City of Long Beach. I dialed the number on an old rotary phone; my heart was pounding and I had a lump in my throat, thinking I had no idea about hydrostatic transmission and why they were better, or tractors and mowers for that matter.

During this time, my husband and I attended a year-long training course, Dale Carnegie Human Resources and Sales. We learned the methodologies of human relations and sales, which paid off in a big way.

During my sales calls I would jot down notes, for example; 'son broke his arm while playing football'. I would never ask for the sale. It was all about building a network of friends. I would ask, "Would it be okay if I called back in a few months just to check in with you?" They all said yes. I would file my index card by the month I was supposed to call back. Every month, I would take out the index cards for that month and make the calls again. I would say, "Hey, how is your son doing after he broke his arm?" So many people would comment on my excellent memory!

It would be cliché to say we were thinking out of the box, but it was more than that, we were thinking creatively. First we contacted all the purchasing agents in every city in California, in addition to Caltrans. We came up with an idea to talk to the men in the field and get them to request our services from their purchasing agents. We decided to attend every event for city superintendents, golf course superintendents and decision makers. We exhibited at trade shows; we had contests, mailers and even made brochures for the company, which was unheard of in our service industry. We did not realize it at the time, but we created a market for our service. More importantly, we built friendships and a network. We knew that when a job was available, they would call us.

We became the most trusted company in our industry and the governmental contract offices would ask us to help them write the specs for the contracts. We monopolized the industry, however, it took over three months to get paid. You cannot run a business with no money for payroll and other expenses. Our next idea was how were we going to get paid faster. We came up with an idea to offer a discount for fast payment 2%-10 days and 5%-3 days. Amazing how many opted for 5%-3 days. This idea was well accepted, and money was always flowing. Business was great! It took a few years to develop rapport, but it has endured the test of time and is a company that is still in existence today, 38 years later! The bottom line for this business is that we never gave up, we had all our eggs in one basket, and we had laser focus. We did not look at challenges as obstacles; instead, it became an opportunity. We never thought that we couldn't do it, we only thought of ideas to make it work.

The principles are designed to work together; Definiteness of Purpose is the starting point. Take your idea and write it down, make it actionable and do something every day towards your goal. Only you can give it life. Your thoughts are powerful; use them to fulfill your dreams. Desire without action is merely a wish.

BIO:

Dori Naerbo, PhD, MSBA and MSc is a University of Liverpool graduate and specializes in stem cell clinical trials, commercialization of cellular treatments and business development. Dr. Naerbo is a successful entrepreneur and author with over twenty years of diverse business experience. She is a health and business coach, stem cell patient advocate, Certified Instructor for The Napoleon Foundation's Philosophy of Success. Naerbo has extensive international experience in business management, consulting, and life science. She speaks English and Norwegian, and holds a Ph.D. in Organizational Psychology, MSc in Business Administration and MSc in Clinical Research.

Her new book, A Woman's Heart Attack: What Your Doctor May Not Tell You is available http://www.dorinaerbo.com

THE UNPARALLELED ANTIDOTE FOR WOE-IS-ME SYNDROME

By: Mike and Jerrilynn Rebeyka

It was a night like many others. He was on trial again; arguing a case with zero possibility of winning. There was no justice; no impartiality. Every aspect of their lives was like a series of experiments in the legalities of marital bliss; the combined results of which determined a measurement of his love for her. She did not understand her motivation for putting them through these tribulations. Nor his incessant need to enable her. She pushed his buttons and then twisted things around to appear the victim she truly thought she was. She concocted the controls and impacted the variables as her observations were made during each testing phase. Where had she been hurt so badly that she continually had to assess whether or not he was going to stay with her through everything? These childish games resembled nothing of the innocence of youth; all simplicity was lost in the layers of rules and multiple objectives. Moreover, now the stakes were extremely high. A fragile, young family was the subject of the long-range experiment; the crucial outcome of which was teetering dangerously close to being labeled "BOTCHED".

Jerrilynn:

I grew up in a small city on the Canadian prairies with two younger siblings. For ten years, my mom traded a teaching career for giving us her presence. She was always on guard for our wellbeing. My parents got involved in our various after school activities where they could add value. My dad was a surveying engineer who frequently worked weekdays away. I was bullied in elementary school. Until high school, I was easily intimidated, even fearing a new teacher's mispronunciation of my name. My dad taught me to smile because then it is hard for people not to like you. He instilled confidence in me by encouraging me to get into lifeguarding. We lived in close proximity to beautiful northern lakes where dad taught us how to catch fish. The campfires, hot chocolate and absence of conflict were as relaxing as the glassy lake. My parents enabled me to obtain a university degree and a career with a local major corporation soon followed. It was a great blessing to have job security, flexible hours, and good benefits while raising a family.

I met Mike just prior to starting university at the sporting goods store where we worked. It sounds a little sappy but we got to know each other over pricing fishhooks! After eight long years of trying to out-fish me, he decided to marry me anyway. We were engaged on a remote northern lake in, you guessed it, Hook Bay.

Mike:

I grew up in a farming community close to Jerrilynn's hometown. I was raised on natural homegrown food, hard labor and traditional Ukrainian family values. My much older brother left home for a prestigious career with the Royal Canadian Mounted Police before I even knew how much I would miss him. With my dad working the fields, grain elevator, and butcher shop, I was left to fend for myself with my mom and three sisters. I was the second youngest so everyone felt the need to tell me what to do. If I was in their presence, I was perceived as a menace. So I spent a lot of time outdoors finding things to amuse myself with and subsequently landing myself in trouble. My intentions were honorable but usually everyone thought I was misbehaving. I grew up feeling like those around me expected me to fail. I felt unsupported and non-directed. No one communicated to me that I could be something bigger than myself and bigger than where I came from. That made it difficult to feel confident and secure in my abilities. I saw the work ethic of my male role models and their dedication to the farming way of life. They believed that their hard work would pay off. Retirements were stable but accompanied by aching backs and arthritis. I knew there had to be a way to work smarter.

Fishing and hunting was an integral part of the social network in my community and triggered my love of the outdoors. When I first met my wife, we spent countless hours on countless lakes fishing with friends and family. At the time of starting my own family, I had a government job with good benefits. I had already far surpassed any expectations set for me as a child. And yes, we introduced our kids to fishing – both from a boat and through the ice in the wintertime.

On this particular night, his anger boiled over into exhaustion; so tired of trying to understand what she wanted. For him it was simple: a wife, a good job, a home, and a healthy family. What more could they ask for? In the recent past, his frustration had grown to anger and resentment; much of it amplified by the depression that had accompanied grieving his brother's untimely death. Within one month after his loss, he had also become a father for the first time. But his heart had hurt so terribly bad that he could not fully give it to his brand new baby. At that time, his wife felt she had begun a solo journey into parenthood; he had been there in body but not totally in spirit. And as this had continued on through the months, she felt deserted and isolated. The mental anguish had begun to affect both of them physically. They used to socialize more but every event, family centered or otherwise, always included alcohol, which tended to amplify their problems. They had re-evaluated their idea of fun and what type of behavior they wanted their children to witness.

Although she would never have admitted it, she had been depressed too. However, she kept going with complete disregard for her body's signs. She had carried a second pregnancy with multiple complications to nineteen weeks; not long enough. Not fully recovered from his first loss, another round of grief had left him aching to fully inhale. She had grown resentful expecting him to get past his pain. The bitterness would reveal itself every time she addressed him. Counseling had proven that time would have been better spent trimming the lawn with the kid's plastic toy scissors. Sessions had rehashed the endless cycle of ill treatment reinforcing in each casualty's mind that their behavior had been warranted. They had breathed some life into their daily routine but just enough to exist. Their house was not a home. The tension and darkness had taken over like some type of oversized, horror film amoeba capable of infecting everything it engulfed in its path. Sometimes she felt like being widowed would be easier. Sometimes he felt so scared then ashamed and humiliated for he was supposed to be the mighty brawn behind this brood. He felt so inadequate that failure appeared to be a step above him on the progression to achievement. He felt alone and without support. He referred to it as a lack of respect. Truthfully it was a lack of feeling loved and sensing that the love he had to share was not being received.

Jerrilynn:

Somewhere I got the message that marriage was a logical step in life; certainly it appeared the only way to have a long-term relationship. My parents wanted me to be financially independent and educated prior to starting a family. I was never discouraged from dreaming but I was not necessarily encouraged that all things were possible either. I only gave myself two options: Accounting or Teaching. It felt like a life sentence decision. I admit I did not follow my heart. When I received my designation, I felt proud of my accomplishment but never once passionate. My parents provided the best guidance they knew how to give. But we want our kids to choose to serve this world in a way that is meaningful and enjoyable to them. We believe that will bring far greater satisfaction. Job security and long term employment with one company are things of the past anyway.

Before being engaged, I identified some must-haves for a long-term relationship: Romance and respect, a true partnership and teamwork, open communication, and common goals. When I began to feel that my marriage no longer contained those elements, I became terrified to end up in a loveless, uneventful life filled with misery and regret.

Mike:

My parents believed it was better to be safe than sorry. The thought of calculated risk might be entertained but a huge leap of faith was not. I was raised with a poverty mentality; not in poverty but with a belief that there was never enough. I received messages like: eat everything on your plate, we can't afford that, seeking abundance is selfish and greedy. My dad was always hoarding stuff for future use. I have had to challenge these beliefs to allow myself to move towards my DMP (Definite Major Purpose). My parents passed information to us as they had received it. Having a DMP was never brought into their awareness.

My mom and dad exemplified everything a marriage should be. They were a team and had the utmost respect for each other. Material wealth did not hold weight. The highest value was placed on family bonds and strong religious commitment. I have never known two more unselfish people both in actions and attitude. Those two went the extra mile for their family and everyone else. Their home was warm and welcoming; even first time visitors felt like family. That which was ingrained became the expectation for my own marriage. Things were not turning out as I had anticipated.

> She was alone now in the room. She knew he would be back for more agony before the night was over. He could never just leave things to simmer. There had to be answers; immediate answers. Her tears were mercilessly stinging her fiercely hot cheeks. Sure enough, he came back, uninvited, spewing more venom. He demanded a resolution even though the words that had carelessly dramatized the last hour of their lives still felt like sticks and stones. He tried to use his size to intimidate her but she knew he would never cross that line. He felt so threatened and insecure; having his own family was the one thing that truly defined him and he sensed it vanishing. How had their marriage come to this? It was not even a fragment of what she had once envisioned. Perhaps they had dreamed different dreams.

Jerrilynn:

I was constantly feeling like there was not enough of me to go around. Our marriage was always on the back burner. Happiness evaded me. I thought it was tied to possessions or something I would become. Yet with each acquisition or achievement it was further from reach than before.

Something was missing. I used to have goals and direction (although I did not call it DMP) but now, just when I was supposed to be singing life's song, I plodded along doing the mundane tasks of my so called "dream life". Why did everyone else seem happy? Why did they appear to have so much (stuff)? I realized later that most material belongings were debt financed. At the time, though, I was angry at both myself (for not knowing how to get it) and at Mike (for not wanting to get it). Aside from material possessions, I also sensed I should be doing more; aiming higher; challenging myself. I got very involved with my community. Although I received much personal growth from the experience, it certainly wasn't my destiny. Why did I feel guilty wanting more than "just" being a mom? Why could I not figure out what I was supposed to accomplish in my lifetime? Was I already living my purpose? It was gnawing away inside; irritating my soul. My life had to have some deeper meaning and significance. I did not want to have regrets at the end. Much of this contributed to the lowest moment of our marriage where I found my head spinning; questioning a higher power. There was a lot of emotion tied up in that one prayer one night.

Mike:

The reality of raising three smiley faces was setting in. We had a responsibility to prepare them for their future but we were in another world. Family and job demands coupled with our relationship troubles felt like running a race that we could not win; not using our current strategy. Financially, retirement looked bleak and then the markets dropped. Co-workers began adding five years to their retirement age.

Like many other people, we were getting caught up in negative situations without even realizing it. Conversations of doom and gloom, gossip, disliking our jobs, hopelessness and general struggles. Oh "Woe-Is-Me" we cried.

I could not comprehend the existence of our marriage problems because there wasn't some huge violation of moral values. I decided this was out of my control. All I knew was I did not want to end up in court trying to win my kids. I spent time at the local fire department where I volunteered. The guys there and the strangers we helped appreciated me more than my own wife.

154

A voice was calling him. It was frightening because he was in a dark place; somewhere deep inside himself he had never been. Everything inside him felt there was something coming. He just did not know whether it was good or bad.

For some months now, she had been imagining a better life. One separated from him. There would always remain a connection due to the children but hopefully he would be reasonable about that. She wished for some kind of mature version of her childhood Prince Charming; someone enthusiastic about building an exciting, memorable life! Little did she know she was already married to him; he just needed to grow and so did she. And the thought never occurred to her that someone new would have issues too; maybe more! Sadly, she did not realize what she needed to learn would cycle again in her life no matter who her companion. All that consumed her now was that it seemed he felt life was done; like all that was left was to grow old together. He would have been happy with the status quo. She had given up imagining what goals they would set together and focused on her own. She felt they could never be close again. Things were too far-gone. It seemed like the happiness they once had were a cruel joke. The failure of a marriage was not something she wanted to add to her life's resume. Her long held belief that children need two parents to grow up healthy and balanced was shattered by the impact of adult disputes spilling over into their naïve little worlds. It was like a disastrous oil slick polluting a vibrant, unscathed ocean. With neither a loving environment nor a sense of security, it appeared the kids were better off with their parents apart. She put a plan in place to leave him. With some indication that at least tonight's hardships were over, she began the process of settling herself. She poured a cup of coffee and wished for more peace for her and her children; the hovering cloud of negativity reinforcing in her mind that she was doing the right thing.

Jerrilynn:

Things did not begin to change instantly, or so I thought. When I look back now I can see that the minute I allowed help, I received. The first assistance arrived, unbeknownst to me at the time, in the form of better coffee. I started feeling more balanced. I was getting better sleep, feeling energized and more mentally clear. My mood became lighter. I recall starting to think intently about whether I had done everything in my power to make my marriage work. I questioned my role in the problems where previously my ego told me I was never to blame. Just as I did not consider myself a negative person, until I started listening to myself, I did not realize I needed a DMP until I lived without one! I had desperately wanted a rich marriage but had lost the controlled attention such a purpose requires. Gradually, with each conflict, I became skilled at choosing a different action from the traditional; one that was unexpected due to its positive tone. The response back from my husband was contrary to my former expectation as well. I realized I had a power here but in a good way. Mike was realizing it too.

Mike and Jerrilynn:

Years later we became fully aware of the root cause of our distress: As soon as our original dreams of marriage and family manifested, we had let our minds become idle. Our lives then went bankrupt on paying the price of idleness. The following quotes describe the cost and antidote:

"If you strapped one of your arms close to
your body and did not did not use it,
eventually it would become limp, useless,

*and atrophy. The same is true of an empty mind left open to outside influences. It will fill up with negativity, tossed and torn by the stray winds of circumstance; fertile ground for the seeds of failure."
"Occupy your mind with doing what you want to do so that no time will be left for it to stray to the things you do not want to do."*

-Napoleon Hill

As soon as we recognized the potential in the product we were drinking, we began to dream together again. We focused on personal and common goals with respect to family and a business. As we worked to a leadership level in ORGANO™, and thanks to the company's exclusive partnership with the Napoleon Hill Foundation, we were prompted to study Think and Grow Rich. We were blessed again when Ms. Marianne Noad, our upline Diamond in ORGANO™, in her unwavering support of our success and of many others, gifted us the Napoleon Hill Leadership Certification in beautiful Victoria, Canada. We attended with the most remarkable people, learned directly from the incredible leaders of the Foundation, and were especially appreciative and honored to go through the course with Napoleon Hill's grandson, Dr. J.B. Hill. We place tremendous value on further applying both Hill's 17 success principles and the ORGANO™ business model in our lives.

Thankfully our marriage recovered; it was DMP incognito. Next, with an understanding now of the theory, it was time to formalize our DMP. Incorporating DMP along with the other success principles was sensible and exhilarating. We learned you CAN control your own mental attitude toward any situation and you have the ability to impress upon your subconscious mind repeated dominating ideas, such as your DMP.

It created an environment so opposite from the mindless, habitual Woe-Is-Me style we had lived for too long.

Mike:

December 2014, my dad passed away. Although he was 85, it was unexpected because he was still being my dad. Knowing the philosophy, I was able to mourn our loss but it did not knock me off my game. My strength was by no means insensitivity; I was just able to keep things in perspective. I delivered the eulogy and it was an absolute honor. Napoleon Hill speaks of the seed of an equivalent benefit in every adversity and I did indeed find several from experiencing my father's passing. Besides learning more about love, I was able to test out the credibility of the philosophy. I proved that I would not crumble when faced with adversity. In March of 2015, my wife was diagnosed with a brain tumor. In October it was removed, and determined to be benign, but she is still dealing with complications of a cerebral spinal fluid leak. All of this happened just prior to my lumbar spine surgery. With the health issues, and death in the family, it would be understandable to revert back to Woe-Is-Me mentality. To the contrary, by staying focused on our DMP, these events have proved to be merely stepping stones towards achieving our ambitions.

Mike and Jerrilynn:

Fishing on the countless waters of the earth, although vast and abundant, sometimes leaves you empty-netted. You know the fish are out there; you've witnessed other fisherman catch. You can complain that your fishing equipment isn't sophisticated or that your bait rotted or that your boat motor trolls too fast. You could go to the grocery store and buy fish although that would not provide the personal satisfaction that comes from fulfilling the sport fisherman's ultimate dream. Or you can decide that you are going to land a trophy catch no matter what and be determined to keep your hook in the water until it happens. Back your desire with self-discipline and sound but flexible planning of such things as water bodies to attempt, funding of excursions, and fishing techniques.

Most people rarely land their "big one". They continually request change but only achieve wishful thinking. Research finds that the number one regret of dying people is not aiming for that "full net":

> *"I wish I'd had the courage to live a life*
> *true to myself,*
> *not the life others expected of me.*
> *This was the most common regret of all.*
> *When people realize that their life is*
> *almost over and look back clearly on it,*
> *it is easy to see how many dreams have*
> *gone unfulfilled."*
> -Bronnie Ware, Palliative Care Nurse
> http://www.mirror.co.uk/news/world-news/dying-peoples-top-5-regrets-5348209

Their entire lives they alternate "what if…" with negativity about their state of affairs like a continuously looping PowerPoint in their heads. It's called the Woe-Is-Me Syndrome. According to urbandictionary.com, Woe-is-me-ing is "the act of feeling sorry for yourself for no particular reason except that you have nothing to keep your mind off your past." We facetiously add:

It's a widespread state of uneasiness and idleness of the non-directed mind causing one to fall victim to the circumstances of life. Highly contagious, it spreads like a grassfire on the wide-

open prairie. The majority of doctors will not provide a diagnosis because either 1) they are sufferers, therefore immune to recognizing the symptoms or 2) it has become so commonplace that patients are considered to be functioning within normal range. Those affected believe their condition cannot be eradicated and will continue to worsen at a rate unique to each individual.

Most people are either not aware or not willing to protect themselves. They merely float through life not even recognizing any deficit or any benefit to becoming knowledgeable. Now that you have read this, at least you are aware.

What if there was a cure that required no special equipment or medication? What if it guaranteed you would not suffer from the number one regret dying people have? The best-known antidote is having the self-discipline to constantly catch yourself in the Woe-Is-Me-ing act when obstacles present themselves. Then re-focus your thoughts from Woe-Is-Me to DMP. Soon it will become such a conditioned response that Napoleon Hill would say Cosmic Habitforce has taken over. Sounds simple but it requires you to become unlike 98% of people who never definitively write their purpose and never gain control of their mind (their most valuable asset) by directing it towards worthwhile causes:

"The greatest sin of mankind is neglect to use his greatest asset."
-Napoleon Hill

Throughout our marriage we have come to see another side of ourselves. The side that is loaded with strength and enthusiasm, energy and spirit. The side that is fearless and humble, peaceful and full of grace. The side that is love. The side that is determined to achieve all

160

that is ours and help others achieve all that is theirs. We are ready to further explore life from that perspective. As fully and as completely as possible in this human existence. We believe everyone proposes to learn to love; to feel the power of the universe flowing to them, through them, and to other people that are put in their path. Work your own purpose from that basis.

Knowing our DMP gives us opportunity where we were limited before. It enables us where we were restricted before. It teaches us where we were stagnant before. It takes us places we were unwilling to go before. What if knowing yours will do the same for you.

BIO

Mike and Jerrilynn Rebeyka are independent distributors for ORGANO™ (OG) - a global network marketing company focused on bringing the treasures of the earth to the people of the world through a variety of premium everyday products including coffees and teas. Their addiction to personal development flourished during leadership training at both OG University and through the Napoleon Hill Foundation.

The Rebeyka's have been married almost 20 years. They have three fantastic and talented children ranging in age from age 10 to age 16. Jerrilynn's background is in Accounting; she has a CMA-CPA designation and 24 years in the Telecommunications Industry. Mike's background is in Corrections and Public Safety; he has over 26 years working with troubled youth in secure custody. With a steadfast commitment to their community, they have volunteered in many capacities including coaching, fundraising, firefighting, and administrative positions for sports organizations and an investment property board. But in their combined years of experience in the workforce/business world, educational institutions, and community, they have never been so changed and challenged as they have with ORGANO™ and Napoleon Hill. This business model and philosophy are perfectly synced leading them on an adventure of a lifetime, growing them as citizens, leaders, business people, and parents. They will be forever grateful for continued learning and for the inspirational people they meet in these two organizations.

Doing something purposeful and with a passion for seeing others succeed is their driving force. They utilize their business opportunity to grow a strong customer base, teaching others how to duplicate this activity to build secure residual incomes. Both see the need to extend Dr. Hill's philosophy especially to the youth of our nation.

Mike and Jerrilynn can be contacted at:

beyondcoffeerow@sasktel.net

beyondcoffeerow.myorganogold.com

ALL ARE CALLED TO FULFILLMENT

By: Brenda M. Dear

In 1998, Barbara Streisand's version of the song "People" with the infamous refrain "people who need people are the luckiest people in the world"; was inducted into the Grammy Hall of Fame. I believe the refrain in People speaks to all of humanity. As we go through life, we realize that life becomes even more fulfilling when we have people to share it with. Many of you reading this can probably remember a time in your life when you felt misunderstood, unappreciated, unloved, or emotionally alone. Streisand's father died unexpectedly shortly after her first birthday. She desperately wanted to be famous but was often told by her mother that she wasn't pretty enough for show business. Despite her mother's warning and criticism, Barbara set the rudder of her ship with determination and personal initiative to become an acclaimed American singer, actress, songwriter, and filmmaker. Her version of "People" transcends generations and reminds each of us how fallible yet valuable our lives are. If valuable, then each us of has a duty to live a life with purpose and meaning. Dr. Napoleon Hill says "Definiteness of Purpose" is the starting point to all achievement. My hope is that the chapters throughout this book will inspire you on your journey to fulfillment. If by chance you have already moved from novice to expert in living a life with definiteness of purpose, I challenge you to mentor others. After all, people who need people are the luckiest people in the world.

Growing up in a large family of eight children, I had a sense that there was more to life than my humble surroundings. I was a dreamer, a book lover, and pretender. Whatever I lacked physically I made up for with my imagination. It wasn't until high school that I embarked on social activities with my peers. That embarking was short lived as I learned of a program to replace afternoon classes with cooperative education work off campus. I vaguely remember high school and when others talk about attending 10-20-30 year class reunions I can hardly recall any real friends I would have like to see again. My focus has always been the future, albeit unguided; I was always striving for what's next. Sadly, I became focused on building a career, and shortly thereafter, raising a family. Life was much too busy for dreaming and imagining how I myself was called to a certain fulfillment beyond the hurried life I allowed myself to become accustomed to. Years began to feel like months, months like weeks, and weeks like days as work became drudgery, and family life was severely strained from all the juggling. A sad tale with a happy ending that is the subject of a book being written by myself and another Napoleon Hill student, who happens to also be my husband.

YOU ARE CALLED TO FULFILLMENT

"If you are depressed you are living in the past. If you are anxious you are living in the future. If you are at peace you are living in the present."
~Lao Tzu

The first two parts of the above three-part quote by Lao Tzu once described how stuck I was in the past, and how I struggled with anxiety about the future. I am happy to say that my days now are more representative of the third part of Lao Tzu's quote. I suspect with good reason that many of my former co-workers are still suffering through the first and/or second parts of Lao's three-part quote. For nearly a decade I suffered needlessly in a career that provided great benefits, a more than generous salary, a home office, while unfortunately leaving me depressed

164

with little to no feeling of purpose. You see when you work five days a week, eight to nine hours per day, in a job that doesn't fuel your real passion or reason for being, your imagination, creativity, and zeal for live dies a slow death. I take full responsibility for becoming disillusioned, disengaged and thus desperate for departure. There were personal circumstances and challenges that left no fertile ground for me to convince myself I could again find happiness in my current career. In fact, it was my community service work supported by my then employer that fueled my real passion for servant leadership. As an employee I was an unhappy zombie, yet as a community volunteer my creativity, energy and zest for life flourished. The struggle then was how to leave my zombie world for the one I desperately craved. It goes without saying the struggle was really about dollars and cents, medical insurance, and retirement benefits. This struggle was the topic of conversation almost daily with my then peers. We all craved the opportunity to earn an honest living doing that which we felt most passionate about. I had to revisit the years of my youth; a time in which I was a dreamer with an imagination well beyond my chronological age of 10. Charles Haanel was dubbed the "father of personal development" and when I came across his dreamer quote I felt compelled to hang it on my office wall to remind me of the power of imagination: "We have come to know that thinking is a spiritual process, that vision and imagination precede action and event—that the day of the dreamer has come."

There are countless writers who speak profoundly of the power of imagination. Ironically, but not surprisingly, most modern day writings can be traced back to the Bible. The final verdict in all writings on imagination is that imagination is the real storehouse of endless possibilities. Imagine if you would the annoyingly endless sound a tiny drip makes from that busted faucet yet to be repaired. Imagine the chirping sound a single male cricket makes who has infiltrated your home during the dead silence of night. Although he remains unseen the calling sound he makes to attract females and repel other males is extremely loud and interrupts your slumber. The sound gets even louder should the male cricket get lucky and thus begin the triumphal song signifying the brief period after a successful mating. Could you go on to imagine any sane human being sleeping through the night despite those interrupting sounds? Well my dear sweet husband could sleep through those and even stranger sounds if they occur between his sweet spot of five-hour slumber. I on the other hand do not sleep through nightly interruptions and so I find myself journaling just to force a return of my slumber. The nightly journal entries soon awakened the dreamer in me. I began getting lost in the uninhibited corners of my brain, which led me to some amazing self-discovery. I also began to explore works by late great writers such as Dr. Wayne Dyer, Dr. Napoleon Hill, Dr. Martin Luther King, Nelson Mandela, Mahatmas Gandhi, Wallace Wattles, and C.S. Lewis; all in no particular order. Suffice it to say that all of their works, though written decades ago, are very much appropriate and needed in the 21st century

As I revisit my personal journal entries I see evidence of influences from these great writers but most profoundly from Dr. Napoleon Hill and Dr. Wayne Dyer. Hill's influence was so great that I am now a Napoleon Hill Foundation Certified Instructor candidate with a burning desire to teach Hill's principles to the homeless, marginalized, unemployed, underemployed, and youth.

Dyer's writings challenged and reminded me to seek daily to live an inspired life. In fact, he wrote a wonderful poem about the awesome benefits of living an inspired life entitled "The Benefits of Living an Inspired Life". I encourage you to seek out and read Dyer's poem. As you read, and hopefully reread, the words, sentences, paragraphs and pages throughout this book I challenge you to glean a message of hope and inspiration. For all writing is art and all art is designed to inspire. I hope you are nudged with the ever present reminder that your life is purposed for that which only you can fulfill. C. S. Lewis wrote that we are not just bodies but rather we are souls with a body. Decide today that you will live beyond your physical body and allow the spirit within you to guide you to a life of fulfillment and Definite Purpose.

THE MYSTERY OF ALL MYSTERIES

The mystery of all mysteries says Dr. Napoleon Hill is the power of the human mind. Hill says the human mind holds the secret to all successes and all failures. While it is the most important subject known to humankind, Hill says it is the least understood of all subjects.

Hill's principle of Accurate Thinking is based on the following two fundamentals:

1) Inductive Reasoning: Based on the assumption of unknown facts or hypotheses

2) Deductive Reasoning: based on known facts, or what are believed to be facts

Hill says Accurate Thinking and common sense are in part the result of experiences. You can learn from your own experiences as well as those of others when you learn how to recognize, relate, assimilate and apply principles in order to achieve your goals. Thus he says the accurate thinker takes the following two important steps in making his thinking effective:

1) Separate facts from fiction or hearsay evidence (one must analyze facts separate from emotions and feelings)

2) Separate facts into classes, important and unimportant

Learn and apply these seven rules of accurate thinking:

1. Never accept opinions as facts.

2. Avoid following free advice.

3. Don't trust information given in a discourteous or slanderous spirit.

4. In asking for information, do not disclose what you wish the information to be.

5. Anything which exists anywhere in the universe is capable of proof.

6. Begin developing your intuitive faculty which enables you to sense what is false and what is true.

7. Follow the habit of asking "How do you know?" Ask for source

Hill further explains that all thought habits come from either one of two sources, both of them hereditary:

1) Physical heredity: one inherits from this source something of the nature and character of all the generations of the human race, which have preceded him. This inheritance Hill says is fixed by laws of nature and can be modified by accurate thinking.

Social heredity: this source consists of all environmental influences, education, experience and impulses of thought produced by external stimuli. The greater portion of all thinking is inspired by the influence of social heredity.

Hill offers the following admonishment: "Study yourself carefully, and you may discover that your own emotions are your greatest handicap in the business of accurate thinking". One such example of emotions becoming a handicap is in Luke 10:38-42; (21st Century King James version); the story of two sisters Mary and Martha who were visited by Jesus:

"Now it came to pass, as they went, that He entered into a certain village; and a certain woman named Martha received Him into her house. And she had a sister called Mary, who also set at Jesus' feet and heard His Word. But Martha was encumbered with much serving and came to Him and said, "Lord, dost Thou not care that my sister hath left me to serve alone? Bid her therefore that she help me. And Jesus answered and said unto her, "Martha, thou art anxious and troubled about many things, but one thing is needful, and Mary hath chosen that good part which shall not be taken away from her."

In the biblical account I believe Mary and Martha found themselves in a private audience with Jesus; both however having opposite experiences. Mary was wise enough to know that Jesus was no ordinary guest and that she needed to give Him her undivided attention. Mary used accurate thinking to relish her special time with Jesus; while Martha was consumed with the emotional and social need to be a good hostess. Martha fussed over Jesus while Mary focused on His every word. Both sisters were anxious; one to learn Jesus's doctrine, the other to be a good hostess. Martha allowed her social heredity to inspire her thinking and influence her behavior.

In those days it was customary for homemakers to care for the feet of travelers thus Martha was consumed with the social tradition of being a good host. Rather than remain focused on what Jesus was teaching Martha thought surely Jesus was getting thirsty and hungry by now. She quickly forgot this was the same Jesus that fed the multitudes with just 5 loaves and 2 fish. Martha shifted from student to hostess and made temporal needs more important than hearing the eternal word of Jesus. Martha even made the awful mistake of asking Jesus to urge Mary to join her in focusing on the unimportant while neglecting the important. Martha's emotional need to be the best hostess distracted her such that being a great hostess became her hardship. Martha became slave rather than master of her social and physical need to be a good hostess. The world is filled with multi-tasking "Martha's" who lack the ability to prioritize the important and the unimportant. Dr. Hill teaches that the principle of Accurate Thinking requires us to separate fact from fiction and the important from the unimportant so that we focus our energy and attention properly. This biblical lesson is still being played out in the lives of thousands of Martha's today that dissipate life's forces and ruin their health moving from one hurried state to another. Men and women, young and not so young are connected 24/7 to multiple stimuli which further inhibits the ability to master Hill's principle of accurate thinking.

I leave you the reader with a reminder that you are called to fulfillment. The fact that you are reading this now should affirm your awareness that you are called to fulfill a purpose designed only for you. I challenge you to continue your journey of discovery. Know that your temporal and physical needs are secondary to your spiritual being. Be guided therefore by your imagination and the callings from your Creator to live beyond your flesh. Use the power of your imagination through repose and meditation throughout your journey of self-discovery and fulfillment. In paraphrasing Romans 12:2 "...be not conformed to this world: but be transformed by the renewing of your mind, that you may prove what is good, and acceptable, and the perfect, will of God." I am, as are the many thousands of other followers of Hill's work, grateful that he fulfilled his role as teacher of great universal truths throughout his earth bound existence. I am grateful that the Napoleon Hill Foundation continues its mission to propagate Hill's teachings. I am humbled and honored that as a student of Hill's work I too can fulfill my passion for helping others discover and fulfill their Definite Purpose in life.

BIO

BRENDA M. DEAR, MSOD, CP-PHR

Founder and CEO of D.E.A.R. HR Consulting & Coaching, LLC (Development, Empowerment, Agility, and Reformation) focused on 21st century HR best practices and continuous improvement. Certified Human Resource Management Professional by the Human Resource Certification Institute-HRCI. Napoleon Hill Foundation Certified Instructor candidate. When she is not coaching clients or consulting with community colleges and universities she volunteers with God's Helpers of Raleigh; a 501c3 in which her husband serves as President. She coaches and mentors women in homeless shelters and youth aging out of foster care to learn and apply Dr. Napoleon Hills 17 Science of Success Principles to rebuild and live their best lives. Brenda also holds a TEFL certification from ITTT and plans to use this training on mission trips to teach English as a Foreign Language.

A SHIP WITHOUT A RUDDER

By: Robert Dear

"Don't' Be Like a Ship At Sea Without a
Rudder..."
-Dr. Napoleon Hill

BEYOND WHAT IF

What if I failed to dream a better environment than that which I was born into and grew up in? What if I allowed my mom and dads failed marriage and subsequent divorce to pit me against the possibility of one day being a great father and husband? What if my mom had not sought a better outlet for my anger and restlessness and instead of sending me to perform work at a Catholic church rectory continued with just corporal punishment? What if this Priest and mentor had said no to his calling to serve; stayed in his homeland of the West Indies and our paths never crossed? What if this priest never thought to ask my parents to be my guardian and allowed my faith in God to grow under this man's guardianship? What if I had not appropriated "applied faith" to overcome the insurmountable to find purpose and meaning in life? What are your what ifs? What keeps you up at night? What dreams are you seeking to manifest? I invite you to find hope and affirmation as you read my story and the stories of my co-authors. May you seek earnestly to discover your definite purpose and help others along your path to purpose and meaning.

THE RUDDER YEARS

Dr. Hill's number one principle in his Science of Success is Definiteness of Purpose. Hill says Definiteness of Purpose is the starting point of all achievement. When my wife became a student of Dr. Hill she was searching for meaning and fulfillment after having raised four wonderful children. I on the other hand felt no need to study Hill's work since I was happily immersed in serving at church and the nonprofit organization over which I preside as President. Little did I know Dr. Hill had warned would be students as follows: "Don't be like a ship at sea without a rudder, powerless and directionless. Decide what you want, find out how to get it, and then take daily action toward achieving your goal. You will get exactly and only what you ask and work for". My wife and I share a home office so there is no getting away from Hill quotes plastered on the walls, Hill's books on the bookshelf, or hearing the audio versions of Hill's Master Key to Success or Your Right to Be Rich series. I have always considered my wife an organized, obsessive planner and goal setter. I relished the fact that I the slacker, non-reader, non-planner had found meaning and fulfillment and she the avid reader, and organized planner was on a massive manhunt. I am convinced that Dr. Hill wrote the admonishment message to me, the ship without a rudder. I soon learned that proximity can cause one to capitulate; and capitulate I did.

I spent the first five years of my life with mom, dad, and my seven siblings living in public housing in the city of New Orleans. The Desire Housing Project was low income housing authorized by the Housing Act of 1969 for poor African American families. Considered one of the largest public housing sites in the country; poor families were strategically cut off from the rest of the city by the Industrial Canal, Florida Canal, and railroad tracks on all four sides. This segregated housing was designed for poor families displaced by urban renewal projects flourishing in other parts of the city. Sadly, this public housing was situated on swampland that had formerly been the site of a landfill. After Hurricane Betsy destroyed our bottom floor apartment, and mom and dad saw that the city was not going to repair the damage, we moved out. My family moved into a two-bedroom shotgun house just across the railroad tracks from the Desire Housing Project. As I write this, part of me is glad that history repeated itself in 2005 when Hurricane Katrina forced low and mixed-income families off this swampland. You can read the rest of the story on how Hurricane Katrina impacted my own wife and kids decades later albeit living in North Carolina at the time. The sad story with a happy ending is recounted in the soon to be published work by myself and another Napoleon Hill student who happens to also be my wife.

At the age of nine I was the most industrious among my peers although, in the words of Dr. Hill, I was truly a ship at sea without a rudder. Hours before heading off to school with my peers I delivered 99 newspapers throughout my neighborhood. Mom worked overnight as a nurse and part-time at a local bar called Twilight. She and dad were like ships passing in the night. When they were home at the same time it was one argument after the other. I remember too many to count arguments mom and dad would have about money and infidelity. Dad was a tall handsome man and spoke with a statuesque soft deep voice. Mom was 5'2 and skillfully yelled colorful four letter adjectives like an army sergeant. My dad would simply take it all in as if he were being scolded by his mom. Then one dreaded summer day, I awoke to find my dad gone. I took the news pretty hard. Dad was an extremely focused and dedicated construction worker. He taught me humility and the importance of going the extra mile. Each parent taught me very different lessons that have shaped the man, husband, father, and servant leader I am today. Friedrich Nietzsche said "That which does not kill us makes us stronger". I can attest that an impoverished childhood and seeing my parents' divorce gave me a greater appreciation for the life I share with my wife and adult children.

I could never articulate my anger and disappointment and, like most kids whose parents' divorce, I misbehaved. I grew up in the 60s and 70s in a community where everyone looked out for each other. I could have easily been a statistic, but I was saved by this close knit incubator community. My mother was determined and worked hard to send me and my siblings to private school where the Nuns did not shy away from disciplining with the paddle.

A child shall lead them. My cousin Larry noticed how capricious and delinquent I was becoming and invited me to go with him to a catholic church called Saint Philip's. Getting to this churched required that we travel on two city buses. The twelve mile journey brought me back to one of the worst neighborhoods in the city of New Orleans called the Desire Projects; where I had actually lived the first five years of my life. I instantly became infatuated with the soulful gospel choir and the West Indies Priest called "Gigi" who masterfully identified God's words as solutions to many of the struggles in our community. The summer I gave mom the most trouble was the summer that my worst punishment saved me from being a ship at sea without a rudder. Mom had become fond of this West Indies priest and the two conspired to teach me a lesson. Rather than endure mom's wrath of corporal punishment I was to complete chores around the church and at the rectory. The priest "Gigi" and my mother had numerous conversations about the many challenges she faced as a single mother and my behavior in school and the havoc I cause by staying out late. I was a handful for a single mother trying to raise seven other children. Father Gigi and my mom created a new ways for me to spend my time by hiring me to do chores as punishment at our church rectory which led my mom to conversion. After my first summer working at the rectory, I began to find purpose in my life. I completed various other tasks so well it led to a summer job at the church's vacation bible school. The cherry on the top of this experience was that I met this cute skinny girl who later became my wife. The story of our courtship despite the fact that mom had given me permission to take up residency at the rectory is retold in a soon to be published book by me and another fellow Napoleon Hill student who happens to also be my wife.

I learned later that I had actually been the impetus for Mom and the rest of my siblings returning to church. Mom began her own mission to provide holiday dinners and groceries to those even poorer than us. I watched mom scrimp and save throughout the year. She started baking and freezing sweet potato pies, asking friends to donate hams and storing canned goods so she could cook holiday dinners for the poorest in the Desire housing community. My brothers and sister provided the transportation logistics by which the dinner deliveries were accomplished. Mama Dear had a way of touching the hearts of so many people to give from what little they had. She taught me and others what it meant to go the "Extra Mile" using "Applied Faith", her "Pleasing Personality", "How to Budget Time and Money", and "Teamwork" all for a "Definite Purpose" which fed about 200 families in the community. I think Mom must have studied under Dr. Napoleon Hill because she clearly employed his principles of success.

Dr. Napoleon Hill's body of work in "Think and Grow Rich" was clearly an important undertaking for my wife. In the spirit of transparency I had never been fond of reading. As the kids got older I found my wife spending her spare time reading more and more. She tried for years to get me to read short articles, short books so that together we would have something to talk about besides work. To her credit, by being lovingly persistent she finally got me engaged with Dr. Hill's work by introducing me to the electronic audio versions. Seeing her dedication to study Dr. Hill's work and having finally listened for myself I became committed to taking the journey of becoming a Napoleon Hill Certified Instructor. The journey has been extremely difficult for me because it requires more reading than I have ever done. The fact that we are on this journey together has really strengthened our marriage at a time most needed as our nest grows empty. I feel I have always known what I wanted to dedicate my life to besides raising a family. Articulation and a written game plan has always been my struggle. Before Hill I had initiative however I lacked a road map. Unlike my beloved wife who wrote and followed a plan, I struggled with the writing part. So much so I found myself not being able to say no because I had no real sense of all that was on my plate. I believed sleep was overrated and found myself rising early and staying up late to take care of home commitments and my nonprofit commitments. Invariably when I got behind the eight ball on either front I solicited her help knowing full well she was juggling a corporate job and helping me raise our children. Tensions had become so high on the home front that I know it is "divine grace" that sustains us. The greatest epiphany I have had since immersing myself in the study of Dr. Hill's principles of success has been in regards to my wife. I have a much greater appreciation for how steadfast and committed a companion, encourager, and covenant keeper she is.

While Hill's 17 principles must be studied and applied in tandem, I will focus on Definiteness of Purpose because Hill's says this is the starting point of all achievement. Unlike my wife, who is also a Hill student, I have always felt led to public service. Because I was a poor planner, and ignorant of Hill's Science of Success Principles, I lacked the ability to say no and to balance the amount of time spent serving outside the home. Although I felt fulfilled in my church and community service, my wife and kids were left with a tired overextended me. Before I began to study Dr. Hill's Principles I spent as much time working my day job as I did serving at church and my community. My ignorance of how emotionally detached I was from my wife of 31 years was so far off my radar that I felt like two people. The perfect servant at church and in the community yet the husband and father whose body goes home while his mind remained disconnected. After years of added stress I know it was only the grace of God that saved and revived our marriage to the healthy state it is in today. I credit Dr. Hill's Mastermind Alliance Principle for helping my wife and I foster perfect harmony for the attainment of our common definite purpose.

"Definiteness of Purpose is the starting point of all Achievement "
-Dr. Napoleon Hill

"I am for doing good to the poor, but I differ in opinion about the means. I think the best way of doing good to the poor is not making them easy in poverty, but leading or driving them out of it."
-Benjamin Franklin.

As President of the 501c3 God's Helpers of Raleigh we use food as the catalyst to provide homeless, unemployed and underemployed men and women with breakfast, spiritual encouragement and a safe place to socialize and receive hope and life building resources. We connect our clients with job resources, community college training, and networks to aid them in becoming self-sufficient. Our mission is not just to meet the physical and temporal needs but to bring hope and resources so they become self-sufficient, contributing members of the community and society at large. I find fulfillment when past clients return to share how our service to them has led them to rise above their circumstance to change their lives. The service I offer to my brethren through God's Helpers of Raleigh is reminiscent of the service I watched my mother provide to those less fortunate in our community. After mom gave her life to Christ I witnessed profound transformation in how she spoke, how she served in our neighborhood, and how she ministered in our church. She had such a glow about her and those who knew how much her life had transformed had so much admiration and respect for her. I knew if my mother could be transformed in her later years that there certainly was hope for me.

I hope the stories in this book inspire and empower you to stay the course on your "Definite Purpose". Whatever you undertake, know that the journey is much smoother and the burden lighter when you employ sound principles and take others along. Dr. Hill says: "No man can become a permanent success without taking others along with him".

BIO

Robert P. Dear, Sr. is President of God's Helpers of Raleigh, a non-profit organization dedicated to helping the homeless community of Raleigh, North Carolina restart their lives.

God's Helpers of Raleigh takes care of client's temporal needs; collaborates with the North Carolina Employment of Security for employment resources, and with local Community Colleges to secure free tuition opportunities to earn a Certification in a service skill area or trade in order to reenter the workforce.

As a Napoleon Hill Foundation Certified Instructor candidate, his vision is to find a location where client's temporal needs can be provided for five days per week along with classroom instructions on Dr. Napoleon Hill's 17 Principles for Success.

Robert's greatest discovery as a Napoleon Hill Foundation Certified Instructor candidate was that in following his passion for service he was erroneously operating like a "ship without a rudder".

He and his wife Brenda now employ Hill's "Mastermind Alliance" principle (and the other 16 principles) daily and are working together to broaden the scope and service of God's Helpers of Raleigh.

Robert has served as VP of Human Resource for Personal Healthcare Inc. as well as Certified Laundry Linen Manager for UNC, Wake, Rex and Duke Hospital facilities in Raleigh/Durham, North Carolina Healthcare System.

He resides with his wife and young adult sons in Raleigh, North Carolina.

Robert can be contacted via e-mail at rpdearsr@gmail.com

A VOICE CRIES OUT AND THE HEART ROARS

By: Apple Suwanna Mitchell

When you reach your goal, what do you intend to give in return?

This question made me think for a while because I had never considered others, or this world, in this way before. Many thoughts came to mind. Why am I alive? Who am I living for, myself or my family? Do other people live for themselves or for other people? If people live for others, what do they gain for themselves?

The memory of a little girl popped up in my mind. She was so young at just eight years old and had a round, short figure; some would consider her homely. The little girl played with her friends all day, far from her house. Some days her mother could not find the little girl when she returned home from work. Her father was a salesman who travelled all over the country and was only home for four or five days a month. That homely little girl walked two kilometers to school by herself every day. She had so much freedom in her life; she played and studied, then played and studied some more. The days passed by quickly. I imagine that she had a very good life, enjoying her freedom.

One evening the little girl returned from school and, like each day, hurried to finish her homework before going out to play with her friends. Her father had returned home and was preparing new goods to sell during his next trip. Soon she heard her mother shouting loudly at her father. The atmosphere was like a war zone and, sadly, was a daily occurrence in the little girl's home. The homely little girl could hear nothing but shouts and exclamations; an eruption of noise as harsh as a storm of bullets. She shut herself away and cried a lot. Then the homely little girl became stronger, discovering her own weapon that allowed her to block out the sights and sounds, repeating to herself over and over that she would grow up to be a beautiful, smart and strong lady.

The homely little girl became a happy teenager. Her family moved north to a province where the weather was pleasant and the traffic was less chaotic, not at all like Bangkok where she had lived for 12 years. Her school was very nice but some of her new friends seemed strange. Most of her teachers were kind, aside from one woman who taught sociology. One day during class, while holding a book in her left hand, the teacher walked slowly from the front of the room and stopped near the girl, pinching her right arm.

The girl immediately stood up and asked the teacher why she had pinched her. The girl had been talking while she was teaching, the woman replied. The girl responded that she hadn't been talking and had never done such a thing during class. She felt all of her classmates staring at her. Suddenly, the teacher walked out of the classroom. "Ah... the class ended because of me," the girl thought to herself. But she was no longer that homely little girl; she had grown up to become a brave young woman, and soon realized that she would have to apologize to her teacher before the instructor would return to the classroom. She went to the teachers' room and told the teacher she was sorry. As she turned away with tears in her eyes, the determined girl made a vow: "If I become a teacher, I will listen to my students and respect their thoughts."

The girl graduated with her bachelor degree, beginning her first job the day after her final exam. She was a workingwoman and felt that she could fly like a beautiful butterfly, filled with the freedom she remembered as a young child. Life was so beautiful. Each day, she travelled by public bus; having to stand wasn't a problem for her since it was a familiar part of her past. But she thought it would be nice to have a car or find someone who could give her a ride every day.

One day, she met a man who would come to be a part of her life. The workingwoman married this successful businessman who owned a Thai company valued at $16 million US. Overnight she became a rich woman.

She settled into married life and the family grew to four with the addition of a son and daughter. One dark night, the rich working woman thought about how exhausted she was, looking after her five-month-old daughter who had been battling a high fever. Beside her, her three-year-old son slept peacefully. Suddenly, she saw her daughter start to convulse and immediately began bathing her with a wet towel, moving so quickly that she almost scratched her little baby's body. The woman's cheeks flooded with tears and she felt like her heart would stop but her mind seemed to take over. "No heart! You can't stop beating!"

The seizure ended but her daughter had to be taken to the hospital. The rich workingwoman quickly packed a bag for the baby and her young son. It seemed like trouble always happened on the days she didn't have a babysitter. She had to wake up her son, holding him with her right hand and carrying her daughter in her left arm, both shoulders weighted down by two heavy bags. She walked up to her husband, drunk and laying on the floor, and tried to kick and shake him awake with no response. It was 2 o'clock in the morning, and she drove to the hospital with two children in the dark, lonely night.

Was life still beautiful? A wife should respect her husband because he is the leader of the house. The rich workingwoman, and mother of two, was living well, acting as a family of three while her husband entertained clients during dinners throughout the week and every weekend. This was the key to the success of his business. But seven years later, his company collapsed. The family now owed $6.8 million US, a "gift" from the Happiness' Drink, or too much alcohol leading to poor business decisions. That was followed by another six years of the Sorrow's Drink, where her husband drowned his disappointment in more alcohol.

Was life still beautiful? No, no, no … not anymore. The sun still rose every morning, shining the light that allows every being in this world to see things clearly. But the rich workingwoman could see nothing; she was becoming poor, the poorest of the world. In the span of seven years, she experienced two of life's extremes: wealth and poverty. She swallowed a palmful of pills and then closed her eyes, the mental pain evident in her endless tears as she felt herself sink into darkness. Her body felt as if it was floating through the air when she heard a voice, "Hey! Miss… wake up, wake up, swallow this to take the pills out!"

Her eyes were still closed; she could hear footsteps and the voices of doctors and nurses. There was a beeping sound coming from the machines. Her chest felt so tight and heavy … it was too heavy … her lungs were working to take in oxygen and pump blood to her heart. "Come on!" her lungs seemed to shout. "Miss … take a deep breath! A deep breath!" a voice shouted. Her body was writhing on the hospital bed, her arms hitting parts of the frame and her legs working to escape the unknown. Her head swayed and bobbed up and down. As the end neared and the darkness continued to close in, an image of her children popped into the poorest workingwoman's mind. Her inner voice exclaimed, "I have to be alive! Breathe! Breathe! Breathe!" and suddenly her heart roared.

The poorest working woman was standing at a small balcony, taking a deep breath as a refreshingly cool wind made her feel better than she had in 13 years. What a peaceful time to be reborn! The poorest workingwoman could go back to being a hard-working woman, enjoying her small online trading business at home, though unable to make much money. The voice inside her heart was always telling her that she had to be more patient, to earn more, to get her children back some day. It kept calling on her to do more and to work harder. Her determination had never wavered as she focused on getting her children back. Her heart roared for a second time.

Time flies by so quickly when we feel happy but so slowly when we're waiting for something. Every drop of sweat, every stressful moment adding up day by day couldn't stop the hard-working woman from reaching her goal. Trading at home, getting up at 4 a.m. to work from 5 a.m. until midnight, and putting up with the men who trolled the cyber world, saying hello to girls and women over the internet. Who can believe in these men? Such a ridiculous approach.

"Hello. We have the same birthday!" "What?! How does this guy know my birthday?" the hard-working woman said to herself. This was a new approach and she spent a long time trying to find out how he knew about her birthday. Her assistant, who had set up her Skype account, said she had no idea but would soon find out. Just keep chatting with him, she told the hard-working woman, while she worked on it.

Sometimes it's God's objective to have you meet someone who is your true soul mate. Although the hard-working woman was a single mom with two children, it didn't seem to matter. After chatting over Skype for a year, the hard-working woman married the American man in Texas and he changed the Thai woman forever.

Her American husband, a retired U.S. army soldier, loved to be deployed to dangerous zones and after his marriage, he continued to work in Afghanistan. One day the Thai wife received a phone call from his colleagues that her husband had undergone emergency surgery and was fighting an intestinal infection. He was medevac'd from Kabul to Dubai, UAE. The Thai wife flew from Bangkok to see him, and was shocked by his appearance. Three medical lines ran from both sides of his neck and many additional lines extended from his stomach. There was an oxygen mask on his face, and yet despite the shock, the Thai wife didn't cry in front of her husband. Doctors said the American husband had a zero percent chance of surviving.

The American husband underwent operations almost every day in the first week. The Thai wife stayed alone in a nearby hotel in Dubai; a small price to pay as the American husband struggled in the ICU for six weeks. That was followed by an additional one-month stay in a Texas hospital and, two months later, hyperbaric treatments three days a week. The American husband, whose doctors said would die, survived. The American husband, whose doctors later said would have to live a controlled lifestyle — unable to lift anything heavy and only walk slowly rather than run — was walking three miles three months later. Those walks turned into three-mile runs and then, a year and a half later, he was back to work in Afghanistan!

It takes a strong mind to make a commitment to live, as Napoleon Hill says in "Think and Grow Rich". The Thai wife was inspired by what her husband had accomplished through the power of his mind, so she took online courses with the U.S.-based Napoleon Hill Foundation and completed all of her lessons in 13 months to become Thailand's only Napoleon Hill Foundation Certified Instructor. In two years, she became an Associate Certified Coach (ACC) of the International Coach Federation (ICF), USA, and is soon to be a Professional Certified Coach (PCC). She has accomplished her goals quickly by subscribing to Napoleon Hill's PMA (Positive Mental Attitude) and using the 17 Principles of Personal Achievement every day.

When you reach your goal, what do you intend to give in return?

That question in Napoleon Hill Foundation's assessment has lived within the Thai instructor since she was a student. Such a meaningful yet simple question — it has changed her life!

The sky is always bright, birds are always singing, the sea is swimming in harmony with man, and the sun, moon, trees and fresh air are all helping life flourish within this world. Just close your eyes and listen to the voice inside your heart. The voice may call you to do

186

something, not only for yourself and your family but also for something even greater. The voice will tell you the right ways to find fulfillment in every step. Daily life is more meaningful when you discover that you can do more for others, allowing you to live a longer, happier life. Call on the beauty and power inside of you to help others and make the world a better place in which to live.

The greater you can be, the greater you can do! Let the voice inside you make your heart roar!

@Coach Apple Suwanna Mitchell with her forever mastermind husband Jim D. Mitchell

BIO

Coach Apple Suwanna Mitchell used to be among the millionaires living in Thailand. Unfortunately, she faced major financial problems during the Tom Yam Kung Crisis of 1997 and ended up in debt with a non-performing loan (NPL) worth more than 100 million Thai baht or $5.6 million US. By combining patience, determination, dedication and diligence with Napoleon Hill's philosophy, she was able to free herself from debt. She completed the Master level of Life Coaching from the Thailand Coaching Academy by Jimi the Coach and became the Success Coach of Success Mastermind Co., Ltd.

Her professional coaching skills and clear definition of purpose helped Apple achieve her Associate Certified Coach (ACC) credential from the International Coach Federation, USA (ICF). Her greatest achievement to date, of which she is so proud, is her designation as a Napoleon Hill Certified Instructor from the Napoleon Hill Foundation, USA. She has adopted Napoleon Hill's mission for her homeland to "make Thailand a better place in which to live". She is the only Napoleon Hill Foundation representative in Thailand and intends to share Napoleon Hill's philosophy while doing the best for Thailand and the world at the same time.

Apple Suwanna Mitchell can be reached at.......

Email: suwanna.m@successmastermind.co.th

www.successmastermind.co.th

FB: Apple Mitchell Napoleonhill Instructor

FB Page: Napoleon Hill by Success Mastermind Thailand

A LIFE GUIDED BY A PURPOSE

By: Eduard Lopez

It was 1942 and there he was, a 14-year old kid trying to make his way up through the staircase in the building where the army had a communications center office in Barcelona. The boy was interested in getting first hand news on how WWII was progressing and he knew he was able to get daily updates there. The army administration used to leave the previous day's reports on a table and nobody noticed a teenager hanging around being interested in such material.

By that time Spain was suffering through the cruelest wave of political repression after the Civil War, which ended in 1939. His father was imprisoned after the war because of being a democrat and fighting against the military coup which brought a dictatorship in Spain that was going to last almost forty years. And, by being really lucky, his death sentence was commuted to a five-year exile, away from the city where he lived with his family. And the young kid went with him for some school terms to help his mom, who was earning some extra money as a dressmaker working from home, raise the other two siblings.

This boy's childhood and teen years were marked by war, post war and scarcity, some of the many examples we still see on TV these days. But, after a few years, the family reunited again and continued the struggle together to keep the kids growing in the best way the parents could afford.

It was by this time when the young man made his mind to have a much better future than the life he was living. To have money and independence to offer his future family much better living conditions. To have respect and appreciation towards other people regardless of their ideals or financial status. It was at that young age when he made his decision and this was going to mark the rest of his life.

It was this time when the boy started being interested in everything that was going on around him and in the entire world. He became an avid reader of the newspapers and magazines that fell into his hands.

Because of the family's situation, and living in a small town, he could not afford to continue a formal education beyond basic schooling so he started taking menial jobs until he went off to the mandatory military service at the age of 18. Because of everything he had learned by himself (for example, he was one of the few soldiers able to write on a typewriter and had basic accounting skills) he was given good assignments during his two-year term at the military.

Upon his return, he looked for jobs. He wanted to start working for himself and become independent, but did not have the money nor the influences to create a business. He was offered a job working as a bellboy in a big bank office. Everybody told him that this was a comfortable job with a stable pay. In those post-war years, nobody in his environment was able to work on a warm place in winter, a cool place in summer and go to work nicely dressed. At the first interview he asked if, over time, he could make his way up to the Bank Office Director. When his supervisor laughed out loud, he quit. This job was clearly not fitting his vision and his purpose for the years to come.

He started working as an accountant for a small factory, manufacturing faucets, where he gained the confidence of the owner and became his right hand man in the business, up to the point that the owner suggested he could marry his daughter and keep the business for them both. Although this looked tempting in the direction of his purpose, he did not want to compromise his feelings and, finally, moved away.

In the mid 1950's, his father, who had been working all his life as a shop attendant selling fabrics (by that time, the pret-a-porter had not arrived yet) opened a small business in the town where they were living. The young man looked at the opportunity and joined his father to grow that business. They did not have money and the customers did not have much money either, so the evolution of this business was really slow. But the great picture, the idea of having his own business burned in his mind. He envisioned having a big shop, employing people and providing the best service to his customers. And he was seeing it in his mind every day when he was going to open the small, rented place; unlike his father, who always was contempt with basic earnings just enough to keep the family's bare necessities covered. They were working together, father and son, at the same small shop, doing the same basic activity, but their thoughts were dramatically different.

In the meantime, our young man continued his self-education. He enrolled in French classes and was one of the very few people in the town with the knowledge of a foreign language. He continued reading everyday about everything: politics, society, science, economy... everything that would help him to enlarge his current environment so he could see the opportunity much clearer when it would arrive.

After few years he married a good lady, a humble person who migrated with her family and was working as a factory operator painting tiles by hand twelve hours a day. The young man managed to place his vision and purpose in his wife's mind. "If you cooperate with me and we both row in the same direction", he told his wife right after marrying, "I will develop a business that will provide our children the future we did not have". And there they went after their common dream.

This called for personal sacrifices. No holiday trips, no luxury, no new cars, no expensive clothes. Every cent they could manage to put aside was kept to be invested in their dream. As years passed, the family grew, and with them so did the living costs. The family lived in a humble apartment, although they could probably afford something better, but the dream of building a business was stronger.

By the late 1960s, the economy in Europe was recovering and this helped speed up the possibility of opening a business, which was getting closer to being realized. By the early 1970s, pulling together all their life's savings, the big opening happened. The young man, then in his mid forties, opened the biggest shop in town, a modern design shop, offering a broad selection of clothes and accessories for men, women and children, employing three other people and bringing the latest trend in fashion to that town.

The man had finally achieved his purpose: he had his own business, it was profitable and it was bringing money into the family to provide for the future he dreamed for his kids who were by that time boys not kids any longer. He could have started relaxing and enjoying life with more luxuries, trips, cars and leisure time. People around him, maybe with much less income and even more debts, were starting to spend more money and displaying a much more expensive lifestyle. So, to keep up with what people in his environment were doing, it was easy to start increasing his standard of living, but his 'education' was telling him something different. He knew that he had no security, and no money backing him up if something should happen to him or to the business itself. So his life continued focused on his business and on securing the future for his two boys. This would have been very difficult if he did not have the continuous support of his wife, always looking for ways of running the house as efficiently as possible to always end up the month with some money saved.

Marvelous things happen when your daily actions are aligned with your beliefs.

The clothes shop business was growing nicely, partially because of the growth in the town population due to the heavy migratory movements by that time in Spain; but it was also growing because the approach this man took with his Customers was fully aligned with his purpose and beliefs.

Most of the Customers were from low-income people, many of them new immigrants who did not have much money to spend. How could the business grow under such conditions? The answer: building trust by giving them credits at zero interest!

Customers could pay in several weeks what they had bought and took with them at the time of the sale. Each Customer had a hand-written credit-debit card with their name close to the shop counter where the new buys (debits) and the partial payments (credits) with a net due amount were duly registered.

Customers (mainly wives) loved this system, since they could afford to continue buying until their husbands' pay day would come to settle part of the debts. This system became very popular in the town so more and more Customers were attracted, increasing the sales in an environment where there was not many opportunities for a business to prosper.

And it was also a leap of faith: the owner had to trust in their Customers and that they would come and settle their debts. And they responded very well; almost everybody always did pay.

Life continued this way for several years, during which the boys kept growing and slowly the family started increasing its lifestyle: their sons were moved to a better high-school, they spent the summer vacation at a nearby beach and a new car was purchased, but it was still a second-hand one. The purpose of this man had not been achieved yet, which was ensuring financial security for his family.

By that time, his father had passed away; and, after a whole life of work and sacrifice, he left behind a situation aligned with his thoughts in life: he never had a car, never took the family on vacation, never owned a house since he just earned enough money to get by. This is all that he asked life for. And this is what he got back.

Then some changes started to come. New malls started opening in the area and people started changing their shopping habits, so our clothes shop's revenue started to decline. But our friend was on-guard. He was in purpose and was not going to quit so easily.

After so many years living with honesty and integrity, he cultivated many friends who had a high opinion about him, so it did not take long before he started developing another business while still running his shop, where he appointed a salesperson responsibility, which gave him additional time to think of other businesses that would keep taking him closer to his purpose.

Tough times were going to come: the family spend was growing, the two sons were already in College, the shop's revenue was steeply declining and our friend was getting older. He feared he was not going to be able to achieve his purpose. But he did.

The last years prior to his retirement, he developed several other sources of income which allowed him to compensate for the declining business results and to keep up with the family expenses, so he proudly retired at the age of 65 leaving two sons married and with enough assets to live comfortably together with his lovely and dedicated wife for years to come. Time to enjoy the life with his grandsons, to play chess with his friends and to continue supporting and serving as a model to his sons.

Our man, my father, passed away at the age of 78 and left behind a legacy. A legacy that cannot be measured in terms of money, although he accumulated assets to ensure that my mom would not have any money worries for the rest of her life.

More than anything he left an example to all of us. The example that you can achieve what you want in life just by focusing on it and following your beliefs and letting your intuition guide you.

He could not have guessed all the different circumstances life had prepared for him, all the needs and traps that lay ahead, but he always saw himself in possession of what he was going after: to be independent and give his children a much better life and better opportunities than the ones he had.

At the time he made this decision in his early teens, he was surrounded by misery, lack of education and hate. Spain had just finished its Civil war (1936-1939) and the country was divided in two: the ones who won and wanted retaliation, and the ones who lost, who were publicly persecuted and ridiculed, with no hope of getting ahead in life with equal opportunities.

Also, the Second World War added more scarcity and impunity to the way the military regime established in Spain was managing the post-war traumatic process.

In such an environment, my father had a vision and converted it into a Definite Purpose. All his life's actions were taken to bring him one step closer to what he wanted to achieve, and this way, step by step, he managed to get out of this environment and, never being blinded by short-term success or failure, his rudder was always in the direction he wanted to achieve.

This is a great lesson that, like everything that comes to us for free, is priceless.

For me, looking in retrospect, and having had the privilege of knowing him, there is something hidden in his story that has impacted me the most and has shaped my and my brother's personality: everything my father did was done with honesty and integrity.

And this is the second priceless lesson I learned from him: to achieve what you want in life you don't need to take advantage of other people's situations, you don't need to lose respect or treat others dishonestly; you just need to have a clear image of how you want to act everyday in alignment with your deepest beliefs. Everything else will take care of itself.

I recall countless personal examples that, today, looking back, I recognize as valuable lessons you can pass to your kids. Without sermons or speeches, his day to day example was sinking into our subconscious mind and made it part of our invisible direction.

When my father died, I had never seen more people attend a funeral. He was loved and appreciated by the whole town and friends he cultivated during his life.

He left behind a lovely family and life lessons for us to profit from.

Dad, I am sure you are proud of what you did. We all are!

BIO

Eduard was born in a small town in Spain from a low-middle class family. Having his parents completed only basic schooling, they managed to be able to save for Eduard's University where he got the MSc degree in Engineering.

Eduard has developed his entire professional career in Multinational companies, from his early days when he joined IBM's ranks as a junior professional, right after College.

IBM's crisis in the 1990s opened a new world of challenges and opportunities where the real Professional and Personal growth started. Always part of big Corporations, succeeding in dynamic and challenging environments was only possible through sustained Peak Performance individuals and teams.

Considered as one of his best decisions in life, Eduard developed his career in three different countries, getting to know how to successfully integrate the cultural differences into team and individual performance.

Knowing how hard developing a career without experienced advice and support is, his Mission has become helping people to accelerate the process of getting what they want to achieve in life. Becoming a Certified Coach by the International Coach Federation and a Certified Instructor of the Napoleon Hill Foundation has set up the base for the successful accomplishment of that Mission.

You can contact Eduard at:

Email: elopezgimeno@gmail.com

Linked-in: https://ro.linkedin.com/in/eduardlopez

Human For Human Consulting: http://www.h4human.com/

WHAT IF MY DREAMS COME TRUE?

By: Gerardo Dominguez

The Battle That Every Man Fights Against His Biggest Enemy.

What if I fail? What if they don't like me? What will other people say? What if my dreams just stay dreams? The same old questions that every man asks himself over and over again.

In The Beginning

Since I was very young I have considered myself a dreamer. For some strange reason dreams were more powerful for me than reality. Those images that move so fast in our minds and make your heartbeat increase within a few seconds had an effect on me and I knew that, for some reason, I had to pay attention to them.

When I was 15 years old I began to observe all the differences among the people around me and I asked myself questions such as:

Why is it that some people are happier than others?

Why is it that some people get what they define as success and others do not?

Why is it that very few people live with a purpose and most live according to "the social system"?

Why is it that, even with a full tank of willpower, most people fail and just a few achieve their dreams?

Was it luck? Was it the old lady we call fortune? Or is it something rare that is inside a few men from the time they were born?

Those questions stayed in my mind for a couple of years and something was telling me that a person requires more than willpower to succeed. Something inside me was telling me that a man needs to follow the steps of other great men to become great. Something was telling me that a man is forged by his choices more than by luck and fortune.

My questions guided me to ask those around me about success and how to achieve it. Coming from a middle class society in Mexico City, the answers were almost the same from every person I asked. I received answers such as:

• Success is to finish school with good grades, go to college and get a good job.

• Success is to expect the best in life and never desire what you know you cannot have.

• Success is helping others and never asking much for yourself.

*These answers were basically the same, one after the other, in various forms.

I knew that something was wrong, that those were not the answers I was looking for and, if I wanted to achieve what some may call a crazy dream, then I needed to find my answers somewhere else.

My Dreams

I have always been a big dreamer. Even when my teachers, my classmates and those around me were telling me that some things were impossible, I kept on dreaming.

I remember when I shared my dreams in a class with one of my teachers and my classmates. They were amazed by the size of my dreams, and it took them a little less than 30 seconds for them to laugh about what I was saying.

"One day I will be able to travel around the world. I will be able to create and guide my own company, and will guide other people to success."

Just those few words were required to get a good laugh from my listeners.

I remember that I received comments such as… "Let me know when you have done it", "Do you really think someone from this school could ever make it big?" and "YEAH RIGHT, Dreams are free".

Some may consider this a bad experience, or even one of those moments that one would like to erase from their lives. But, for me, it was one of the best moments of my life.

This experience, that took only a few minutes, was one of the best moments that helped guide my steps. It was at this moment that an intense emotion raised up inside me and I made the decision to make my dreams come true at any cost. It was this moment when I said to myself the words:

"I AM GOING TO DO IT,
WHATEVER IT TAKES".

My Biggest Enemy

I remember the first time I heard my biggest enemy's voice. That voice that whispers in your ear and tells you every single thing that may go wrong.

What if you get criticized?

What if you fail?

What are they going to say?

What if I lose?

What if this is not my opportunity?

I had just made the decision to make my dreams come true and, like every single person that wants to achieve something great, I encountered my first challenge. A challenge that is very common but exactly where most of the dreamers get stuck. A challenge described with the question:

"Where Should I Start?"

It is true that dreaming is easy, but defining the path and the plan to achieve your dreams can be a challenge. This is right where most entrepreneurs, dreamers and those who want to achieve something great get stuck.

Since I was young, and my dreams were big, I was really lost as to how to achieve them and it was here when my enemy was awakened.

The first time I listened to him he spoke to me in a gentle and even logical way. He told me: "What if it is all only a dream?", "What if you were born for something else?" Words that I still remember today and I believed them for a few days.

The second time he spoke to me it was a little more aggressive, since my actions were not aligned with my dreams, but my mind was still dreaming all the time. The second time I heard the words "What if you are criticized by everyone?", "What if you make a fool of yourself?", "What if you waste your time and never achieve anything?"

It took me a while to admit that my worst enemy was my own inner voice and that he talked very similar to me. Honestly, I let those voices control my thinking for a few years. At the same time, I never stopped dreaming. For some reason I kept on dreaming and expanding my ideas just because they felt good. I stopped believing for a while but never stopped dreaming.

The Revelation

When I was 17 years old I was in a library and the title of a small book caught my attention... "Think and Grow Rich"

Just the title caught my attention. "How can anyone think themselves into riches?" I asked myself as I grabbed the book. I have never enjoyed literature before, but something inside me told me that I should give this book a try. This was the first time I remember that I used the same power that was stopping my dreams, but to my advantage...

"What if I give it a try and it works?"

I was changing the way I spoke to myself and I was translating it into the right actions.

The first time I read Think and Grow Rich I was amazed by the stories it contained. Examples of the information applied by Henry Ford, Andrew Carnegie, Rockefeller and Edison, among others, were opening my mind to new possibilities. I was reading stories about people that built the world as we know it today and who made our way of living possible thanks to their ideas.

The famous phrase "Whatever the Mind of Man Can Conceive and Believe It Can Achieve" was starting to create an impact in my brain and I started to understand the amazing power that every person has in their own mind.

I realized that everything I was doing before reading Think and Grow Rich was conceiving ideas and for me to achieve these ideas it was necessary to start believing in them. Once a man believes in his dreams and his ideas, they can be translated into desire, and there is nothing more powerful than a man's desire to achieve something in life.

The Process

As I was reading, I was constantly battling against my own thoughts. Every new idea I was able to create was attacked by this old friend that I like to call "The What If Syndrome".

I realized that going from little belief in an idea to complete belief was hard to do so I developed a game that started to quiet this voice and started to increase my belief in my ideals.

Every single time I heard this voice in my ear, telling me "What if…" I translated the belief into one of my own. If the voice was telling me "What if you fail", I repeated a few times "What if I Win". If the voice was telling me "This is JUST a Dream", I repeated a few times "What if my dreams come true?"

This exercise helped me increase my belief level step by step and it started to reprogram my brain to what I wanted it to do and believe.

At the beginning it was a little hard, since these limiting ideas were kind of a habit but, after a few days, it started to become easier each time.

The Outcome

Playing this game may sound a little silly sometimes, and even when I shared it with a few people around me they laughed about the idea. I wasn't bothered about it and when anyone would make a joke about it I was able to play the same game once more: "What if I am different because I want different things?"

After some time, once I started to increase my belief about what I wanted to achieve, some very interesting things started to happen. I was introduced to people that were living the lifestyle I wanted to achieve. I was guided through businesses and achievements by people that created them one after the other. I realized that it was all available to me thanks to the process of taking care of my thoughts, and that every single opportunity was designed in my mind even before it happened.

I kept on applying this science for quite some time. I started to understand the importance of creating a detailed plan after developing a desire, and even more important, to be clear on what you are willing to give in return for what you want. It took me a while to understand that there is no such thing as something for nothing. When I was able to apply this to my life amazing events kept on happening.

The Adversity

I was having such a great time understanding and applying this information for a few years that I forgot one of the most basic concepts. I stopped taking care of what was getting into my brain. I started to use the same power that was opening doors and creating results against myself.

I started to develop difficulties instead of opportunities; I created fights instead of new great relationships. I started to focus obsessively on what I did not want instead of what I did want.

It took me a while to realize that all of these adversities were being created by me. It took me a long time to learn that every single thing that happens in my life, good or bad, is my complete responsibility. Once I realized this I started to focus once again on what I wanted to achieve.

The Lesson

Many would say that going through this rough process was a misfortune or even a bad time but today I am able to understand that every single moment that I do not like in my life is a great time to define what I do want. From that moment, each time that I encounter a bad event or a negative situation I am thankful for the opportunity of noticing what I do not want so that I can focus obsessively on what I desire.

Going through negative situations of every kind has taught me that life is a constant process of creation, and once you decide everything is going to go well you have to make it happen that way. There is no moment in which you can go to sleep and let good things happen by themselves, you have to create them constantly.

One of the greatest lessons I have learned is that we humans are just like plants in nature, we are either growing or dying but we are never still.

By constantly defining where you are going and what you will do to get there, you are able to use your own brain for what it was designed to do, create everything that happens in your life.

The Constant Practice

Life is a process of continuous creation and definition. Each time you use your brain you are emitting a frequency that creates every single scenario in your life. You can take control of everything that goes on in your life by taking care of what is created in your mind, or you can just let everything from the outside world take control of your mind and life.

We can all control our thoughts and how we respond with constant practice. Playing the "What If Game" has been my method of taking charge of my attitude and my own way of thinking. Anyone can practice it and over a period of years it has helped myself and other people take control of their way of thinking.

"It all starts with a dream and, once you believe it, you are able to develop a desire for its achievement."

BIO

Gerardo Dominguez was born and raised in Mexico City, Mexico. From a very young age he was guided through the Napoleon Hill philosophy and mentored in various aspects of business and personal success. His studies and understanding of the material pushed him to start teaching them from a very young age.

He is the creator of various educational systems that guide and help the modern business man and entrepreneur to achieve more with their life and business. He has created brands in the personal development industry in Latin America and has been able to help other personal development speakers and authors to achieve better positioning in their market.

He is the Co-Founder of "Mastering Your Life Institute" a research and educational institute that gathers and teaches everything related with the science of the mind and the science of personal success. He has changed the life of hundreds of thousands of people in Latin America by delivering systems, conferences, programs and private consulting.

Get to now more about Gerardo and his current endeavors, visit:

www.GerardoDominguez.com

SOLVING THE LIFE PUZZLE WITH DEFINITE MAJOR PURPOSE

By: Tachanat Bhatrasataponkul

Life is like a jigsaw puzzle. Much of what we have been exposed to sometimes makes sense some years later. Much of what we have experienced sometimes yields fruitful results at a later age. Apparently, the course of life does not seem like connecting the dots as Steve Jobs told us and yet many desirable things arrive randomly in time at different points of life. This is one important lesson life has taught me throughout the years.

Everyone attempts to solve their own life puzzles individually and draw their own legends beautifully. We keep collecting and combining those in-hand and in-coming jigsaw pieces into our life puzzles. We need to figure out where things can match up and fit into the picture hidden behind the puzzle. However, there is an essential key in solving the life puzzle. That is your own definite major purpose in life. It will fundamentally serve as the big picture, which you desire to create.

One may have different strategies in solving their life puzzle. Here I will share one strategy based on my true stories and life lessons. Although this strategy follows common steps, like playing a jigsaw puzzle, it is also practically applicable in solving the life puzzle. There are basically five steps as follows. First, imagine the desired picture. Second, choose your work corner. Third, assemble the edge pieces. Forth, sort pieces into color groups. Fifth, continue filling in the gaps.

Imagine the desired picture.

I have been living in academia throughout my life. People usually thought I was the cream of the crop in my classes. Honestly speaking, I struggled a lot during my undergraduate study. I was placed on academic probation during my first two years in college until I almost got kicked out because of my unsatisfactory cumulative GPA. One reason was that I entered one of the top universities in Thailand by skipping grade 12 in high school. This caused a lack of basic background knowledge in many science subjects. Also, I could not adjust myself to independent college life due to immaturity. I should have enjoyed the last year in high school with friends. It could have been an unforgettable moment in my life.

Until my first year in college went by, I still did not know what major I wanted to continue for my study. There were more than 20 science majors to choose but I did not have many options due to my terrible grades. I decided between geology and oceanography since these two majors offer many opportunities for field trips and field excursions. The only motivation was that I just wanted to escape my parents as often as possible. To me, going out on shipboard field observation sounded like a good excuse to live away from home. That is what I was thinking. Then I finally chose to major in physical and chemical oceanography. It turned out that I struggled a lot more as this major required core courses in both physics and chemistry, which I was never passionate about. I cannot believe I survived those horrible years.

During my senior year in college, I had seen several professors in the department dealing and handling with numerous pressing environmental problems at both national and international levels. They included a wide variety of issues in marine resource and coastal zone management such as water pollution, habitat loss, coastal erosion, overfishing, natural disasters, El Niño–La Niña impacts and the 2004 Indian Ocean tsunami tragedy. Their expertise played a great role through with the media and society. I then realized that my country still lacks professionals in various branches of ocean sciences. That was my first time I thought about my future career path. I told myself during my senior year that I would like to be a professor with expertise in physical oceanography. I often imagined myself as a renowned professor. That made me truly feel a great sense of accomplishment as if I had already attained it. I kept that desired picture spinning in my head as a self-affirmation. This is my definite major purpose.

Choose your work corner.

Soon after setting up my definite life goal, I was planning and thinking of what could help me achieve it. First of all, I needed to have a PhD and gain more experience abroad. However, I realized that I could not afford further study at a higher degree in a western country by myself. The only possible way was that I needed to earn a full scholarship to go study abroad. There are a number of funding agencies out there where full scholarships are available each year. In order to make it happen, I needed to have an excellent academic background and very good proficiency in English. These were all clues to a treasure trove acting as my road map.

Apart from a nautical chart, navigating a ship across the ocean also needs a compass. I still had a broad range of interests. I kept asking myself which area in ocean science I actually was passionate about. Then I jumped into various aspects of marine science beyond the classroom and curriculum whenever possible. I got my hands dirty in an attempt to explore some practical insights in every single area. Later on I found out that I was particularly interested in ocean-atmosphere interaction and satellite remote sensing. This is one subfield in physical oceanography that I wished to dive deeper and deeper into. Accordingly, I did my summer internship at the Marine Meteorology Unit at the Thai Meteorological Department. There I learned a lot about ocean weather forecasting using numerical models.

I realized that I could not go abroad right after I finished my college degree. I needed to become well prepared so as to be qualified for a full scholarship. What should I do with my poor academic background? I decided to continue my master's degree with the aim of regaining my confidence and potential in academic research. My student life in graduate school went very well. I completely retrieved myself as the cream of the crop. I had a lot of patience with strengthening my English skills in academic writing and presentations. I joined many international conferences, workshops, seminars and training courses. In the long run, I became more determined with a strong passion for ocean and climate research.

Assemble the edge pieces.

While searching for a full scholarship to go abroad, I looked for every single opportunity and put all my effort into improving my English communication skills. During one summer semester, I served as a volunteer guide at the Bangkok Youth Hostel. There was a help desk for foreign travelers asking about things to do and places to go around Bangkok and beyond. That was the way I learned the art of starting conversations and became familiar with talking to foreigners from different cultures. I met and talked with travelers and backpackers from around the world. To be honest, I used to be an introvert but this experience totally changed me. It also broadened my perspectives on various aspects of life.

I became hyperactive with interests in a wide variety of volunteer works and youth affairs. I joined numerous extracurricular activities outside the university in an attempt for self-improvement in all aspects. I was selected to participate in many competitive programs regarding international youth activities, e.g. UNESCO youth camp (South Korea), ASEAN youth exchange (Japan), APEC youth forum (Thailand) and YMCA work camp (Thailand). I gained more and more confidence with my English communication skills. I was officially awarded the national outstanding youth award in recognition of my excellence in the area of youth development and public welfare. I consider this award a key jigsaw piece that brought me many other great opportunities later on. Most of all, I became much more self-empowered in many aspects of my life.

Soon after I finished my master's thesis, I applied for a full scholarship to the Royal Thai Government to pursue a PhD study abroad. I was blessed to be one of the finalists to be awarded the full scholarship. Unfortunately, the scholarship required me to continue a PhD study in environmental engineering with a specialty in wastewater treatment but my passion is to dive deeper into physical oceanography. That is the only burning desire, which fuels my energetics and enthusiasm. It was a tough decision to make as I had been waiting for this opportunity for my whole life. Eventually I decided to resign that scholarship contract.

Life is fair enough and always moves us to a more desirable place. I passed a selection process among a number of highly qualified candidates to a tenure-track teaching faculty position at one leading university. Since people in the field of physical oceanography are an extremely rare species, I could be a potential candidate even though I only had a master's degree. Surprisingly, I became a university lecturer when I was 24 years old. What I had imagined suddenly arrived earlier than I expected. The university campus is located in a remote area surrounded by the mountains and close to the sea. I loved this place.

Sort pieces into color groups.

There I taught many classes related to oceanography and meteorology. I enjoyed teaching and supervising students through their research projects. I loved my job and I found that the passion and pursuit of helping others achieve and make them become better than the person they were the day before has been more rewarding than anything else. I still wish to pursue a PhD study abroad. Unexpectedly, opportunity came to knock on my door again. The Royal Thai Government awarded me a full scholarship for PhD studies abroad in whatever field of study I wished to pursue. I applied and I was accepted to many top oceanography schools in the United States and some European countries. At this point, I was ready to start the journey I had dreamed about.

A harsh reality soon set in which I did not anticipate. I felt heartbroken again. I was not allowed to live abroad because I was diagnosed with immune thrombocytopenic purpura (ITP). It is an autoimmune disorder in which the immune system destroys blood platelets that are necessary for normal blood clotting. It has no cure. Treatment with modern medicine was made by continually giving a high dose of steroids that suppresses the immune system. This subsequently brought me even worse and worse symptoms affecting the malfunctioning of other organs (i.e. lung, liver and kidneys). It was very challenging to maintain a positive mindset when faced with physical illness. It took two years to fully recover using alternative medicine.

I looked back upon my life and then realized that I should have been well balanced in all areas of my life. Throughout those two years of medication, I was on my quest for the meaning of life. I read many books. I studied Tao and Zen and various methods of holistic healing. I went to meditation retreats at many different places. I learned how to maintain mind-body-spirit fitness. I now understand and appreciate the rhythms of life. Life has taught me that imbalance habitually brings about some form of physical ailment. In the long run, it is sometimes worth it to pause to sort out the puzzles of life, so that you can find meaning in your life and ultimately fulfill your destiny.

Continue filling in the gaps.

I almost lost my hope of going abroad to study. Fortunately, the scholarship contract allowed me to travel once I was fully recovered. I decided to choose the oceanography program at Florida State University, as many professors there are legends. So far I have been in the U.S. more than five years. I have traveled to more than 40 states and 50 countries mostly through academic events like conferences, seminars, workshops and summer schools. Living in academia does not always seem nerdy but rather facilitates borderless learning opportunities through travel, which considerably makes my life both enjoyable and intellectually stimulating.

It has been a long journey to where I am today. I could have never reached this point without my definite major purpose. It acts as an essential key in solving my life puzzle. I am currently working toward my PhD in physical oceanography and I am almost there. I really cannot wait to resume my position as a professor in my beloved motherland. Last but not least, life is like a never-ending jigsaw puzzle. Every single jigsaw piece can elucidate our gloomy path and bring us one little step closer to our ultimate goal. Undoubtedly, we have to continue filling in the gaps.

To this end, solving the life puzzle depends primarily on how we live it. With definiteness of purpose, we focus on what truly matters and life eventually becomes so much brighter.

BIO

Tachanat Bhatrasataponkul is an oceanographer, meteorologist and climatologist by educational background and professional training. He is currently working towards his PhD in physical oceanography at Florida State University. He is originally from Thailand where he holds a post as a teaching faculty member at a leading university. He joined the Napoleon Hill Leader Certification class onboard the Celebrity Summit cruise in the Caribbean Sea in late 2015.

Tachanat is truly a self-made lifestyle-preneur and world wanderer having been to more than 50 countries by his early 30's. While living in the United States, he has traveled to over 40 states including Alaska and Hawaii. He loves backpacking, trekking, diving and exploring different aspects of the world and nature. He has learned several foreign languages including Chinese, Japanese, German, Italian, Spanish, and Russian. He has about 5,000 followers on his Facebook fanpage where he keeps sharing inspirations, stories and lessons learned in life.

Tachanat can be reached by email at tachanat.buu@gmail.com.

HOW I CHANGED MY LIFE WITHOUT CHANGING MY CIRCUMSTANCES

By: Bereah Al Shanqiti

I must say that life has been good to me. I have a loving and supportive family, a great education, a great job and I recently moved to Canada. I am blessed to have been raised in an upper middle class family, and to have obtained an education in the best universities in Jordan and England. I have landed excellent jobs in the best telecommunication companies in the region. So in essence, I am grateful for the life I have been granted.

Nevertheless, have you ever felt that life is going too fast? Where you are running between work, kids, activities, cooking, appointments, housework, school, etc. It feels like you are in a "rat race" that never ends and by the end of your day you just go to sleep out of exhaustion and fatigue only to start the same cycle the next day.

Have you ever felt like you have a long to-do list that keeps on expanding? What about all the things you wish you had the time to do? Have you ever thought that reaching your goals can make you happy only to be surprised that happiness was momentarily and overrated? Have you ever felt that you are always looking forward towards the summer or the winter vacation to get out of your daily routines? You work hard for months dreaming of the perfect upcoming vacation, only to find that time passed too fast or your expectations were too high and from there you start the planning cycle again?

It is as if you are always preparing the grounds for a better tomorrow but what if tomorrow does not come? What if tomorrow comes with its own struggles that you have not prepared for? And what about today? What is wrong with today? On a scale from 1 to 10 where 1 is bad and 10 is perfect, how would you rate today? Would you rate it above 7? How would you like today to be?

That was exactly how I felt. I was running, planning, doing something all the time so I could have a better tomorrow. I am a high achiever who exerts pressure on myself and everyone around me and pushes them towards success. I felt like I was always in the planning and executing mode. Planning for the next trip, planning for the next thing to do, planning for the next activity and, since I was never a procrastinator, I always followed through with my plans. In essence I was doing well but I felt tired, exhausted, and consumed. I started feeling the stress of being in control and everyone around me found it easier to ride along, since I decided to take on that job.

Looking around me I saw a lot of friends who had similar symptoms, once we reached home after a long day of work, we wore the hat of Sherlock Holmes and got into the commanding and investigating mode. Once one task was finished, we would initiate the next one. "Please tidy up your room. Can you stop playing on …? Go take a bath. Did you finish your homework? How did you do on your exams? Did you tell your teacher to….? How many times do I have to say do…?" And the list goes on and on… until we are perceived as the house-officer with a never-ending to-do list. In the end you end up being the witch everyone is trying to avoid.

Was this the life I imagined for myself when I was young? Was I supposed to be rushing to do things all the time? And if so, how could I change myself to enjoy the tasks rather than just mindlessly finishing them?

As an example, I enrolled my kids in lots of activities; swimming, karate, art, drama, jewelry making, Kumon, tailoring, languages… you name it. Any activity I felt would be beneficial for their future I managed to find a time slot to enroll them in. The kids were engaged in one or two after school activities daily and so, in addition to my full time job, chores, and appointments, I was running with them to and from the activities. My intentions were noble. I wanted to expose them to new and useful activities that could sharpen their talents. In addition, I was driven by the guilt most working mothers have. A super mom is what I wanted to be.

In the end, all of that came at my own expense. I was exhausted, tired and easily agitated. I was not the fun loving mom I wanted to be. I forgot my hobbies. I was always the "party pooper" or the sound of reason and that is the worse feeling a woman and a mother could have. We are supposed to be the love, the joy, and the free spirit. We are supposed to be the warm heart, and the voice of passion.

There comes a time when you seek change. You decide it is time to stop running this mad race and start thinking what is next.

A quote that always resonated with me was:

"Stop doing and start being"

I made the decision that things had to change. My family welcomed that decision. It released them from their endless attempts to please me. Knowing that, if I changed, the whole dynamics within the family would change too was revolutionary to me. I decided it is time to stop trying to control the outcome of a situation or having a plan B all the time. When I decided to change, everything else, my entire outlook towards life changed. I started by imagining what kind of life and family dynamics I wanted. I filled in the details of my vision with what was important to me and I wrote down my definite major purpose.

To build a life that is rich with love, fun and fulfillment. Be the inspiration for others to adapt a positive mental attitude in all aspects of life starting with myself, family and friends by modelling and embracing the principles of success I learned.

My motto:

"Live by design and not by default"

Once my goal was set, I decided on a time frame and a general plan to achieve that goal. I did not have a detailed plan of implementation. I had a rough idea of the whole scenario and what I wanted however, I always knew the next few steps that had to be followed. Putting the plans into action was not easy as I had to change my mindset towards everything first. I made multiple mistakes but I always learned a lesson from each downfall. One lesson I found fascinating was that once you decide on something the whole universe comes to assist you in order to achieve it.

The initial step was education. I knew I needed to educate myself, so I resorted to reading lots of self- help books and listening to audios. I also looked for coaching, but decided that, rather than hiring a coach, I would learn how to become one and so I enrolled myself in the University of Toronto for Solution Focused Brief Coaching program. It is a great method of coaching that focuses on what is more results oriented rather than problem solving oriented. I also studied NLP, Neuro Linguistic Programing, which was another tool to focus my mindset and harness my aspirations.

After thorough studies, I was convinced that most of these tools/programs/books were based upon Napoleon Hill's principles of success. Taking one item from his teachings and expanding it, I decided to further study Napoleon Hill's principles and become a Certified Instructor with The Napoleon Hill Foundation. It is a journey I am currently enjoying immensely and can't wait to teach it to other people.

So what tools did I implement at home that had the biggest affect?

First was defining what I wanted.

"Whatever your mind can conceive and believe your mind can achieve."
-Napoleon Hill

It was not easy to define what I wanted and so in the beginning I focused on what I did not want in order to figure that out. I knew I did not want to be angry. I did not want to feel like a slave. I did not want to be tired and exhausted. I did not want to be agitated and certainly I did not want to be in command mode all the time.

From there, I started figuring out what is it that I aspired to be. I wanted home to be a relaxing environment with lots of laughter, fun and appreciation. I wanted a home that was neat and inviting and I wanted every day to be an enjoyable day filled with love and hugs. I knew I did not want to keep running between activities so I reduced the number of activities the kids participated in every semester and I opted for the ones with minimal transportation time. I also ensured that there was ample time to reach the activity without being stressed for time.

Gratitude Journaling

I started a gratitude journal along with my kids. Every day each of us wrote three things that we were grateful for. We also wrote down an act of kindness someone did for us, and one we did for others. The practice was very therapeutic in focusing our attention towards appreciating what we were blessed with. We started noticing that more things were coming our way every time we acknowledged our fortunes. The kids got engaged in this exercise, which was a great nighttime activity we did before going to bed. I know a lot of people write journals about their day and focus on what went wrong, expressing their distressed feelings which ends up making them feel worse and victimized. I would rather focus on what I desire and write that down instead of the unfortunate events in my life that make me feel down.

One day, my husband was distressed due to some unfortunate events at work. Getting him out of that mood was hard, so I resorted to telling him a story I heard but could not recall its source. "Imagine six men were invited to a meeting. On the door each was advised to write down the adversity he is facing. The first one wrote; facing terminal illness, the second wrote; coping with a cancer-sick child, the third one wrote; have a debt of 1 million dollars, the forth wrote; dealing with sick parent, the fifth one wrote dealing with the death of my wife and raising kids on my own, and the last one wrote; migrant from war zone area and living in a refugee camp". After the meeting they were all given the option to change their adversity, to leave the one they had and pick a new one. What do you think they decided? After looking at all the challenges, they all opted to keep their original misfortunes due to the fact that they already were able to deal with it. Although these circumstances might seem hypothetical, there are people all around us each facing their own challenges in life and dealing with them. Unless we are grateful for what we have, we will not notice the blessing bestowed upon us. Since then, every time my husband is faced with a challenge, I hear him confirming that the situation can be managed and it could have been worse and always looking for the silver lining in that situation.

*"Every defeat carries the seed of an
equivalent benefit"*
-Napoleon Hill

Focusing on fun activities that can be done together.

When the kids started having more time at home, they became more creative. They started their own projects and expounded their curiosity. Time was spent playing board games, going for bike rides and engaging in small exploration trips to different cities in Canada. We try to incorporate fun in everyday activities such as cooking together, singing, dancing and keeping it light and fun. We still have our chores to do and we implemented a no internet policy unless and until we finish our tasks, so we rush to finish what we need to do.

Napoleon Hill spoke in one of his lectures of a motto that he saw at Dr. Frank Crane's office.

"Don't take life too DAMN serious"

...i.e. You will be damned

In addition to adventurous activities, we engaged ourselves in retail therapy, which is quite entertaining, especially when you have young ladies. I enjoy spending lovely moments with them; shopping for them and myself as long as it does not damage the budget.

Praying and meditation

Connecting to God and the universe was an important pillar in my transformation. I have always been a conservative/religious person. I do believe in God and always accepted whatever happens without anger and complaints, knowing that if I did not get what I wanted, then there must have been a good reason or maybe something better would be coming my way. During this process, I knew I needed God to support me in growing and learning to be a better person. Praying and meditation was a great tool to stop the chatter in my mind and to always think positively.

Changing my Attitude towards chores and tasks

There are a lot of chores and tasks that I need to do around the house. I decided I wanted to change my attitude and to enjoy performing these tasks, so I resorted to being present while doing them. When I am washing the dishes, I start thinking of the water or the smell of the soap. When I am doing some cleaning, I put some music on and dance. I also try to engage the kids in some of these tasks and make it fun.

Previously, when I used to come home after a long day at work, the house would be in a total mess. I used to get so frustrated. Now I still come to a messy house, but my attitude is completely different. I go in thanking God that the kids are safe and that they were able to take care of themselves while I was away working. Now they greet me with hugs and kisses. Then I take a 30-40 minute break to relax, shower, change and pray. After taking some time off to build up my energy, I engage everyone in preparing dinner and tidying up the house. It stopped being my chores and it became OUR shared chores.

Everyone feels more relaxed and comfortable and we all share the responsibility of tidying up. Being present as much as possible while doing tasks results in completing the task on hand rather than thinking of the next thing to be done. I try to focus on one thing at a time rather than multi-tasking. I started enjoying my tasks more and always focus on completing them before moving to the next one.

Giving love and appreciation and celebrating small achievements

Celebrating any small achievement is a great tool to bring home the fun loving atmosphere. This can be a good mark, a promotion, a school reward or anything that needs to be acknowledged and that can be celebrated. Giving hugs and kisses as much as possible is great as well. Now, my younger one comes to me when she feels depleted and she says she needs my hugs, which recharges her when her batteries are low.

I also have incorporated writing a message on the bathroom mirror to each of them to encourage them and show how much I appreciate having them in my life. It is a tool I learned from one of the colleagues in Solution Focused and has proven to be very successful. I focus on finding something nice about them every day and bring it to light. Some days they even surprise me by writing me messages expressing their love and appreciation.

Unfortunately my Dad passed away at the end of January 2016. It was one of the most difficult episodes in my life, but I chose to focus on what I received from him rather than what I am missing. I was blessed with a great dad that provided me the love, appreciation, and security any child would need. I was fortunate to have lots of good memories and my kids are blessed to have had the greatest granddad anyone would wish for, although I miss him a lot and was not fortunate to say goodbye. Those happy moments I had make me grateful for what I was blessed with. In my mind I believe my dad's life and death taught me how to live. Thank you dad for being who you are. I love you.

Now I feel much happier, even though my circumstances did not change, my attitude about life did.

What I learned

• I learned to empathize with others and not be judgmental, keeping an open mind all the time.

• I learned that when you do the right thing you are at peace, even if the other party does not act accordingly.

• I learned to act according to my values, rather than react to a situation. When someone pushes my buttons, I try to be patient and decide the way I want to act rather than just being angry and in retaliation mode. I know this is not easy and I still react sometimes but, with practice and awareness, it gets better every day.

• I learned that it is okay for things not to work out all the time. The lessons learned from failure are more powerful than the ones learned from success.

• I learned my attitude is contagious so I opted to spread a positive one and try being optimistic all the time. I also try to focus on positive thoughts and eliminate negative ones.

• I learned that the only person you can change is yourself. So to influence a situation, I opted to change my attitude and reactions, rather than work in vain to try and change others around me

• I learned we need to slow down to appreciate the beauty around us.

A friend once told me "you are doing a lot but somehow you make it sound so easy." I know it was not easy but I feel it comes naturally now. I do not feel the burden of doing things any longer. I feel I am just going with the flow and not fighting to find my way anymore. I feel happy, relaxed and content and deep down, I know better things are yet to come. I still have lots of dreams and plans that I want to achieve, but I will accomplish them one step at a time. I am no longer in a race. I am lucky to have examples in my life that enforce the positive mental attitude that I work to always maintain. I am not suggesting that it was always smooth sailing. I had to go through some difficulties and losses but I am not here to focus on what went wrong, or what I did not have. On the contrary, I choose to focus on what went right and how I grew from there.

You can be the change you want to see in your life. Do not wait for others to change or to make you happy. If you are not satisfied with your current situation you have the power to change that.

I hope my story inspires you to implement some of these steps. You can always contact me if you need more insight or support in your journey at Bareah.shankiti@gmail.com

BIO

Bareah Al Shanqiti is a happy spirited woman born in 1971 in Jordan to a loving family, amazing siblings and supportive group of friends. She studied in Jordan and England completing a master's degree in information systems from the London School of Economics. In 2000 Bareah got married to a very ambitious man from Pakistan and was blessed with two wonderful girls aged 9 & 13.

She lived in Jordan, Dubai, Kuwait and Canada and has always worked in the telecommunication sector. She took some teaching jobs while living in Dubai and is currently working towards having a coaching practice to spread the Napoleon Hill principles of success.

Bareah is certified from the University of Toronto in Solution Focused Brief Coaching and NLP. She is currently working to complete The Napoleon Hill Foundation leader certification course.

Bareah believes in people's ability to create the changes they want when they want to. She loves focusing on bringing the best in other people.

Her best times are when she makes someone feel good about themselves.

WHICH FUEL ARE YOU USING FOR YOUR LIFE?

By: Diana Ascente

"Great minds have purposes; others have wishes. "
-Washington Irving

Since both ways are used to propel your life, my question to you is, which one do you habitually use?

I believe that we are all created equally in the image of God, each of us unique, and yet we choose to operate at different speeds and strive for different things. We each have a story we are wrapped up in while we are continuously seeking our purpose in life. We all have received the same instruments and gifts at our birth, but we employ them to be the reflection of those around us, rather than to be ourselves. We are given the opportunity to interact with the beautiful waves of life's problems, which starts helping us discover who we are. I watch my toddler interacting with problems. He has a lot of wisdom because he knows not to go headfirst when he wants to get out of bed. Something in his mind tells him to turn around and safely land on his feet by sliding on his stomach. He also manages to climb stairs, eat, walk and run. I do not have to teach him these things because it is all instinct and self-taught. All I have to do is create a safe environment in which he can explore his capabilities and learn from testing his surroundings. Problems are great opportunities because they help us develop the thoughts that take us from curiosity, to wishing, to desire and finally to purpose.

I am a problem solver as much as a problem creator, and if I had not had the blessings of the problems in my life, I would not have been ready to discover the benefit of operating using the fuel of purpose in my life at a very young age. The thought we are having at any given point is the key that turns on the engine, and the manual of operation is very clearly stated by Napoleon Hill's words. "Keep your mind on the things you want and off the things you don't want." Below I will introduce you to one of my first problems that helped me learn the difference between riding life with purpose versus wishing.

Forming a strong desire and living for that desire only.

It was a strange morning for me when I woke up to an unusual noise and found out that an ambulance had shown up at our home. It was the winter of 1984, and I was 12 years old. Mom did not respond to us and yet she had breath that smelled like acetone, a diabetes symptom, a problem we never know she had and also signs of a heart attack, with a large bruise over her heart. Everyone from my family thought that we had lost her and they started to express their thoughts on how life would be without her. However, what happened in my mind was very different. I somehow pushed this reality away. I made my decision that this was not true. I was too young to be taken in the ambulance with her and be close to see what happened next. Instead, my brother went with her, and I stayed at home with my father who was paralyzed on the right side and moved heavily around the house showing his nervousness. I cannot remember what I told my dad, but somehow I managed to leave home and go to the nearby church. The same church in which I was baptized I found out later. I was baptized as an Orthodox Christian when I was 18 months old. I found two priests available to talk to me, and I urged them to let me know what to do because I did not want her to die. I was crying and had a desperate feeling in my body but at the same time, I know I had made up my mind to refuse what happened. They told me to pray; I asked how? And they said from my heart. They asked me what prayers I knew, and I told them two, one being The Lord's Prayer. They told me to whisper in my mind from my heart. They told me that everything would be okay, and I believed them. I left the church with a different emotion in my body. That was the first time I felt charged inside with a burning desire to make this nightmare disappear, a confidence that this was what was going to happen. I knew she would be just fine. I returned home with a different demeanor and spoke to my father to give him faith that everything would be ok and that she would come back home.

Mom was in the hospital for more than three months, including six weeks in a coma. My family and I visited her daily and, each time we went we heard from the doctors that she did not have much time to live. It was the best hospital in town, with the best doctors. The same doctors that a few weeks later said that they could not explain how she recovered as all her vitals returned to normal. The doctors and their science were challenged by the power of GOD and this miracle. I remember going to see her at the hospital with my sisters and brother, all of who were much older than I was, who were getting ready for her imminent death. They even brought candles with them and they were getting ready for their last moments with her. My family was intrigued by my quiet spirit and the fact that I was not crying at all. They explained my behavior as being too young to understand. My thoughts were just a continuous prayer with a simple request to God for her to be healed and restored to her previous condition. I felt I had conversations with God, which made me stronger in my beliefs that she would be okay. Saying those prayers many times a day, I was patiently expecting the miracle to happen. After three months she returned home, and I was as happy and pleased as I could be, feeling better than a winner, feeling like a miracle maker. I registered in my mind at that time that this was not a wish but something deeper. At that point I could only name it a burning desire, something which I chose to believe during those three months.

Understanding what makes us live or die.

When my mom came back from the hospital, I had a conversation with her and she told me that she had a dream while in the coma that she saw her family while she was deceased, and that she saw a little angel asking her to come back to life. She said she knew that it was me that did not let her go, but somehow I realized that she was not happy about this, and I was right. She told me that she did not want to live anymore, that she was out of desires. Somehow at that age, I understood her. She felt that she had nothing to fight for, and unfortunately many people experience the thoughts and emotions. I could have said more than I said at the time. My answer was just a quiet understanding of her need, and a realization that she gave up. She died exactly one year after her recovery. As hard as it is to lose someone so close, I had total peace in my heart. I understood and respected what she wanted. I moved on with my life and kept conversing in my mind when I needed her. I never thought I was alone. Even when I was physically alone, I felt that she was next to me. I asked questions and received answers. I guided my life and managed not to do crazy things other teenagers would do because she was closer to me than I thought possible. I grow up guided by a voice that was in my head helping me to make the right choices, the same voice that made me go to church that morning. Teaching me that life is about the choices I make. I learned to take responsibility for my actions and go with my instinct and when I messed up, having a learning experience, was when I doubted myself, or I did what others around me were doing. Interestingly enough, given what I know now about how our brain works, I realize that all this experience was nothing else but my thoughts and the choice made to keep my mom close for as long as I needed.

Examples learning by contrast

I owe a great deal of who am I to my grandfather who I refer to as my father because he was the one who picked me up from an orphanage when I was 15 months old. He brought me home, and my grandmother became my mom, my natural father my brother and my aunts my sisters. I was fortunate that he gave me the example of how to fight in life. He worked long hours every day after his stroke and recuperated a great deal of his independence despite the fact that all the odds were that he would be in bed or a wheelchair most of the time. He proved the doctors wrong by being able to take care of himself for 20 years after my mom passed away. He continued to enjoy and love life thinking it was a gift that he could not give away so quickly. His example was in contrast with what my mom's desires were. However, both of them contributed to shaping me as they provided me with the environment in which I spent my first years of life.

Outputs

Today, I have my family, and three kids, I love to serve others, and I know what a miracle is, and most importantly, how to create one. I am getting charged with the burning desire that may start with a strong wish but ends up propelling my future actions to achieve the reality I design.

I see a definite purpose as a state of mind in which miracles are cultivated and occur. It is that state of mind that brings you compliments about being hardheaded, never wanting to give up and always finding a way, simply because you know anything is possible. Mark 10:27 from the Bible reads "for all things are possible with God." I remember telling friends about looking inside to see what they wanted, but also why they wanted what they wanted. If the reason for why is not strong enough and does not feel like the right choice and does not serve anyone else but yourself, then the fuel is not truly purpose; therefore, the results are not miracles. A wish is serving your ego while a real purpose is serving your soul.

I learned to listen to my intuition and develop my actions around this magnificent voice that helps guide my life. When I became a mom, I tapped into it a lot, as well as in all unknown situations, realizing once again that listening to that is what proved to me what I could call the truth. It becomes clearer to me that we are born with wisdom available to be accessed when needed and, we should learn how to preserve that connection for the rest of our lives.

Like the stories we make in our life are an output of who we decide to become, so are thoughts the agents of change in our life. The path from being curious, to developing a wish, and then a strong desire, is to me a redefining moment of our purpose, and it has been used many times and will continue to happen as long as we enjoy life and the journey through fantastic opportunities called problems.

A great mind is cultivated and carefully crafted for the beautiful possibility of exploring the great potential of human nature. The creation of opportunities occurs inside first and then manifests in the exterior world via the story we choose to make up. Therefore, we need to be careful what we allow in by keeping our mind on the things we want and off the things we don't want.

BIO:

Diana S Acsente is a transformational life coach, working with individuals who love tapping into their entrepreneurial spirit to design and create miracles in their lives.

Her expertise includes problem solving and creating opportunities for growth and innovation. She worked in various small to Fortune 500 corporate and government consulting environments as a dynamic Knowledge Management and Information Technology professional who blended strong technical expertise and a high degree of business acumen to optimize organizational performance. Today, she is taking all she learned in the past 15 years to a more personal level, working one on one with clients creating extraordinary futures together for their lives and businesses. She has enjoyed this new journey, discovering the highest potential of the human nature, since 2012 when she attended The Napoleon Hill Foundation Certified Instructor program. She holds Doctoral degrees in Engineering Management from George Washington University and an MS in Computer Science from American University.

She can be contacted by Skype email: dacsente@gmail.com. Website: www.disand.com

TRANSFORM YOUR CHALLENGES INTO OPPORTUNITIES

By: Codruta Bala

Life started...

My grandfather from my mother's side was born in the Autumn of 1929. He was born in a small village in Romania, very close to the Hungarian border. Nobody could have predicted what his life would look like. He was one of 3 boys. Another two boys, twins, had died at a very young age.

Life in Romania at the time was very difficult. There were many basic things that people had to live without a no way to know what was happening in the country or the world. My grandfather was very smart ever since he was a child and always got good grades. He loved math and his teacher thought he would lead a successful life.

In today's world, getting support from social programs, scholarships, Non-Governmental-Organizations (NGO's) with the advantage of today's technology a bright future would be expected from a child like that. Opportunities are 'easier' to be found in today's developed countries than they were in the 1930's in Romania.

This situation still persists in many parts of the world in the twenty-first century, and that encourages me to look for opportunities to help those brilliant kids develop a better future.

The entire family, mother and father plus the 3 boys, lived in a one-room house but nothing stopped my grandfather from continuing to study while still working in the fields. Everything was happening in the usual way for a family living in a village in Romania until the year 1945. It was a fatidic year, where the Second World War had reached the heart of Europe and was making things more difficult for those already suffering. Things started getting worst and worst for poor families and day to day life became a real challenge.

Life gave him a huge challenge…

1945 was also the year when both my grandfather's parents died. He was only 16 years old and his brothers were 8 and 3. That was the reality, which he had to face as a young teenager. He became the parent of the house. His brothers started to look to him as a father so his responsibilities grew practically overnight.

They continued to live in his parents' house and he started to work hard in order to earn money to support the family. Unfortunately, he was not able to continue school but his definite purpose in life became the survival of the family and education of his brothers. He had to support them going to school while he was taking care of them and ensuring they had everything they needed. Nobody ever heard him complain about anything, which was admirable since he was doing things which other kids his age, and even some adults, were not doing.

"Any idea, plan, or purpose may be placed in the mind through repetition of thought".
-Napoleon Hill

Responsibilities increased...definite purpose became clearer...

He started to work in construction and was paid daily. He did not have a stable income but this did not stop him from working. He was just a young man who became mature overnight. He woke up early every morning to feed the animals, which remained after his parents died, 2 goats, 1 cow and 20 chickens. These animals had to provide the food for them to survive.

After his morning routine, he walked few kilometers to the place where his work in construction was. He did it every single day. It did not matter if it was -20 or +40 degrees Celsius. His thoughts were occupied with his brothers who were waiting for him at home and the promise he made at his parents' cemetery every time he visited them; "Mom, Dad, I promise I'll take care of them and you'll be proud of all of us, don't worry".

On one hand they were lucky that authorities did not take them to an orphanage and split them up. They had an aunt who visited them once a week to bring them some food and see if they were alright, but most of the time they had to take care of each other. If they were sick, nobody was there to take care of them. They only had each other and they realized this more and more every day. They learned that they had to count on themselves because nobody else was there for them. They had to learn from their mistakes because nobody was there to give them advice.

He wanted to give a purpose and a life to his younger brothers and to give them the wings for a better life. Keeping his promise to his parents became his burning desire. It did not matter that he was just a kid. He wanted his brothers to have a better life. He started to live for their success.

First love and the fight to make it happen or how to transform your dream into reality?

At the age of 19 he fell in love with my grandmother. She was even younger than he was, around16 years old. At that time life was very difficult. My grandmother's parents wanted her to marry a boy from a rich family and did everything possible to make it happen. They made an agreement with the boy's family and they sent her to his house.

My grandfather was very sad and, while splitting his time between work and being a parent for his brothers, he was also looking for a solution to his "problems of the heart". He never accepted defeat and was looking for solutions to fix this challenge. He was visiting her by stealth to steal a kiss with her. This gave him all the power he needed to survive all day. My grandmother was also in love with him so things looked easier and they put together a plan on how to be together. One day, when it was dusk in the village, my grandfather went to kidnap my grandmother from her future husband's house. They succeeded in leaving but my grandmother's parents were really upset and did not want to speak to her any longer. They could not accept my grandfather because he was from a poor family and had his two brothers to care for.

"Man, alone, has the power to transform his thoughts into physical reality; man, alone, can dream and make his dreams come true".

A new beginning as a family...

My grandparents did not care about what others were saying and started their life in my grandfather's house. My grandmother started to be a mom for my grandfather's brothers and took care of them like they were her own kids. The family started to live a better more complete life. My grandfather supported one of his brothers, (the other did not want to continue his studies) by providing his university costs and he eventually graduated.

That brother came home from boarding school every weekend and the rest of the week he was away. My grandfather instilled in him the desire to learn, develop and grow continuously. Although he himself was not able to get a university degree, he was living life more practically, learning from day to day activities, successes and failures. He was so happy that he told everyone he met about his brother's success. He was celebrating the victory and achievement of his younger brother who became a chemistry engineer, which was not common in this small village.

Bigger family…more responsibilities…

Meanwhile my mom and her sister became a part of the family. My grandfather spent a lot of time with his daughters and he loved them with all his heart. He worked hard to provide them the proper conditions in which to develop and grow. His initial definite purpose extended to his daughters and he wanted to see them become successful and happy in their lives. He wanted them to enjoy a better life than he had. He fought all his life to give his family a better life than he had himself.

But even with all the previous challenges in my grandfather's life, there were more challenges ahead.

Collectivization period…

In Romania from 1949-1962, during communism, was the period of collectivization, which was the confiscation of almost all private agricultural properties in the country and their conversion to state-run

239

farms. This included my grandparents farm around in 1960 or 1961. The idea was for the government to own everything and bring benefit to the state more than to the people whose fields they confiscated.

My grandfather remained with only the house and the land behind the house. It was another period of constant fighting to survive in a world where everybody was for themselves. He got a job as brigadier in the state run farms. He was responsible for the stables for the animals. The majority of the people were working for this "company", were working their own fields, which were not theirs any longer and now belonged to the government.

"Opportunity often comes disguised in the form of misfortune, or temporary defeat".

The hidden talent came back to the world...

The fact that the communists took his land did not get my grandfather down. Instead he started to look for alternative and this revealed to him a hidden talent from his childhood, which was working with his hands. My grandfather seemed to be very talented with his hands ever since he was a kid. He worked building houses and his imagination was really good. More and more people started to ask him to help them build their homes. He could also make brandy and wine barrels...or you might find him doing joinery work using all kind of different tools including axes and chisels.

"When your desires are strong enough you will appear to possess superhuman powers to achieve".

240

My grandparents never gave up. They continued working in the fields and raising the girls.

New beginning...

They bought land close to his parents' house, which he sold and then split the money between them and his brothers. He started building his own house when his daughters were approximately 6 to 9 years old. Finally, his dream of having his own home became true. At that time, it was common to invite people for a dance in your new home before finishing it in order to pave the ground. This helped in finalizing it before it was completed. At that time there was not any specialized equipment to do this and people were creative about finding different solutions while socializing and enjoying.

He also built a house for one of his brothers who had started his own life by getting married and having kids.

During communism there were things, which now cannot be imagined. For example, there was only one shop in the village where people could "buy" things they needed but this was mainly done as barter without using money. My grandfather tried to motivate my mom to get good grades at school. If this happened, she was allowed to collect the chickens' eggs and go to the village shop where, based on the weight of the eggs, using a specific tool, she could take money but instead exchanged them for wafers, which she loved. People did not have many material things but they were able to survive that period of time.

"Desire is the starting point of all achievement, not a hope, not a wish, but a keen pulsating desire which transcends everything".

His influence on me…

"Until you have formed the habit of looking for the good instead of the bad there is in others, you will be neither successful nor happy".

I remember my grandfather like it was yesterday. I was young and restless while spending time in their house. My parents could not take care of me due to their challenging jobs so I spent my first years in my grandparents' house as well as all the summers. I remember his soft touches, his stories about war, his words about how important it is to study and develop. He motivated me to learn a lot and rewarded me with small gifts or money when I finished school with very good grades. He remained for me an example of how you can succeed in life even when you are facing many challenges. If you have a definite purpose and you keep your positive attitude you can move mountains. He inspired me with the idea of being on my own feet and not depending on others but at the same time helping others with everything I could which would help make this world a better one in which to live.

When you have a Definite Purpose and start where you are, life will help in unseen ways along the way. Despite his very poor beginnings, all my grandfather's actions were aligned with his definite purpose of raising a healthy and happy family in the midst of poverty and misery. He did not only achieve his purpose but overachieved it by helping his brother get a University degree when nobody in his village knew what that even was. He was also able to influence his second generation, planting in my mind the seed of honesty, independence and personal initiative, which, in retrospect, I realize has shaped my actions in life.

"Victory is always possible for the person who refuses to stop fighting".

With love,
Codruta Bala

BIO

Codruta has 15+ years experience in human resources area that was accumulated by having different roles during her career in big multinational companies from IT, FMCG, EMS or automotive industries. She is passionate about personal development since she was a kid and the proof is all the training or seminars she attended during all these years and continues attending.

She is motivated by transforming the others in a better version of themselves which she continues doing it in her professional and also personal life. Her definite purpose in life is to change the world in a better one where people will be living their lives with Positive Mental Attitude and Going the Extra Mile without expecting anything in exchange. She is involved in many social responsibility projects and was recognized as a pioneer in this area at regional and national level, being an example for the others around.

Her involving with the Napoleon Hill philosophy and coaching has given Codruta's work a different dimension to create an inspiring environment that can impact other people in their professional and personal lives.

You can contact Codruta at:

Email: codruta.bala@gmail.com

Linked-in: https://ro.linkedin.com/in/codrutabala

Human For Human Consulting: http://www.h4human.com/

SEEING BEYOND THAT...

By: Hillary Vargas

"I am the master of my fate, I am the captain of my soul"
– William Ernest Henley

"Your brother will not survive".

These were the words told to my mother and I as we were sitting in the doctor's office.

I will never forget how I felt. It was a mix of emotions including anger, betrayal, sadness and hopelessness. You see what the doctor did not realize is that this was my little brother and, even through his depression, attempted suicide, and self-mutilation, I still saw beyond what the doctor and society saw in him. What did I see, you may ask? I saw an extraordinary young individual who would impact and leave a huge legacy on this earth.

I knew at that point my brother did not see that and I believe a part of him believed all the negative words everyone was telling him, but I knew that it did not matter what other people said. I had to fight for what I saw in him and his potential, when everyone else wanted to give up on him. I would never have known that the next 10 years of my life would be the most challenging I would ever have to face and, at the same time, it would be the foundation of me discovering my definite purpose and lead to me to becoming Ms. Hillary.

I always thought I knew what my purpose was but God had a much more important purpose for me on this earth. I always had a knack for business and had a great deal of interest in it and so when I went off to college that was what I focused on. I worked really hard to build a name and gain respect in an industry where women are not always looked on equally.

I had many great opportunities and worked for many amazing people. I always thought that I wanted to get a good job with good benefits, and work 9-5. Truth be told, that was nowhere near what my true purpose was. After graduating from college I had job opportunities with 6-figure salaries and the whole 9-yards. It was everything I had strived and worked so hard for, or at least I thought. And yet I was not content. There was something missing and I knew if I had followed that path, although on paper it would have sounded great, I knew I would have been unhappy.

While I was in college in Rhode Island, I started volunteering at local schools and organizations that were located in very underprivileged neighborhoods. I started seeing kids who came from families with major struggles and I started seeing the patterns of teachers, and family members saying that these kids were simply not going to make it. I found myself again in the doctor's office when they told me my brother would not survive. I realized that people were lacking vision and faith, and so they were projecting onto their youth that there was nothing beyond their circumstance or what they were told. I started showing them how to have a positive mindset and, as Napoleon Hill once said, "Whatever the mind can conceive and believe, it can achieve".

I decided to turn down a lucrative job offer and sign up with AmeriCorps for an urban charter school in Providence, RI. I continued to work at different schools, year after year and the same pattern repeated itself over and over again. People only saw the exteriors and the mistakes made by these youth instead of seeing beyond that and asking themselves if this kid could be the future President of the United States. In that journey of working in those schools, "Ms. Hillary" was born and I discovered that the true definite purpose that God had for me was more extraordinary than I could have ever imagined. Ultimately, that was to become an advocate, educator, mentor and a voice for these youth.

I would go on to mentor hundreds of kids who were seen as lost and helped them to break barriers, becoming top of their class, graduate and be accepted to top universities. As I continued to work, I began to see the unfairness in the educational system. I wanted to do more and I knew that my purpose was bigger.

I came up with the idea of a mentorship program for life that would instill a sense of family, which was lacking in many of my mentees' lives. The idea was so big that it frightened me but I knew in my heart it was my calling. Many people said I was crazy to try and pursue such a dream. Why should I place so much effort in helping "urban, underprivileged kids"? "They are a lost cause, why even bother?" I had already seen and proven that with the right mentorship and mindset, their lives could turn around. My health was a concern since I had battled rheumatoid arthritis since I was a toddler and my symptoms had intensified during this time. Many cited this as a reason it might be too difficult and thus unattainable, although I knew in my heart that to pursue this, I initially had no idea how to begin.

It was during this period that I became fully versed in the principles of success taught by Napoleon Hill. I developed the right mindset and knew I would accomplish my dream of founding a nonprofit that would serve and believe in our youth. I had no experience or knowledge about how to establish a nonprofit organization and this was another reason many people emphatically told me that I could not do what I was planning. All those people saying it was impossible just emboldened my resolve.

Mahatma Gandhi once eloquently said,
"Be the change you wish to see in the world".

I was determined to be that change and plunged right into following my definite purpose.

Despite the naysayers, I would go on to create my own nonprofit organization called "Ms. Hillary's Kids". The organization's mentoring program is designed to help youth establish social, emotional, academic and spiritual balance in their lives. Mentees get to network with some of the most successful individuals in their respective fields and obtain opportunities that will enable them to move forward toward their dreams. I believe in empowering each of my "Kids" to reach for the highest star and in teaching them that they, not their circumstances, determine their future, and the effect they will have on the world. By joining the organization, students are committing not only to themselves, but to their future selves. They are committing to their peers, their families and to me. They commit to dream big, show up, do the work, and make it happen. Our youth are our future. They are our future leaders, doctors, politicians, engineers, musicians, entrepreneurs and artists. To help them accomplish their dreams, I teach my students the success principles of Napoleon Hill. The principles taught in Napoleon Hill's book Think and Grow Rich are an enlightening lightening rod of empowerment. Adhering to the principles has helped mentees break free from the challenges and mediocrity of their lives and follow their purpose and they are well on their way to accomplishing great things. Mindsets of "that is impossible" are gradually evolving to "What if?" What if I believe in my purpose and myself? What if I pursue my dreams? What if I can change my circumstances? What if I am successful?

Dreams and goals that seemed impossible are now possible. It all begins by simply educating our youth on the power of their mind and the success principles from Think and Grow Rich as the tools to pursuing their purpose. Applied properly, anything is possible. Their only limitation is whatever is placed in their minds. One such Mentee's story of changing his mindset began by asking "What if?" and then slowly achieving when others said it was impossible. His name is Miguel Patxot and I would like to share his story.

What If I Conquer...

Conquer your limits! This is my motto and it has been developed through failures and hard work. It came from the moments where I had fallen and needed to fight to get back up. The origin of this motto came from a life-changing quote by the great Bruce Lee,

"If you always put limits on everything you do, physical or anything else, it will spread into your work and into your life. There are no limits. There are only plateaus and you must not stay there, you must go over them."

Limits are meant to be challenged, they are meant to be broken and worked out how you want it worked out. Doubt spreads into your life like a fog that never goes away, but it is important to remember that every step you take through the fog is another step closer to getting out of it.

Growing up I had no self-confidence. I was always quiet and kept to myself. I let very few people into my life and even fewer into the life where I was suffering deep down. I was overweight and constantly getting picked on by people at school and even my own family. I kept to myself knowing it was safer to bottle up those feelings because other people would not understand the battle I was fighting with myself every time I looked in the mirror. Those scars were carried into my college years. It was baggage that I did not want to start a new chapter in my life with but, like the fog that never goes away, I kept it there because it was all that I knew. I was living my life day by day with no purpose or drive. I was trying to accomplish what others wanted from me but I could not figure out what I wanted for myself.

Change came in big ways during this chapter in my life. I was introduced to the gym and weight lifting for the first time. From that moment on, I fell in love with fitness instantly. I became obsessed with changing my body to the way I wanted it. I felt deep down that the more I was working on my body, the better I felt physically and mentally. My confidence was boosted tenfold. I was getting involved with the community and allowing myself to let others in because I was beginning to accept the man in the mirror. I began to see the light beyond the fog. Compliments began to flood into my life and I wondered if my true purpose was to help others become someone better, to become someone who they could look at and be proud of.

Life has a way of challenging you, and that curve ball came my way like a meteor. I was stricken with an infection called Methicillin-Resistant Staphylococcus Aureus (MRSA) and, at the same time, I was facing a financial situation that kept me from finishing my education. Since I was at the top of my game, this was the last thing I needed because, in a heartbeat, my light was swallowed up by the fog once again. This time the fog was thicker because I was raised with the knowledge that college is the only way to make it in life. I fell down hard, and with every fall came the judgment from others. I was immediately rejected by my parents and family because, in their eyes, I became a disappointment. At my lowest point I gave up entirely. I gave up on everything that I thought I had control of including my education, my social life, and fitness. I did not know what else to do with myself. I was staring more and more at the mirror wondering what went wrong.

A year and a half later I had the chance to reconnect with a friend of mine who was creating a name for himself as an entrepreneur and who was also beginning a startup fitness company. He wanted me to join him on this journey in the fitness entrepreneur world, and I accepted. The life he is living and pursuing is the life that I am yearning for. His lifestyle and growth cemented in my mind how I wanted to become an entrepreneur myself, not for the money and luxury, but because of the legacy that I can create for myself.

Running in the fitness entrepreneur world also brought up old weaknesses that needed to be tuned. The biggest one was leadership. The snowball effect continued and brought into my life a mentor who has guided me in finding my purpose and discovering who I truly am. She showed me that my passion and purpose have been in front of me the whole time, but the excuses I created for myself blinded me. I realized that I was meant for fitness and for uplifting others because I was great at it. I learned that no matter what curveball or roadblock that presents itself in life, it will not be enough to keep me down. I must conquer my limits because there is more to life that I yearn, and that alone is enough for me to keep fighting through adversities.

So what is my purpose in life? I am a firm believer in balancing my physical and mental strength. These two components are my yin and yang, and it is what has been keeping me hungry for more in life. I believe that these two components are my keys to changing the world. Life is about being consistent, being able to push yourself harder than the day before. Through wear and tear there is growth. Through consistency there is desire, and through knowledge there are questions, visions, roots, dimensions and values. As an individual who has spent their life fighting the man in the mirror, fighting to conquer adversities and limits, fighting for my purpose, fighting to grow, I desire to use everything I have learned throughout my life and use it to live. Use it to conquer my limits and rise above them. Use what I learn to be happy, healthy, and to live a prosperous life, to embrace my adversities and use them as weapons to overcome life's challenges. My purpose is to spread my knowledge and help uplift those who surround me because I do believe that I will change the world.

Every day I wake up with a purpose and every step I take have a driving force of passion and motive behind it. I think about my past and I embrace it because of the lessons I learned that brought me to where I am now. "Troubles never really end for any of us—they are woven into the human experience...as long as you have hard work and a positive attitude to fall back on, it doesn't matter how many times you get knocked down. You'll always know how to get back up," said actor Dwayne Johnson. Never give up, but always fight to get back up.

As I continue to progress with Ms. Hillary and Ms. Hillary's Kids, I see that I am evolving into something better. My mindset, personality, and ethics, have all changed. I am taking every step now with purpose and motive. I am methodically becoming who I really want to be in this world. Through every step with Ms. Hillary, I am expanding my network, breathing in inspiration through others, expanding my knowledge through the teachings of Napoleon Hill, and breaking my shell to share my story in order to inspire other people. As I continue my mentoring with Ms. Hillary, I am methodically taking my throne into the entrepreneurship world.

Legacy

Each one of us has a purpose that has been assigned to us. It is sometimes not what we expect, what we might have wanted or what we might have planned. It is, nonetheless, important to know that our purpose is extraordinary and we have a responsibility to fulfill it. If you have a dream, never lose faith and know that, no matter what, no one can ever take away from you the gifts you were born to give this world. You ultimately have control of your mindset. Your mindset holds the key to establishing a path forward toward your goals. Naysayers and negative mindsets are irrelevant. In the spirited words of William Ernest Henley, no matter the obstacles or challenges, you are the master of your fate; you are the captain of your soul. Dare yourself to follow your own path towards your dreams and leave a legacy.

BIO

Ms. Hillary Vargas is a life coach, motivational speaker, entrepreneur, youth mentor and educator. She is the founder of Ms. Hillary's Kids, a non-profit organization designed to support and empower young adults with learning disabilities, behavior challenges or who come from rough or underprivileged backgrounds, as they reach their full and highest potential. She aids them in seeking out the richest soil they can find and planting the seed of their dreams. As they care for the seed, with Ms. Hillary's guidance, they slowly see it begin to grow. They care for it, and nurture it, until one day it blooms like a rose from a crack in the concrete.

Ms. Hillary has also served as an educator in several urban schools in Rhode Island and New Jersey, teaching and engaging teenage students in a myriad of topics. Her true passions are teaching and mentoring, and investing in our youth, as they are the seeds of our future. She has a BA in Marketing and a minor in Psychology from Johnson & Wales University. As Mahatma Gandhi once eloquently said, "Be the change you wish to see in the world", and Hillary Vargas endeavors to change the world through her students and each person she encounters, one at a time.

If you would like to get more information please visit www.mshillaryskids.org or email mshillaryskids@gmail.com

FROM DARKNESS TO LIGHT/LITE

By MageshKumar Venkatesan

The moment I saw the title "Think and Grow Rich" the first thought that came to my mind is "Ha..!!! I am going to become rich, meaning becoming a multi-millionaire. Now be honest, how many of you thought the same way I did? Well, there's nothing wrong with that, but there are many other riches that you will come to know just by reading the book and applying it every day. I am going to provide you with a few simple lessons that I have learned through my journey so far, and I am hopeful that there are one or two resonate with you so that you can use them to create a better life for yourself. I am still a student learning during every moment of life.

PEOPLE ARE YOUR GREATEST ASSET

As it may have happened with many of you, I received the audio CD of Think and Grow Rich through one of my friends when I was searching for a purpose and in a very down and depressed time of my life. At that time, I had to commute 3 hours a day. So, I listened to whatever I could get a hold of to keep me motivated and to learn new skills in life. The moment I popped in this CD and listened to the first 30 minutes, I could not stop listening. I have lost count of how many times that I listened to that CD now. After listening many times, I called The Napoleon Hill World Learning Center to enroll myself in the Leader Certification course they offered. I met some incredible people including; Judy Williamson, Uriel "Chino" Martinez and Alan Chen and of course our own Tom too tall Cunningham, who I refer to as Mr. Awesome!

I also had the chance to meet Dr. Hill's family members, including Dr. J B Hill and his sister Terry Gocke, grandson and granddaughter of Napoleon Hill. They further strengthened and motivated me so I can keep moving forward. I am so thankful to them and will always remember them in every walk of my life, especially when I am in trouble and need to reach out for help. There are millions of people who are waiting to help. I am sure you all agree that it is getting harder to trust people and you might not be sure how to go about trusting them. Well, my little wisdom says that you trust people fully. There can be only 2 outcomes, one they become one of your life long friends to lean on, or two they provide you a life long lesson to learn from. Either way, you WIN!!

WHAT IS BEING COMPLACENT?

So I am very sincere, hard working, down to earth, very loyal and a person with high integrity. I was flying so high at my work managing a wonderful team of Engineers and projects that were very critical. I was convinced that I was invincible. The day you feel this way, rest assured that it is a warning sign! So the day came where I lost my entire team and didn't know where to turn. I wondered what had happened to me, and the question in my mind was 'How can this happen to me? Is being good not enough? Apparently "not" was the answer. Everything happened for no apparent reason. Can I say that? No, not any longer, because I am now wise enough to understand that whatever happens to us, we must take responsibility for our lives. We can control our destination if we choose to. All along my routine was go to work, come home, login to my computer and work again and sleep. This cycle repeated for a solid 20 years with no break. I experienced incredible growth until that day came along. This was the day where I was trashed from Hero to Zero. I was devastated and felt deflated like a balloon.

My take on being complacent is that when you do not learn any new things in life, then you are being complacent and for sure life will teach you one day not to be so. To me I did the best I could in every way at my work, but the world is in constant change and, if you do not align and grow with it, you will certainly become complacent. I strongly urge you to learn one new skill a year. It could be as simple as learning a new game that you could play with your kids, gardening, bee keeping, flying kites or taking a course at college. Everything counts. The bottom line is to be a life long learner.

I am glad in a way that the situation happened to me the way it did, because if it had not, I would have perished with boredom. That was the moment I decided I was going to take control of my life, but at the same time I did not know how to go about it. When we do not know where to go and where to start, my guru always said that the best thing is to completely get 100% involved in whatever you do and the 'how' will present itself. That's really how I became and remain that way today. I involve myself completely in whatever I do. I attended every free seminar that was available. I explored with an open mind opportunities involving network marketing, real estate, financial seminars, tax liens, land management and others. I ran pillar to post to acquire knowledge and figure out what was the best fit for me.

WHICH DIRECTION DID MY COMPASS TURN?

Finally, two things stood out, one was related to stock market options trading and the other was investing in real estate. The learning curve was so steep that I learned more than I had in all 16 years of schooling. I spent all my savings on getting educated and becoming a better person. It was intense and many compromises were made. I missed my son's birthdays, our anniversaries and many family events. Nevertheless, I was determined to find my footing. I soaked up as much as I could from these seminars. Thank God my wife, Rupali, was completely supporting me all through this time. It is not easy to deal with somebody who says one day that I want to become a real estate broker, another day a motivational speaker, and another day a stock trader. She had incredible patience dealing with all my crazy ideas and behavior. I can only speculate that she knew that I was desperate to figure things out for our family and myself.

When you learn something new, you need to apply it right? Sure, but it is not always the wisest thing to do, particularly trading in the stock market. After attending numerous seminars, I thought that I knew everything and started trading. With my primitive trading and investing experience I was getting hammered in the market. I lost my shirt but thank God, my pants were spared! I should write a separate book on the mistakes I made with that venture.

AN IDEA AND HOW INCREDIBLE SIGNALS WAS BORN

Then an idea came to me. Why not build a team and a system to trade? That is how my Mastermind team came together. I spoke to several friends who were all incredibly talented. We all worked together at some point in time. They knew nothing about the financial markets, but were great engineers and great computer programmers and architects. I started teaching them every week for nearly 2 years that I learned through various seminars and curriculum.

Then slowly they started to get a feel for what I was planning and my vision for us and the company "Incredible Signals Inc." was born. We developed an incredible stock trading system that focuses on Nasdaq, S&P 500 and Dow Jones stocks for both up and down market directions. We tested the system a great deal before we released it to the public. When we did, we had some amazing feedback from our users. We spent anywhere from 4 to 12 hours every day and all weekend for 5 years. Come rain or shine I made the weekly call with my team, most of them who were in India. I remember that one of the weekends we had to travel as a family and we got stuck in traffic. My son, Pranav, who was 3 years old at that time, and I had to pull into a parking lot to make the call. During the 2-hour call my family was patient with me and my son was so well behaved that he didn't even make a single noise. I was so thankful to be blessed with such a wonderful family. There were so many hardships that we had to face, not only myself, but also my team members. Our chief architect's father passed away, my father passed away, and a programmer's health was affected during those times. Nevertheless, the team stood together to march through the challenges. We tested millions and millions of combinations to achieve optimized and consistent results. We did not change a thing once we implemented the trading system.

Today, we have systems that we created that are the best on the market. That was the real taste of satisfaction. This is what I call richness and happiness in life. A sense of creating what did not exist before is very rewarding and satisfying. Whether we make millions or not is secondary. I believe it is just a question of time before everyone recognizes how cool our system is. Money does not make a person happy. Money only amplifies your state of mind. If you are happy, then it amplifies your happiness and if you are sad then it only amplifies that feeling. You can have all the money you want but if you cannot stand yourself as a person what purpose does it provide? Please spend a moment to think about this deeply.

The question is; Do you have to do something big to be happy and have a sense of accomplishment? Not really. There are many simple things and ways to enjoy life and achieve the same satisfaction.

Here are some of the techniques:

1. Play more often with kids 6 years old or younger. The more time you spend with them, the better your life will become. You can learn a lot from kids. They live in the moment. If you place an expensive

diamond and a $2 toy next to each other and have the kid pick, they will pick the $2 toy and completely ignore the diamond. 99% of grown ups will pick a diamond for a better tomorrow while missing the present. One may not even live to see another day but they will pick a diamond thinking that it is going to be used for retirement.

2. Be grateful for every day that you are alive. Ensure that your first thought is a positive one when you wake up. The important words are "first thought". Just a simple 10 seconds can make a big difference. It could be a statement such as " I am going to have a Wonderful day today" or "I am feeling Great". Try it for 60 days.

3. Spare 2 seconds to think about millions of people around the world who are not fortunate enough to eat a meal that is in front of you.

All these things may not take much effort, but they can be incredibly rewarding. Don't believe me? Try it for yourself to see the results.

Am I a Hero now? You bet. I am a Hero from my own perspective. All along I was a Hero who became a Zero from other people's perspective, and now I don't worry what others think about me. As long as I am centered and understand who I am and where am I traveling, that is all that matters to me. Nobody should tell you that you are good, bad, great, etc. That is not worth anything if you love yourself for who you are. When you do this, things will definitely turn around for you.

There were many incidents that I applied this philosophy to in order to achieve success in what I did and accomplished. While I would like to share many things with you, I will keep it short. You can however always reach out to me through the email address in my bio.

I also want to acknowledge my spiritual Guru, Sadhguru Jaggi Vasudev and of course "Dr. Napoleon Hill".

I want to thank my family who have always supported in whatever I did. I believe that we have met through this book and I am looking forward to meeting some of you in person or through social media.

BIO

Magesh hails from a very simple and humble family. Born and raised in India, he migrated to the United States in 1998. He feels lucky to have the best of both East and West. He lives with his wonderful wife and two adorable sons aged 9 and 1 at the time of this writing. He possesses credentials in Electronics Engineering and Business administration.

Magesh has always been associated with Quality in some way, which he says was inspired by his Dad. Three things that he believes in are; Integrity, Loyalty and Sincerity. He learned this wisdom from his father.

He has had many different roles as part of his career with Quality being the common theme. He is a Lead auditor for both Quality Management System ISO 9001 and Environmental Management System ISO 14001.

Magesh co-founded Incredible Signals Inc. along with his friends to create a system that can be easily used by everyone. He spent so much time and effort developing it to gain an edge that he is willing to share it with the world. He practices ISHA yoga, which provides him a perspective to see the world as is and approach it with gratefulness.

Magesh can be reached at magesh@incrediblesignals.com or at 707 775 0776.

Website : www.incrediblesignals.com
Gratitude to www.Ishafoundation.org and www.naphill.org

THE WIRE LOBSTER TRAP

By: Andrew Knott

Using Definiteness of Purpose to Start a Company and Change an Industry

This is a story about how a family started a business and changed an industry, which had been using the same technology for 100 years. In the story, I will describe how the family set a Definite Major Purpose to achieve a goal and how the family overcame, over a period of several years, numerous obstacles changing the minds of the target customers and developing the business. The story covers a period of twenty years, from 1976 – 1996, but parts of the story began to evolve a decade earlier. It is my hope that people reading this story will come to understand they can have anything they want from life by taking possession of their own mind, developing a Definite Major Purpose backed by Applied Faith, creating a Mastermind Alliance and using Self-Discipline to move forward, when faced with adversity.

The Market Opportunity

The Northern Lobster (Homarus americanus), inhabits the chilly waters of the Northwest Atlantic, from Newfoundland, Canada to New Jersey. Lobsters have been harvested by man for food since the early 1600's. In colonial times the Lobster population was so "Thick" that a person could wade into shallow water and literally pick up Lobsters off the ocean floor. In the early 1900's fisherman began building Lobster traps with locally harvested hardwood, mainly Oak. The traps, constructed by fisherman in many different sizes and shapes, were weighted down with heavy rocks, until the wood absorbed water and sunk on their own. The traps, baited with discarded fish, were attached to wood buoys with rope. The buoys were painted different colors and designs unique to each fisherman.

By the late 1930's coastal states and the Canadian government enacted laws to protect the Lobsters from overfishing. A minimum size was established and Lobsters caught under the minimum had to be thrown back. Female Lobsters bearing eggs were also protected. Fisherman caught breaking the law were subject to heavy fines and loss of their fishing license. By the mid 1960's, dozens of companies along the coast were selling traps to fishermen. It was estimated that there were about three million traps in use in the USA and a similar amount in Canada. The average trap lasted five years. This suggested there was an annual market of 1.2 million new traps per year.

In the early 1960's people began experimenting with new trap designs, made from different materials. One company, Marcraft, developed a trap made from steel, welded wire mesh, coated with Aluminum, to resist rust. Fisherman tried the traps and many fishermen had success with the design. Marcraft began to grow and, after about six years, were selling over fifty thousand traps per year. They were the largest producer of traps made from alternative materials in the world.

At the same time, my father, Jim Knott Sr. developed a method to apply a thick, tough plastic coating to galvanized steel wire mesh. He gave samples of the mesh to fisherman to wrap around the wood frame of a trap. This eliminated the need for heavy wood laths on the side of the trap, which made the trap lighter on the boat and easier to handle. Fisherman soon found other advantages: Water currents would flow through the steel mesh better because the surface area was much less than the all wood trap, which meant in times of storms the traps were more secure on the bottom. The steel mesh was tough and didn't break as easily as the wood. These advantages translated into better catch rates for the fisherman. However, the plastic coated wire on the frame of wood never really obtained much acceptance, because the "All wire" Aluminized traps were available and they worked pretty well.

Our family lived in Gloucester, Massachusetts. Gloucester, originally settled in 1623, is the oldest fishing seaport in the USA. Large wooden schooners (125 ft.), with huge sails powered by the wind, brought fisherman to the grand banks off the coast of New England. The fisherman would leave the schooner in small dories, set long lines in the water with hooks to catch Codfish. Much has been written over the years about Gloucester's storied history in the Fishing industry, including its role in the Lobster industry.

At age nine I obtained a license to fish for Lobster. With the help of my parents, I started a summer business to catch and sell lobsters to people in the neighborhood. By age thirteen I had forty traps. Part of the agreement I had with Jim Sr. was that in exchange for the help he gave me starting the business and using his boat, I kept meticulous records of how different trap designs performed. This included the type of bait used, where the trap was located and how many days it was set before each haul. That year, Jim gave me five large traps he designed, made and sold to try. The traps were very large, 48" Long x 28" Wide x 18" High and they weighed about 100 lbs. At that age I could barely pull the trap to the surface of the water. Once I got it there I had to stand on the side of the boat, bend my knees and fall back to pull the trap into the boat. One day, when I was hauling the last trap and after getting it into the boat, I couldn't believe my eyes. There were several large Lobsters in the back of the trap. Not wanting to touch the catch, I brought the boat onto the beach. Jim came down with his camera. There were eight large Lobsters, the biggest one being 15 lbs. (The average Legal Lobster at the time was about .9 lb.) The total catch was 42 lbs.! Jim took pictures of the trap and the catch and made it into an advertisement. He thought there could be a large, "Undiscovered" amount of big Lobsters close to the shore and a huge demand for the big traps. It turned out that I never had a big catch like that again, although those big traps did occasionally catch Jumbo Lobsters.

264

My Dad, Jim Knott Sr. was an inventor and innovator of in the field of plastics and applying plastic coating to metals. He started his first company, Coatings Engineering Corp. (CEC) in 1956. One of the inventions he made was a method of applying plastic coating to steel, welded wire mesh in rolls. The rolls, 48" wide by 500 long, were pulled through a large tank of liquid coating and then into a long oven to cure the coating. The coated wire was rolled up and cut into 50 or 100-foot sections. The wire was (and still is) sold for backyard fencing and gardening and for fencing around above ground swimming pools. Five years later, Jim sold his company to The Gilbert & Bennett Mfg. Co. (G&B) one of the country's largest manufacturers of Steel wire mesh. G&B had seven factories in seven different states and about 800 employees. G&B, one of the oldest ongoing corporations in the USA, dated it roots back to 1818. After the sale Jim was named President of the new subsidiary (CEC). He remained there until the fall of 1978.

The new owners of CEC didn't give Jim much encouragement and support to develop the market for the wire Lobster trap. They had several large customers doing millions of dollars of business, including Sears, Ace and the True Value Hardware chains. They looked at Jim's efforts to develop the trap as a hobby and a waste of time.

Now, fast forward to 1976. Early in the year, the company making the Aluminized mesh for Marcraft, Armco Steel in Kansas City, MO, decided to shut down their production line. Marcraft had to scramble because Armco was their sole supplier. A competitor of Armco's, Bethlehem Steel from Bethlehem, PA, was the only other company producing Aluminized wire. They agreed to supply Marcraft. It turns out that the production process used by Bethlehem was slightly different than Armco's. The Aluminum coating on the steel reacted with the salt water. The wire quickly developed a white film and the traps began to "Fall apart." Class action lawsuits were initiated against Armco, Bethlehem and Marcraft. Six months later, Marcraft filed for bankruptcy and a few years later some fisherman received a settlement from Armco. This created an opening for a new kind of wire trap.

In the fall of 1977 I started my junior year at Boston University (BU). I was on a Liberal Arts track, majoring in Economics. For a variety of reasons, I was not really happy in college. I spent four years in high school at a small boarding school in Northern NH, Kimball Union Academy (KUA). The boarding school environment was good for me. We had to participate on a team sport every season and wear jackets and ties to dinner. We had classes Monday – Friday and Saturday morning, until 11:30 am. I was an average student but could earn an "A" whenever I wanted, if I liked the subject. I learned the value of Self-Discipline at a young age.

Back to BU. It was big, unstructured and there were lots of distractions compared to KUA. In the first week of September in 1977, I exhibited the wire Lobster trap at the World Fishing Exhibition in Halifax, Nova Scotia, Canada with J. Pike Bartlett, the owner of Friendship Trap Company in Friendship, Maine. Over the course of five days, twenty-five Thousand people visited the show. Countless Lobstermen, some who had been Lobster fishing for fifty years, came by the booth and ridiculed me. I heard comments like: "That trap won't catch no damn lobsters, the wire will "Sing" in the water and scare the lobsters away; after the first storm the trap will be flattened like a pancake; they are too expensive compared with wood, no one can afford them; You are wasting your time; You are crazy." For every fifty people who had a negative comment there was one person willing to listen and show some interest. Of course, based on my personal experience I knew better! Unfortunately, that week in Canada set me behind at BU.

THE CHRONICLE-HERALD

THE MAIL-STAR

Tuesday, September 7, 1977

On August 1, 1978 I left BU, two courses shy of fulfilling the requirements for graduation, to take a full time job at CEC. My title was Marine Products Manager, reporting to the VP of Sales, who reported to Jim Sr. My territory was the East and West Coast of the USA and Atlantic Canada. My major goal was to sell Plastic Coated wire mesh for marine applications and to specifically target the Northwest Atlantic Lobster trap market. Sales in these markets were about $400,000. Two months later, in a major shakeup, Jim Sr. left CEC. He came into my office, shook my hand and said he had quit. When I asked him where that left me he said, "Hang around and find out." The President of G&B appointed the Plant Manager of CEC to the position of General Manager. Late in the day I met with the new GM and my boss. They told me the President of G&B said Jim told him he intended to start a new company to produce Plastic Coated wire for the marine industry. The President wanted the GM to fire me but he left the decision in the new GM's hands. He decided to keep me aboard until such time that he made a move to become a competitor. We agreed we would discuss my status at the CEC if Jim Sr. decided to get back in the business. Two years later, on August 1, 1980 I left CEC to join my Dad and younger brother, Jim Jr., to form a new company. When I left, CEC was on track to do $2.2 million in sales.

The Formation and early years at Riverdale Mills Corporation (RMC)

Jim Sr. used personal funds to purchase an abandoned and dilapidated mill building in the village of Riverdale, located in the town of Northbridge, Massachusetts. I remember the first time I visited the town to see the building. I thought my Father had lost his mind. The building was huge. Located directly on the Blackstone River and set on 71 Acres, it contained about 140,000 sq. ft. of space, about four times what we needed for the business. Almost all the windows were boarded up. The roof was sagging and in some areas had collapsed. The floors were wet from numerous leaks in the roof. One day, Jim and I visited the fire chief and informed him that we were starting a new business in the building. He put his hands on his head and said: "Oh my god, thanks for letting me know, I had an agreement with my men that if the building ever went up in flames I wouldn't make them go in and fight the fire."

We had to come up with a name for the business. Like many owners of family businesses, we thought about using the family name for the business. We decided against using our name because many people either misspelled or mispronounced the name Knott. We settled on Riverdale Mills Corporation (RMC) because the building was known locally as the Riverdale Mill, it was easy to pronounce and spell, and it was unique.

To get the business going, Jim Sr. got a loan for $250,000 from a local bank, to construct a new plastic coating line and for working capital. Jim Sr. had to personally guarantee the loan against all the assets he owned. Before Jim Sr. got the loan I loaned him $25,000. This was almost every dollar I had saved, from working for years in the Lobster business, in high school and college and at CEC. Jim Sr. paid me back with interest in six months, after he got the loan from the bank.

Most of the money was used to construct a new, state of the art Plastic Coating line. The main difference between this line and the system at CEC was the Plastic (PVC) was in powder form, as opposed to a liquid. The powder coating had several advantages over the liquid system for marine use. The main advantages were that the coating thickness was uniform on each side, the thickness could be controlled much easier and the coating was solid. The liquid system produced a thin and thick side and when the coating was "Cured" solvents were burned off, which created small air pockets in the coating and weakened its strength.

The line was 8' wide and 200' long. Nine major elements made up the line, including two large ovens to pre-heat the wire mesh and cure the plastic after coating. Every effort was made to save money building the line. For instance, steel plates needed to build wash tanks were pulled up from the 2nd floor of the building, where they were not needed. Some parts of the oven were purchased at a local junkyard for pennies on the dollar. The line was capable of coating a roll of mesh measuring 6" up to 90" wide by 500' long.

Starting a business is a leap of faith. You have to possess an unwavering belief in what you are doing. I took an 80% pay cut to join the business. RMC purchased my company car from CEC, because I needed it to commute to RMC and to visit customers. We talked about stock options and it was "Understood" that someday, if we were successful, Jim Jr. and I would be compensated for our effort's, by getting an ownership stake in the business. This was a family business and there was implied trust and loyalty that we were working together for a common objective. When you work at a startup, it's all about survival.

The Definite Major Purpose of the business was to produce and sell plastic coated wire mesh to construct Lobster and Crab traps used in Salt Water. We estimated that the combined products had an annual market potential of $15 million, in 1980 dollars. We registered the trade name AQUAMESH to differentiate our products from our competitors.

RMC from 1981 – 1989

By 1983 we had 20 full time employees and hired part time people when needed. That was the year I married Jayne Fifield. We bought a house in Northbridge, 7/10 of a mile from the Mill. I could walk or ride my bike to work, which was helpful, because I was working 12 – 14 hour days. Jayne worked in Boston. RMC purchased an IBM PC and software to run the business. It sat in the boxes unopened for six months. One day Jayne took the software manuals on the train with her and read them. Over the next few months, in her spare time, she set the system up in the basement of our home. By then we had hired a bookkeeper, Jan Carter. Jan worked at the house part time and our basement became the first official office at RMC. Thirty-two years later Jan still works at RMC. Jayne and I are happily married and are blessed to have three children, Jennie, Andrew and Nancy. Jayne is the #1 member of my Mastermind team.

The Lobstermen were slowing converting to wire traps and our sales were growing but we were barely profitable. Any money we made was plowed right back into the business. We were at a competitive disadvantage because we purchased the rolls of wire we coated from other manufacturers and our primary competitor, G&B made their own wire and mesh. In 1985 we took another leap of faith and raised $3 million dollars to fund the purchase of equipment to make our own wire. There was no turning back now. We would either make the business a success or go out of business.

Over the years I wore several hats at the business: office mgr., inside sales and customer service mgr., personnel (human resources), purchasing, logistics (shipping and receiving) credit, finance (with our bookkeeper and accountant) and outside sales. Jim Jr. had more of a technical background than me and he ran factory production and equipment maintenance. Jim Sr., still the sole owner of the company oversaw everything. He made the final decisions when there were disputes. Jim Sr. always enjoyed having several projects going on outside the business. This meant that Jim Jr. and I had lots of autonomy to make decisions, which was good for our learning.

There were several obstacles we had to overcome which would take an entire book to describe. Some highlights are:

• The technical challenges of making a consistent quality product for marine use were daunting. Running the coating line was part art and part science. In 1985 I toured the factory of a supplier in the UK. They had a coating line similar to ours and they let me look at it. I came back from the trip with two ideas for improvement and I described the ideas to Jim Sr. and Jr. and our people. We implemented the changes and over the next few months problems that plagued us for years were solved. Annual savings were huge and those savings went directly to the bottom line.

• In 1986, shortly after we installed an automatic mesh welding machine to make our own wire, Jayne and I noticed that the lights in our house were blinking at the same rate that the welder operated (about 70 welds per minute). On one hand, I could tell if the machine was running without leaving the house! On the other hand, the blinking lights were annoying. It turns out that the electrical line feeding the mill installed in the 1930's was small and couldn't handle the electrical requirements of the machine without causing the blinking. A few hundred people who lived on the line got the same blinking and they complained to the Dept. of Public Utilities. The Power Company wanted RMC to pay $500,000 to run a new line to service RMC. Of course we had no money for this kind of thing and a legal batted ensued. It turned out that the power company had other customers with similar machines in different parts of the state. We argued that as part of their grant to have a monopoly they had to serve the public. They threatened to disconnect us from the power grid and they made good on the threat a few weeks before Christmas in 1989. When they did, all forty employees on the 1st shift walked out of the Mill at once. The next day, the entire story with pictures was on the front page of the Worcester Telegram & Gazette. We went to court and got an injunction to force them to reconnect us to the grid. About six months later a new line was installed in the street without any cost to us, other than time, trouble and legal fees.

•While we had the expertise to make the best-coated wire for marine use, every manufacturer of wood traps wanted nothing to do with our wire mesh. They viewed us as competitors. It took the help of a few wire trap builders to convert the rolls of wire mesh into saleable products for Lobstermen. Bob Ketcham of Ketcham Trap & Supply in New Bedford, MA started in 1975 and was an early pioneer in building wire traps for Lobstermen. J. Pike Bartlett, the founder of Friendship Trap Co. in Friendship Trap Co. developed many innovations to enhance the efficiency of the wire trap. These people and countless others helped accelerate the industry.

By the end of 1989, RMC had sixty employees and was operating two or three shifts, depending on the needs of each department. Sales reached $6 million but profitability was still low. Jim Jr. and I had increases in salary but for the hours we were putting in the pay was well below market rates for similar jobs in other companies. Our younger brother Jeff joined the business upon graduation from BU in 1983. He was helpful in developing the Canadian Lobster trap market as well as other markets and products. He ended up pursuing other interests and, for a variety of reasons, did not stay with the company. I have one other sibling, my older sister, Janet. She had a successful career as a staff photographer at the Boston Globe. She never worked at RMC but always remained interested in how we were doing. In the very early days my mother Bette was the company bookkeeper. Whenever Jim Sr. traveled for business she usually accompanied him. She was always a source of inspiration and support for the entire family.

RMC from 1990 – 1996

Our major competitor, G&B, made the decision to exit certain markets, including the market for Marine wire. A 3rd competitor, Shepherd Wire Products of Houston, TX had entered the market but they had an inferior quality product. With G&B's leaving the market this left two suppliers. This had the immediate effect of bringing new customers to RMC and allowed us to slightly increase our prices. Fortunately, we had added production capacity with the addition of a new welding machine, so we had the capacity to handle the new business.

Late in October 1991, an epic and now famous storm hit the coast of New England. The events of the storm became a famous book and movie called The Perfect Storm. The storm hit at the height of the fall Lobstering season. Because the storm went largely unpredicted, Lobstermen were unprepared. Hundreds of Thousands of traps were either lost or destroyed. After the storm, the industry shut down and sales to the Lobster market dropped precipitously. However, in the spring of 1992, demand skyrocketed. Production at the plant was increased to three shifts, seven days per week. By the end of the year, sales increased to $14.8 million. EBITDA (a measure of profitability) exceeded 30%. Both Jim Jr. and I received an increase in salary and a year-end bonus. The Company made a significant contribution to the company profit sharing plan, which had been set up a few years earlier, for all employees.

In December 1992, Jim Jr. and I received shares of stock in the company. The Corporate Resolution signed by Jim Sr. on December 31, 1992 stated:

RESOLVED: IN RECOGNITION OF THE VALUABLE SERVICES PERFORMED BY ANDREW M. KNOTT AND JAMES M. KNOTT, JR. FOR RIVERDALE MILLS CORPORATION DURING THE YEAR 1992, AS WELL AS

PREVIOUS YEARS WHEN THE CORPORATION WAS FINANCIALLY UNABLE TO COMPENSATE THEM ADEQUATELY FOR THEIR CONTRIBUTIONS TO ITS GROWTH AND SUCCESS, IT IS HEREBY RESOLVED THAT THE CORPORATION DOES DECLARE A BONUS TO EACH OF THEM PAYABLE DECEMBER 31, 1992. EACH BONUS SHALL CONSIST OF SHARES OF COMMON STOCK OF THE CORPORATION.

In late December 1993 we received another bonus of shares of common stock.

Until 1996, company sales grew an average of 25% per year. RMC had an 80 – 90% share of the Lobster trap market and almost 100 employees. We could see that once the Lobster trap pipeline was full, our only hope of further growth was to find new markets for the wire. I was appointed to the newly created position of VP of Sales & Marketing and Asst. Treasurer. Jim Jr. was appointed VP of Manufacturing and later COO. In the new role, I gave up the purchasing and human resource roles and focused full time on existing sales and new product development. We found new customers in the Construction and Agricultural markets. We had achieved our Definite Major Purpose set back in 1980, by using Applied Faith, the Mastermind Principle and Self-Discipline.

In 1994 I was accepted into an executive education program at Harvard Business School: OPM-24. The program was for Owners, Founders, CEO's or senior executives of companies with sales between $5 - 100 million per year. A requirement for acceptance was each person had to have an equity stake in the company. There were eighty-two people in my class, representing twenty-nine countries. The class ran three weeks per year for three years. It was like an accelerated MBA for people who started and ran companies without the formal training. I thrived in the program and loved every minute I spent at Harvard. My wife and children attended my graduation ceremony in August 1996.

One day, in the spring of 1996, my Father in Law, Dick Fifield visited our family. He had just come back from a trip to New Brunswick, Canada and he gave me an article from a local newspaper. The article was a long interview with a Lobsterman who was eighty-two years old and had been fishing since he was a teenager. There was a big picture of the Lobsterman with a large pile of wire traps in the background. He said the only reason why he was able to continue fishing at that age was because he switched to wire traps ten years earlier. The traps were easier to handle and easier to repair. A tear came to my eye. Who knows, maybe he was one of the people who told me I was crazy twenty years earlier at that show in Halifax.

BIO

Andrew Knott is President of AVO Fence & Supply, Inc. (AVO), a manufacturer and distributor of custom fence systems located in Stoughton, Massachusetts. Andrew attended Boston University and is a graduate of OPM-24, an executive education program at Harvard Business School. Andrew began his career at Coatings Engineering Corporation (CEC).

After CEC, he co-founded Riverdale Mills Corporation (RMC) with his family and worked there for 27 years. In the early years he did just about every job including machine operator, fork truck driver and receptionist. As the business grew, he became VP of Sales & Marketing and Assistant Treasurer.

RMC is the nation's leading producer of specialty welded-wire products for marine and industrial use. Andrew acquired AVO in 2012 with two partners. He is the proud husband of Jayne F. Knott and father of three children, Jennie, Andrew and Nancy. He is an avid squash racquets player, loves sports and politics and is active in his local church. Andrew can be reached at: amknottsr@yahoo.com or through his website: www.avofenceandsupply.com

A MOTHER WITH A PURPOSE

By: Nick Nicholson

I was 15 years old, my father had just died from a heart attack, and three months later my mother moves the only son left at home from Michigan to the desert of New Mexico. I was shocked. The thought of leaving friends, the potential of going to Michigan State University and becoming a State Trooper was exploding in my mind. The hopes and dreams of a teenager shattered! I thought . . . "What am I going to do? How am I going to "fit in" with these kids? I don't even speak Spanish!"

The saving grace, similar to Dr. Hill's childhood experience, was my mother. Her concern for a proper upbringing and devotion to me during those years started me toward truly understanding what Definiteness of Purpose meant. With little formal education and absolutely no training on the Principles, my mother possessed a "what-if" mentality. She uncannily was able to get an idea of how we would live in our new surroundings. She thought "what-if I go to the bank and get a loan to buy a house to rent so we can have extra monthly income?" I thought . . . "No way! A single mother with a teenage son, in a new city and no previous credit line. She only has a full-time job managing a retirement facility, and her monthly social security check." Well she did it. Unbelievable! Even my two older brothers couldn't believe she had done it. They had never known her to be any more than mom, the lady who loved them, fed them, and made sure they had clean clothes. I saw her determination and ability to take an idea— literally a dream—and make it come true.

As I began to learn from her I developed my own sense of wants and desires—who I wanted to be, the things I wanted, and the people I wanted to meet. In 1975, I joined the United States Air Force (USAF) as a Security Policeman, now referred to a Security Forces. It was during this period of my life I found my first motivational publication, Think and Grow Rich. What caught my eye were the people who had endorsed the book, especially Mr. Wrigley of the Chicago Ballpark fame. His unequivocal endorsement was all that I needed to read the book. I read each chapter, trying to figure out how to do all the things Dr. Hill said you needed to do. There were times that I drifted due to other prevailing interests, such as going on dates, staying out late, and working double shifts, or the typical military activity "unannounced recalls." The one thing I knew, if I was willing to establish a Definiteness of Purpose through what-ifs, I could get what I wanted.

After my tour of duty in the USAF I knew exactly what I wanted, to be a Michigan State Trooper. So I began to visualize myself in the uniform, seeing myself going code 3 (emergency with lights and siren) to an accident, and helping people. That's all I needed, the what-if moment kicked in—"what-if I move to Michigan and apply for the position and go through the process?" I did, along with a baby and my wife, we returned to our home state ready to meet the challenges of a new job and career. Well not so fast. It was the 1980s and the previously flourishing Detroit big car days had just hit a brick wall. People were being laid-off, local governments couldn't meet the fiscal challenges without increasing taxes, and here sits a veteran with a family, trying to go to college during the day, and working as a security officer at a local hospital while going through the extended application process to be a trooper.

Ah yes the day finally came—I did it, the process completed, acceptance to an academy class assured and our lives would be happy forever. Well not so fast. Although I had received a letter, it was shortly followed up by another letter, stating that the academy class I had been selected for was now cancelled due to funding issues. In other words, thanks but no thanks. No way! Unbelievable! I was so close but what now? Then Dr. Hill's words shouted out to me, "every adversity, every failure, every heartache carries with it the seed of an equal or greater benefit." Well OK, I'm ready . . . where's the benefit, I mean let's go . . . I've seen the worst, so now I need the best. Um, nothing happened. So I sat, I thought, and said . . . call mom.

I did, and her words were clear and distinct. She asked a few questions and suddenly said, "What-if you were to come back to New Mexico? I know they're hiring sheriff's deputies." I immediately responded . . . That's it! But what would it take, would I have to do all of the same written, physical testing, and medical exams? Yes of course, why should I be treated any differently? The agency needed to know without a doubt I was ready to do the job!

After weeks of Academy training I graduated and went full force into the field, where I arrested bad guys, helped people, and made a dent in the blatant crime wave throughout New Mexico! Well not quite. I was unsatisfied with my job, my wife had left me for someone else, and I had sole custody of two young boys. What happened, why did this happen to me, what did I do to deserve this? After several weeks of sulking I found my old Think and Grow Rich book in a box I had stored at mothers before going to Michigan. I dragged it out, thought a minute about reading it, and decided why not— it always helped me feel a little better, and I definitely wanted to feel better.

Shortly after rereading the book, guess what? I found a new police job at a local community, and after a couple of years I was promoted to sergeant and looking toward lieutenant. Well this must be it, on top of the world ready to conquer anything that comes my way! Well not exactly. The Chief of Police was about to make his stepson the lieutenant. I thought, "No way! This is not happening!" So I cleared my desk and went to find a new position. I was out of there and good riddance!

Depressed and frankly not sure what to do, I turned to the only person who might be able to help me through this world tragedy, which no one else had ever experienced, I called mom. In her supportive old sage manner, what I heard was the familiar, "What-if you applied for that federal agent position you used to talk about?" So of course I did. I went through the training, received my assignment, and after a few months immersed myself in learning the skills of a supervisor. As a new supervisor it was mandatory that I attend a two week training course in Utah. So off to Utah I went in the middle of winter. But I quickly learned that the teacher was going to be Stephen Covey. Within thirty minutes of his opening presentation, he was quoting Dr. Hill. I had long admired Dr. Covey and now he's quoting my first tutor on the principles of success.

It was during this class I decided that Definiteness of Purpose meant more than thinking of the what-ifs and just going for it. I began a concentrated effort to again reread my favorite author and seek out any other writings that would help me understand the depth and breadth of the study of success. So what did I learn and how can that help others?

Although my faith in God (my infinite intelligence) has existed since a young boy, it's only been in the last five years that I've drawn closer to Him. Through studying my faith, combined with years of formal education and training on leadership and success, I've come to a few conclusions that hopefully will help encourage others. First, the amount of material that one can acquire to learn the various principles of leadership and success can be listed in the thousands. I once had an assistant go to a local chain bookstore and count the number of publications available on the subject of leadership and success. Her response was "too many to count." So what text should you select to start with? Sounds like a rhetorical question but it shouldn't, especially when there are so many to choose from. My current research indicates that the Principles of Success first developed by Dr. Hill provides the basis for most leadership books written in the past 25 plus years. Although other authors predate Dr. Hill's work, his was one of the first to identify a comprehensive set of principles, but at the same time offered the reasons why one couldn't be successful if they allowed themselves to be distracted.

Next, I learned how to be successful in applying the principles. It's an everyday effort —studying, reviewing, and thinking about each principle, and determining how to apply it to your daily activities. I'm currently working on a leadership book focused on the 17 principles and their relationship to the all-time favorite leadership books ever written. Although the research isn't completed, I feel confident enough at this point to make this statement:

"Of the top ten best-selling books on leadership as identified in the Washington Post, the basis for each has a significant genesis from Dr. Hill's original material in the 1930s."

In fact, most of the publications quote Dr. Hill's works and those that don't, probably should, since it's obvious that only a word or two was rewritten from the original Hill quote.

As a leadership educator, trainer, and consultant I believe learning actually takes place when the knowledge being received is reflected on and put into action as soon as possible after the learning experience. This concept was written about numerous times in Donald Schon's books on learning systems and their effects on an organization. Typically illustrated as:

Learning = Knowledge + Reflection + Action

One of the best ways to achieve success in applying this formula is to write down what you're learning and think about what you wrote. Dr. Hill clearly identifies this technique in his early video (recordings) by showing the little notebook he carried around to record the key moments he wanted to remember.

Most people find it difficult to take the time to "reflect" on a recent training event. We know through studies that if the skills learned are not applied in the first 24 hours after the learning event as much as 70% of the information received will be forgotten. So it's imperative that you find time to retreat to a place where you can meditate, and reflect on your recent acquisition of knowledge.

One of the best means to retain information is to put it into action. When studying the Principles, identify one principle you'll work on during the day or even a week. Find ways to incorporate the language of the principle into conversations, repeat key phrases, and if appropriate tell others about the principle. As an example, I selected, "Going the Extra Mile" as my focus principle for a week. I took every opportunity to tell those who I saw demonstrating the principle that they, "definitely went the Extra Mile on that one!" I asked several colleagues what "Going the Extra Mile" meant to them and how would they recognize the behavior that constituted the Extra Mile. Just discussing the principle with people I worked with started them thinking about the principle in depth, whereas they had never considered it before. Eventually the term became part of corporate culture and found itself on the organization's performance evaluation form as:

"In the past 12 months, identify what you've done to Go the Extra Mile, describe in detail what you did, who benefitted from your efforts and what the outcome was from your efforts."

Obviously, this type of acceptance across a whole organization isn't typical, but it demonstrates the level of influence that can be achieved.

After years of studying the Principles and other supportive leadership and motivational material, I've refined my Definitiveness of Purpose to a trilogy involving my mind, spirit, and body. The following is an excerpt of my trilogy.

Mind

Keep my mind from wondering to thoughts that are negative and fail to promote a caring genuine attitude of love and concern for others. Always be cautious of my addictions and avoid those things that trigger those thoughts.

Read instructional material that promotes open thought and consideration, not biases and prejudices. Read and listen to publications that I can learn from and receive joy in thinking about. Learn something daily and record the results in my journal.

Help me seek new relationships that take me to a higher level of understanding in life and business.

Body

Put things in my body that promote good health. Avoid excessive carbs and avoid alcohol in excess. A drink occasionally can taste good but never eat or drink anything that doesn't please the palate. Think about calorie and carb intake before every meal and snack. Try new healthy foods.

Exercise daily even if it is only good stretches. As my body gets older it needs more activity. Work through the pain in the morning and the rest of the day will go just fine.

Spirit

LORD help me achieve these things through prayer and YOUR guiding light. My spirit and heart is held for YOU, my family, and friends. Help me always-express gratitude for the things I have, and provide the guidance and wisdom needed to serve YOU, those around me, and YOUR Kingdom. Let YOU be the first thing I think of in the morning and last thing at night.

By most measures I've been successful, but I realize that regardless of your age, background or any other inhibitors or excuses you use, your ability to achieve success is dependent upon your desire to follow the steps outlined in the 17 Principles. My story has been repeated over and over by thousands of people, but the true question is, will you be one of the those who will go beyond the "what-if" or remain a timid soul as described in Theodore Roosevelt's speech he delivered at the Sorbonne in 1910.

It is not the critic who counts, not the man who points out how the strong man stumbles, or where the doer of deeds could have done better.

Credit belongs to the man who is actually in the arena, whose face is marred by dust and sweat and blood, who strives valiantly, who errs, and comes up short again and again: because there is no effort without error or shortcoming, but who does actually strive to do the deeds, who knows the great enthusiasms, the great devotions, who spends himself in a worthy cause, who at the best knows in the end the triumph of high achievement and who at the worst, if he fails, at least he fails while daring greatly.

So that his place shall never be with those cold and timid souls who know neither victory nor defeat. . . .

Only you can decide, so what's your answer?

BIO

Larry "Nick" Nicholson received his B.S. (1990) & M.S. (1994) in Education from Southern Illinois University, and his and Ph.D. in Police Administration from St. John's University in 1997. He is the Founder and Senior Partner of The Nicholson Group, LLC, a Leadership and Risk Management consulting firm located near Williamsburg, VA.

Prior to his retirement from federal service in 2008, Dr. Nicholson served as the Special Assistant to the Assistant Director of the FBI Academy. He has held numerous senior leadership positions to include Director of the Center for Civil Force Protection (a National Institute of Justice project) and US Department of Energy (DOE) as a Special Agent.

In his last assignment with DOE, he was the Special Agent in Charge of the Standards and Evaluation Section. Other law enforcement positions include the Bureau Chief of Training for the New Mexico Department of Public Safety, and Narcotics Commander for Rio Rancho Police Department, New Mexico.

He is a graduate of the FBI National Academy Session #176. Dr. Nicholson is nearing completion of the Leader's Certification process.

http://www.tngsolutions.us

WHEN THE FOG CLOUDED MY NORTH...

By: Ana Laura Quesada Rodríguez

I must say that for most of my life things had have gone well for me. Everything that I have wanted to achieve in life, I have achieved in one way or another thanks to going the extra mile and focused effort. I dedicated my years in school and college on studying, who came very naturally to me; I had the passion and motivation to achieve the goals that I have decided upon.

I had the mental clarity and willpower to bury myself into any definite purpose that I wanted. In addition, I had the example of my father who, before I was born, was already fond of Napoleon Hill's success philosophy, so I had seen throughout his life, why he - who had a definite major purpose in life - was in fact, a successful man.

But then, something happened. Suddenly the plan I had outlined for my life was not satisfying me. I was not finding the happiness and success that I had both longed for, and for which I definitely had struggled so much to achieve. I had achieved balance in my life in the eyes of the people around me. I had goals that were forcing me to grow more than any other time, but still, I didn't have the energy and the enthusiasm that had characterized me in previous years.

Many would have thought that I was about to face a crisis because I was turning 40. Although my age was approaching an important decade, I looked forward to it since Napoleon Hill stated that most of the successful people he studied became successful after the age of 40.

That's when I started thinking I needed more, I needed a goal that defied any of the previous goals I had set. I had read that those who aren't happy usually lack a definite purpose.

A purpose that according to Napoleon Hill, is "the starting point of all achievement, a definite objective toward which you strive".

So I concentrated my efforts on that, and I started to push myself more and more, until finally, I was presented with such a dazzling opportunity that I felt it in every bone of my body I sensed it in my whole being. Literally, I almost fell when it was presented to me.

Like most good opportunities, I recognized it through instinct, however, it came in disguise, and I didn't imagine, at least at that time, the challenge I was choosing. It was so unlike anything I had ever done, and it required me to perform, from many points of view, a fairly radical change in my life.

I started working on myself, following the six steps of gold, given by Napoleon Hill in his book Think and Grow Rich. I wrote my statement in which I specified what I wanted to do, and what I was willing to give, to achieve the goal that I had decided upon. I was totally committed.

I read my statement day and night, to start inducing my subconscious mind toward my purpose. Gradually, I introduced in my mind new concepts. Using repetition charged with emotions, I was changing the old habits and creating new ones. I had to change many paradigms and break several terror barriers, but from the bottom of my heart I believed that any change was worth it. Moreover, I was sure to be all in, because the reward was so worthy it would pay much more than any effort that was put into it.

So every day I was getting ready. I faced each of the challenges in my path. I clearly visualized the goal, and I had the excitement and the energy needed to make the changes I wanted. Nothing could stop me. I knew the risk was high, but I was not willing to lose. In fact, at that time, I never thought I was not going to win.

Despite doing work that could be considered well below my knowledge and skills, I perceived a wellbeing that I had not felt in years. I was personally growing in giant steps and I was happier and more motivated than ever. I was looking to overcome every challenge, and sought the next to come.

Like everything in life, I was also experiencing very difficult moments, but still, I had the required energy. But it was then, when the truly big obstacles began to appear, as time passed that I began to see how the barriers of fear that I had to face got bigger, the path became more difficult, the costs required an increasingly extra mile, but I was not willing to give up. Not yet. I was too committed and too passionate.

But time was going by, in fact years passed and things didn't change, and I saw the goal farther and farther away. The effort was becoming more demanding and I had never worked so hard for something in my life.

That's when I started to feel a little defeated, my fears were taking over my hopes, and negative thoughts were occupying more and more of my 50,000 to 60,000 daily thoughts. The road became narrower, and my fears seemed like trees around a dark road, its branches were sinking deeper into what had once been my path to success.

It was then that I began to manifest my own fear; that I was walking away from the goal I wanted. My actions were increasingly inconsistent and it was difficult for me to take control of my emotions and my thoughts.

As if by magic, I started to create and to live just the opposite of what I had wanted. I felt like a weather vane taken over by circumstances. It seemed that I had no control over my actions, and I made futile efforts to get out of the situation I was in.

I went to talk to my mastermind partners, but my mind was so blurred that the ideas that were generated, rather than bringing me something positive, looked like rain, almost a storm in a pot, which had more turbulence than ever.

I was living a constant internal battle between the reason, past education, recent experience, the opinions of others and what I really wanted from the bottom of my heart.

In fact, little by little I really forgot what I wanted and where I was going. My process of change, and my desire to win, had been so intense that somewhere along the way I forgot who I was and what I was made of.

After literally wandering in my life for many months, one day with my dad, analyzing a situation in the company, after he heard my opinion, he said to me ... "I don't want you to tell me anything other than the goal we want!" And bang, it woke me up...

I was not getting the results I wanted in my life, because I had lost my North, in fact, it was so foggy because of my fears that I could no longer recognize it. I didn't know what it was and I knew with regret that I had lost it.

In the past months, rather than listen to what I really wanted, instead of focusing my gaze toward the goal I wanted to reach, I had focused on my fears. I had let my dominant thoughts be my terrors. I was giving so many energy to my fears that I empowered them in such a great way that they wouldn't let me move. It was like being caught in the same situation, without anywhere to go. It was obvious and perceptible why I had not achieved success.

I seemingly had forgotten to concentrate all my efforts on my goal. I forgot to use my persistence over time to accomplish the things I wanted. In my mind, it was easier to choose to return to my comfort zone. I was back to the paradigms that had always governed my life and the people around me.

I once heard Bob Proctor say: "If you are going to be safe, you are going to be sorry." And that's exactly what happened. I went to a safe place. I did what needed less effort, I did the "right" thing according to my internal paradigms. The paradigms that I couldn't discard completely the same ones that prevented me to succeed. Hence, like Bob Proctor predicted I was sorry.

So now what? Now, it was time to learn from defeat...

I would like to tell you, that my goal is achieved, and I managed to accomplish the success I dreamt of, but the truth is, I'm still learning from the lesson. What is certain is that I clarified my North, and I now have a much bigger and much better defined purpose. Of course, it had to be this way.

The critical situations in life all have a reason, but it is our duty to find out what those reasons are, and to learn from them. Today I am definitely not the same person I was. My awareness is much higher than before my 40th birthday (yes I am over 40 now). I learned a lot from the experience. I met new people and discovered new ways of doing things. In short, I grew up.

To conclude, one of the greatest lessons I have learned is to never ever again let my fears take hold of my mind and cloud my North. Don't you ever let your definiteness of purpose go away. Don't you ever cease to look at it at every moment!

I will never stop going after what I really want. Because, after all, you only have one life. There are no trials, and what you experience is what you get. I learned that I must take control of my thoughts, and direct them to what I want to accomplish. I should not let my North perish. Sooner or later the light will come and your North will appear bigger and more amazing, and with the greatest satisfaction you could ever imagine.

Success is a journey and life is a process that leads to learning, in which we must never give up, never stop fighting and never stop looking for what makes us live. What makes us want to be better and what our inner self is always trying to expand through us.

Enjoy your journey and don't ever lose your North!

BIO

MBA. ANA LAURA QUESADA

Napoleon Hill's Certified Leader and Life Success Consultant

Ana Laura Quesada graduated with an MBA from the University of Costa Rica and is the Financial Director for her family's company in Costa Rica. Her father gave her a copy of "Think and Grow Rich" by Napoleon Hill when she was 15 years old and she became very interested in the Napoleon Hill philosophy. At the end of 2010, she contacted the Napoleon Hill Foundation and organized an International Seminar in Costa Rica. Since then, she has helped the Napoleon Hill Foundation with several projects and became a Certified Leader in 2012, the first person in Costa Rica to achieve that prestigious certification. She believes it is her duty to spread the Principles of Success to as many people as she can, as taught by

Napoleon Hill, in order to help them achieve their purpose and dreams, just like it has for her.

Ana Laura can be reached at ana_laura_q@hotmail.com

Napoleon Hill BIO

Napoleon Hill
(1883-1970)

"Whatever your mind can conceive and believe it can achieve."
- Napoleon Hill

American born Napoleon Hill is considered to have influenced more people into success than any other person in history. He has been perhaps the most influential man in the area of personal success technique development, primarily through his classic book Think and Grow Rich which has helped million of the people and has been important in the life of many successful people such as W. Clement Stone and Og Mandino.

Napoleon Hill was born into poverty in 1883 in a one-room cabin on the Pound River in Wise County, Virginia. At the age of 10 his mother died, and two years later his father remarried. He became a very rebellious boy, but grew up to be an incredible man. He began his writing career at age 13 as a "mountain reporter" for small town newspapers and went on to become America's most beloved motivational author. Fighting against all class of great disadvantages and pressures, he dedicated more than 25 years of his life to define the reasons by which so many people fail to achieve true financial success and happiness in their life.

During this time he achieved great success as an attorney and journalist. His early career as a reporter helped finance his way through law school. He was given an assignment to write a series of success stories of famous men, and his big break came when he was asked to interview steel-magnate Andrew Carnegie. Mr. Carnegie commissioned Hill to interview over 500 millionaires to find a success formula that could be used by the average person. These included Thomas Edison, Alexander Graham Bell, Henry Ford, Elmer Gates, Charles M. Schwab, Theodore Roosevelt, William Wrigley Jr, John Wanamaker, William Jennings Bryan, George Eastman, Woodrow Wilson, William H. Taft, John D. Rockefeller, F. W. Woolworth, Jennings Randolph, among others.

He became an advisor to Andrew Carnegie, and with Carnegie's help he formulated a philosophy of success, drawing on the thoughts and experience of a multitude of rags-to-riches tycoons. It took Hill over 20 years to produce his book, a classic in the Personal Development field called Think and Grow Rich. This book has sold over 7 million copies and has helped thousands achieve success. The secret to success is very simple but you'll have to read the book to find out what it is!

Napoleon Hill passed away in November 1970 after a long and successful career writing, teaching, and lecturing about the principles of success. His work stands as a monument to individual achievement and is the cornerstone of modern motivation. His book, Think and Grow Rich, is the all-time best seller in the field.

The Seventeen Principles

1. **Definiteness of Purpose**
2. **Mastermind Alliance**
3. **Applied Faith**
4. **Going the Extra Mile**
5. **Pleasing Personality**
6. **Personal Initiative**
7. **Positive Mental Attitude**
8. **Enthusiasm**
9. **Self-Discipline**
10. **Accurate Thinking**
11. **Controlled Attention**
12. **Teamwork**
13. **Learning from Adversity & Defeat**
14. **Creative Vision**